DATE DUE

'Andrews is ferocious and brilliant and absolutely indispensable.'
Junot Díaz

'Andrews takes the concepts that underpin so much of our woolly, contemporary talk about blackness, structural racism, pan-Africanism and – most of all – radicalism, and does the hard, essential work of re-inserting meaning and critique into the debate. An unflinching and authentic contribution.'
Afua Hirsch, author of *Brit(ish): On Race, Identity and Belonging*

'No more timid, liberal bullsh*t or empty jingoism. Kehinde Andrews is a brilliant, black British intellectual who searingly and expertly reveals the meaning of real change, for those willing to face it. In a time of flux, doubt and uncertainty, Kehinde provides a clear and lucid voice. *Back to Black* is an important book for anyone interested in real change and what that is likely to cost.'
Russell Brand

'Andrews pulls no punches. His concept of black radicalism is raw and powerful. This book is sure to provoke, and will gain him adversaries – both black and white – because of the home truths it exposes.'
Femi Nylander, Rhodes Must Fall

'A timely and important book capturing an important political moment in north Atlantic culture.'
Robert Beckford, BAFTA winning documentary filmmaker

Back to Black

Retelling Black Radicalism for the 21st Century

Kehinde Andrews

ZED

Back to Black: Retelling Black Radicalism for the 21st Century
was first published in 2018 by Zed Books Ltd, The Foundry,
17 Oval Way, London SE11 5RR, UK.

www.zedbooks.net

Typeset in Haarlemmer by seagulls.net
Index by Kehinde Andrews
Cover design by David A. Gee
Printed and bound by CPI Group (UK) Ltd, Croydon CR0 4YY

A catalogue record for this book is available from the British Library

ISBN 978-1-78699-278-9 hb
ISBN 978-1-78699-279-6 pdf
ISBN 978-1-78699-280-2 epub
ISBN 978-1-78699-281-9 mobi

For Assata, Kadiri, Omaje, Ajani
and
the people in the struggle

Contents

Contents

Acknowledgements

Writing this book has been a collective process with me drawing on influences, experiences, conversations for years. Foremost of those influences have been my parents, Carole and Maurice Andrews, whose activism, dedication and book collection on the Black liberation struggle made this book possible. Also a big thank you to my sisters Nzinga and Zakiya for always challenging me to think beyond the surface. I, of course, could not have written the book without the unconditional support of my wife, (Dr) Nicole, who challenged me to rethink the concepts and ideas, while also taking the strain of the hours I had to be out of the house or in the office writing.

A big thank you also has to go to the Black activist community in Birmingham, in particular the African Caribbean Self-Help Organisation and all the people who have been involved with Harambee Organisation of Black Unity. Thanks also to anyone who has come to talk, a meeting, volunteered, or who I have met a conference, taught in class, or bent your ear over a coffee or having a drink. Every interaction, conversation and argument has gone into crafting the book. We may not have agreed (and this will be obvious in the book) but I couldn't have written it without you.

Finally, I am indebted to those people in the Black liberation struggle who organised, struggled, fought and even died for freedom. There is no book without those sacrifices and I dedicate the work to all those who have gone before.

Prologue

Reclaiming Radicalism

'Black Lives Matter', 'No justice, no peace' and even 'Black Power' were chants bellowed by the crowd of protestors. The killings of Philando Castile in Minnesota and Alton Sterling in New Orleans sparked a mass reaction. Watching Castile bleed to death on Facebook was bound to provoke a response. Thousands of people poured out onto the streets to demonstrate their anger and disgust at the slaying of yet more Black bodies at the hands of the police. As the march settled outside the police station, speaker after speaker stepped to the mobile podium condemning the racism and brutality of the 'pigs'. Family members of those who had died in police custody gave impassioned calls for justice. Tension on the streets of Birmingham crackled through the crowd. When Malcolm X spoke of a 'racial powder keg', it was this kind of scene he had in mind. Close your eyes, take in the crowd and you could well be in Alabama in the 1960s. But this is a protest in the second city of Britain in the twenty-first century and the picture tells us how little things have changed in the last fifty years, and speaks to the global nature of racism.

Crowds of Black people came onto the streets following events that took place thousands of miles away because they related directly to our experiences. Just as in America, the

police are often seen as 'an occupying force' in Black communities in Britain. There is a long history of over-policing,
harassment and brutality. To be Black is to be a suspect. To
live in a Black neighbourhood is to be a target. In the 1980s
the situation came to a head, with large-scale rebellions taking
place across the country in cities like London, Birmingham
and Liverpool. Communities tired of the police taking advan-
tage of the 'Sus Laws', where they had the power to arrest on
the basis of suspicion, to crack the head of a 'darkie'. Despite
changing laws and police reforms, if you are Black and in
Britain today you are up to eighteen times more likely to be
stopped and searched by the police. You are more likely to be
charged if arrested, and subject to a longer prison sentence
if found guilty. The criminal injustice system means that in
Britain, compared to our numbers in the country, Black people
are actually more overrepresented in the prison population
than in America. We only make up 3% of the population but
account for 13% of prison inmates. Black people also represent 9% of deaths after police contact that were independently
investigated.[1] The protest in Birmingham was actually a
pre-arranged march for justice for Kingsley Burrell, who died
in police custody after a chain of events that started when *he*
had called the police. At the march the families recounted the
names of Demetre Fraser, Sarah Reed, Mark Duggan and
many more. You are unlikely to be shot by the police in Britain
because the majority do not carry guns. But if you are Black
you are more vulnerable to death after police contact.

Black Lives Matter protests sweeping across Britain
were not just about the shared experiences of police abuse.

The shootings in America drew a much larger protest than the typical marches for justice for people killed in Britain. To understand the depth of feeling in Britain to slayings in America is to grasp the connections of Blackness, which cannot be contained by national borders. When we see Philando Castile bleeding out we are not looking at a distant stranger. We are seeing our brother, our father, our cousin, our friend. His killing happened to Black communities in Britain as much as it did to those in Minnesota. It is that connection, that pain, which drew the largest Black mobilisations for years onto the streets of Britain.

Black Lives Matter has re-energised Black political movements across the globe. In both Britain and America the battles and hard-fought victories for recognition and legislation have lulled us into a false sense of progress. Landmark gains for civil and voting rights in America, and race relations bills in Britain opened up the dreams of inclusion and equality for Black so-called citizens. The sad reality is that fifty years after these apparent gains racism is as embedded in the fabric of society as ever, coded into the DNA of the system. There may have been a Black man in the White House for eight years, but under his rule the value of Black life depreciated. The poverty rate, wealth gap, evictions and food stamp usage all went up under the watch of the first Black president.[2] It was truly a case of a Black man, White house. Meanwhile, the police continued to bring the hammer down on Black communities, providing the horrifying footage that relit the sparks of protest. Now that the fires of protest have been lit the question is what direction they will take.

There is no such thing as a unified Black politics. Mobilisations have taken forms so wide-ranging they have led to violent confrontations. Black people have disagreed with each other as to the way forward as much as, if not more than, we have with White people. One of the most frustrating rewrites of history is the common description of Malcolm X as a 'civil rights leader'. Nothing could be further from the truth. In fact, Malcolm was perhaps *the* fiercest critic of the civil rights movement, its tactics and its leaders. He famously called the showpiece 1963 March on Washington a 'farce', denouncing it as a 'circus with clowns and all'.[3] Though he and the figure he is most tied to, Martin Luther King, were active at the same time, they only ever met once, very briefly. We should not be surprised given Malcolm's public scorn for King, including calling him 'a twentieth century, or modern day Uncle Tom'.[4] These disagreements were not some personal squabble between two men; they were based on a fundamentally different view of the world. Malcolm and Martin did not have the same goals; they did not even see the problem through the same eyes.

Broadly speaking, Martin Luther King and the civil rights movement represent a liberal tradition in Black politics. Liberals acknowledge the problems of racial inequality but put them down to a lack of access to the system. So Black people are poorer because we do not have equal access to the job market. In order to get equal access it is seen as necessary to reform the system through legislation that outlaws discriminatory practices. A barrier to these laws being passed is that we also lack access to political power, and so it is necessary to get

Black politicians elected to bring about reform. This is the logic that made '69% of African Americans believe that Obama's election mean that King's dream had been fulfilled'.[5] It is also the logic that leads to campaigns for more Black police officers, chiefs and commissioners. The system is not the problem in this analysis, just the fact we are not fully part of it. If Black faces were in high places then of course a different set of decisions would be made and equality would emerge.

In stark contrast, Malcolm represents a radical tradition in Black politics. He was never interested in being part of what he called the 'American nightmare'. In the radical tradition the system is *the* problem. There can be no reform, no adjustments and we as Black people should not waste time daydreaming of equality. When Malcolm proclaimed 'we want no part of integration with this wicked race of devils',[6] he was not attacking individual White people but condemning the system of the West as being evil at its core. So the battle is not to get good jobs or to be elected, but to end the system of oppression and create the world in a new image. No amount of Black faces in the police force will make it anti-racist. As the hip hop artist KRS-ONE pointed out, during apartheid (and after) it was the 'Black cop killing Black kids in Johannesburg'.[7]

Black radicalism therefore calls for an overturning of the system that oppresses Black people, and for nothing short of a revolution. The aim of this book is to reclaim that tradition of Black radicalism because it has been widely misused and misunderstood. Radicalism has become a dirty and even dangerous word in the current climate. It has been distorted in association with violence and most usually Islamic extremism. But radicalism and extremism are actually completely opposite concepts.

Extremism is based on taking the fundamental principles of an idea to the extreme. Making them solid absolutes, with no room for flexibility or different interpretations. The terrorism we are seeing across the world in the name of Islam is extremism, taking the principles of Islam so far that they become destructive. But as Angela Davis explained, 'radical simply means grasping things at the root'.[8] Radicalism is based on rejecting the fundamental principles that govern society and creating a new paradigm. So one of President Trump's favourite phrases, 'radical Islam', is completely nonsensical. A radical version of Islam would do away with the principles of the religion and cease even to be Islam. The Jihadists who are wreaking havoc in the Middle East, Europe, Asia and Africa follow in the footsteps of a long line of extremists. Just as there was nothing radical about the Nazis, or Christian fundamentalism, there is nothing radical about Islamic extremism.

For the goals of the Jihadists to be radical they would need to be based on overthrowing the existing social order. Sharia law may seem radically different to us in the West but the Middle East is made up of many countries observing conservative Islamic principles. The Jihadists are simply following a well-worn path of taking these to the extreme. In many ways this rise of extremism is in direct correlation to the decline of truly radical alternatives to Western domination. Once you give up on overthrowing the unjust social order it is easy to fall into the trap of trying to find spiritual salvation. For all of the rhetoric about fighting the infidels in the holy land, the main beneficiary of the chaos caused by extremism is the West. While Muslims are killing Muslims there is no prospect of the region uniting to challenge imperialism. The ongoing conflicts are a money-making machine for the war and reconstruction industries. Even if an Islamic caliphate were installed across the Middle East there is nothing to suggest this could not co-exist with Western interests. Saudi Arabia is governed by extremist principles and is one of the West's closest allies.

Radicalism is confused with extremism because we incorrectly conflate what is radical with what is violent. This confusion is dangerous and has helped to spread the contagion of Islamic extremism across the African continent, in particular. In Professor Robert Beckford's excellent documentary *The Great African Scandal* he chronicled the impact of Western trade policies on Ghana.[9] Rice farming was one of the successes of the post-independence economy, because it was supported by government subsidies and there was a ban on foreign imports. In the 1980s the country wanted to improve its rice production by developing irrigation systems, so it turned to the West for a helping hand. The International Monetary Fund (IMF) and World Bank loaned Ghana the money but on the condition that it 'liberalise' its markets to help boost the economy. Liberalise meant open its market to free trade, and therefore the end of government subsidies to rice farmers and of course no more banning of foreign imports. The inevitable happened when the West gets involved in Africa. Much cheaper and higher quality, mostly American, rice flooded the Ghanaian market. Worse still, America subsidises its rice farmers, in the way that the

Ghanaian government was now barred from doing. Even with the development from the loan, locally produced rice had no chance to compete and the deal with the devil ended up destroying rice production in the country. The first president of Ghana, Kwame Nkrumah, was right when he said that the relationship between Africa and the West has an 'Alice in wonderland craziness' about it.[10] Beckford's documentary highlighted the poverty that the collapse of rice farming had caused and the resentment of the people in Ghana. In a chilling and telling section of the film, one of the former rice farmers, who was living in poverty, showed Beckford that he had a picture of Osama Bin Laden as his phone's screensaver. He explained that 'he is the only one fighting the West' and the system that had caused the destruction of his livelihood. The decline of radical liberation movements on the continent have left a space that is being filled by the violent rhetoric of resistance presented by Islamic extremism, and to deadly effect.

Critical to understanding Black radicalism is to completely untangle its politics from the tactic of violence. The key distinction between Malcolm X and Martin Luther King was not whether to use violence or not, it was the diagnosis of the problems in society. Non-violence makes sense for liberal movements for racial justice because they want to be part of the system and therefore do not want to alienate the mainstream society. Malcolm objected to non-violence because he wanted to overturn the system, so was not interested in placating White officials. As radical politics is based on overthrow it is more than likely that a revolution would involve violence. But this is not because radicals are bloodthirsty and seeking violent confrontation. It is because the system of oppression is unlikely to give up its power without suppressing the struggle through violence. Black radicalism promotes violence only for self-defence and liberation, and recognises that the liberal forces of oppression are defined by violence. The hypocrisy of defining 'political violence' as the possession of the radicals, or the extremists, is truly frightening. Liberalism, upon which the West is built, is the most violent system that has ever existed on the planet. The West is founded on the genocide of 80% of the native people in the Americas. Once they had exhausted the native population they then brutally enslaved Africans for three centuries, murdering tens of millions of people. Colonial regimes were dominated by horrific violence; for example, it is estimated that Belgium killed half the population of the Congo during its rule. The legacy of underdevelopment and continued exploitation, like that which Beckford saw in Ghana, is a world where a child dies every ten seconds because of poor access to food.

Violence is not a choice that Black radicals want to embrace. In fact, in one of Malcolm's most famous speeches he gives America the chance to have a 'bloodless revolution' by offering either the 'ballot or the bullet'.[11] The ballot represented America deciding to give its Black population equal citizenship, and if they refused then the bullet would be the violence that erupted across the nation. But Malcolm understood it was a fantasy to pretend that you can overthrow the murderous beast of the West without engaging in violence. This is why he was so scornful of the civil rights 'love thy enemy' approach. Malcolm X's most famous quote is 'by any means necessary', but this actually distorts the importance of his legacy. Radicalism is not about the means (violence/non-violence), but the ends (reform/revolution).

Reclaiming Black radicalism is vital because it is one of the few politics that presents an alternative to the iniquitous system of the West. In the words of Kwame Ture, 'a true revolutionary must provide an alternative, not just rhetoric condemning the existing system'.[12] There have been any number of false prophets clothing themselves in revolutionary rhetoric. But there are true radical politics that live up to Ture's challenge, that provide a blueprint for overturning the system. In 1963, Malcolm warned that 'many of our people are using this word "revolution" loosely, without taking into account careful consideration of what it actually means'.[13] So starved are we for radical politics that Beyoncé's performance at the Super Bowl, the very pinnacle of commercialism, is being hailed as revolutionary.

Even if you do not believe in the politics of Black radicalism, its revival is essential. Without the radical alternative putting pressure on the state, even the liberal demands fail to be met. As Malcolm explained, 'at one time the Whites in the United States called him a racialist, and extremist, and a communist. Then the Black Muslims came along and the Whites thanked the Lord for Martin Luther King'.[14] Black radicalism changes the nature of the debate and opens up space for liberal 'progress'. Malcolm expanded on the complementary relationship between radical and liberal politics in a meeting with Coretta Scott King in Selma. Martin was furious that Malcolm had visited directly before he was due to speak, feeling he was trying to upstage him. Against her husband's wishes Coretta took the opportunity to meet with Malcolm, and she recalls that he explained: 'I want Dr. King to know that I didn't come to Selma to make his job difficult. I really did come thinking I could make it easier. If the White people realize what the alternative is, perhaps they will be more willing to hear Dr. King'.[15]

A lot of credit is given to the civil rights campaigners for the legislative gains but it has to be recognised that the authorities were terrified of the alternative to supporting non-violent leaders. You will see a correlation between rebellions in the inner cities and civil rights legislation, as those in charge looked to the civil rights leaders to cool things down. It is also no coincidence that the initial police reforms in Britain followed urban rebellions. The uprisings in the 1980s led to the Scarman Report and acknowledgement of police racism, as well as the formation of the Police Complaints Authority, which significantly boosted the powers of independent investigations into the police. Anti-racism has stalled in the present day, and even reversed in America, without a radical politics to force the debate.

More important than trying to achieve the illusory goals of the liberal project is to re-engage with the politics of Black radicalism. Black Lives Matter has caught the imagination of a younger generation who understand the system has failed them. The thousands who came onto the streets across the world to protest need to choose the kind of society they want to fight for. The last thing Black Lives Matter needs to become is the new civil rights movement. The legacy of civil rights struggle is the current system, which has opened up enough for some to 'make it' and receive some of the food from the table. However, the majority remain locked out, left to fight for the scraps. If fifty years of so-called progress has taught us anything, it should be that 'this system can never provide freedom, justice and equality' for Black people in the same way that 'a chicken can never lay a duck egg'.[16] The West is built on and maintained by oppressing Black people and this oppression cannot end without overturning the system.

We need to reclaim the politics of Black radicalism, connecting the struggles today to the long history of Black freedom movements. In doing so, we should stop thinking of Black radicalism as a tradition and start to understand it as its own political ideology. The aim of the book is to lay out the basis of this politics and how we can re-engage with Black radicalism in the twenty-first century. Essential to this project is to debunk the myths and distinguish Black radicalism from the various other forms of Black politics is it often confused with. The first misunderstanding that will be debunked is that Black Nationalism equals Black radicalism. In order to do this, we must undo the ugly caricature of Black Nationalism as 'divisive, fanatical, dangerous, unprincipled, racist delusional and even mad'.[17] We must also distinguish between radicalism and the many different forms of nationalism, most of which are narrow and regressive. Black radicalism has always been based on the connections that cannot be contained by national borders. We will outline the radical concept of 'Black is a country', which links the Black Lives Matter protests across the globe.

Another important idea to detach from our understandings of Black radicalism is that of 'cultural nationalism'. In Los Angeles in the 1960s there were actual gunfights over the differences between the revolutionary Black Panthers and the US cultural movement headed by Maulana Karenga. The Panthers rejected the idea that any salvation could be found in wishing ourselves back to Africa, culturally or spiritually. With the decline of radical politics, cultural nationalism has been confused with an actual radical politics of resistance. Much of the resistance to embracing Black radicalism is in truth a reaction to the restrictive forms of cultural nationalism. We will severely critique the limits of cultural nationalism and explain how Black radicalism is in part built on a rejection of fixed, regressive ideas of Africa, gender and the Black family. Blackness emerged as an identity rooted in the liberation of people of African descent, and has never been closed off because of gender, ethnicity, sexual orientation or any of the other differences within the Diaspora.

In terms of charting a way forward for movements today, the Black Panther Party is important both in America and globally. One of the key debates in Black politics has been the issue of class and Black Marxism has often been viewed as *the* Black radical tradition. While Marxism is certainly radical, we will explore the key departures of this politics from Black radicalism. We will consider the contradictions of the Panthers, who were Marxist in their rhetoric but Black radical in their activities. For all the talk of the Marxist revolution, most of the members were engaged in 'survival programmes', providing support for Black communities that the state would not. This is a crucial lesson for movements today: as romantic as the idea of Marxism may sound, it can never provide freedom for the African Diaspora. We will explore what the Black revolution has historically looked like and imagine what that means for the politics of today.

When it comes to outlining a vision for Black radicalism today, it is important to critique the limitations of my own position. I work in universities, spaces that are historically and structurally overwhelmingly White. Universities were culpable in producing the very racism that Black radicalism emerged to combat. Those of us privileged enough to enjoy the benefits of being part of the system have a complicated relationship to Black radicalism. In fact, it is not really complicated; Black academics have tended to take one of three options in the situation I find myself in. Complacency is common, where we enjoy the spoils and ignore the problem. Becoming complicit in the system of racism by denouncing radical alternatives from our pulpits is also a favoured route. But the most harmful has been what I call liberal radicalism, where academics embrace radical theory but reject revolutionary practice, calling out the system as inherently racist and then pretending there is nothing we can do about it. If the system is the problem, then the university cannot be decolonised, so we are basically fighting to be part of the oppressive machine.

One of the biggest problems with mobilising around Black radicalism is that the analysis can make the issues we face feel insurmountable. If nothing can change without revolution, and the overthrow of the West seems unimaginable, then it easy to lose hope, to get stuck. We will end with tying the bigger issues into a programme of local action. All global movements are based on local groups coming together on the national and international stage. The struggle for Black liberation starts in your home, your community, your school. Black radicalism has always offered a concrete politics of liberation, and a blueprint to struggle where you are. Fifty years of so-called progress, false promises and symbolic change have meant we have moved away from a political programme that can lead to liberation. If we want freedom, justice and equality we need to root the next generation of mobilisations in the politics of Black radicalism.

Chapter 1

Narrow Nationalism

A veteran campaigner against police abuse in Black communities, Stafford Scott was in many ways the ideal person to keynote the first major Black Lives Matter (BLM) conference held in Britain, in October 2015. He battled through the notorious Broadwater Farm rebellion in Tottenham in 1985, which were sparked by the police killing Joy Gardner; and, as he explained in his keynote speech, he has been 'supporting the people who are receiving the hard face of racism' for decades. After a day of listening to speeches in solidarity with the movement that started in America it was jarring to hear some of his scepticism about how BLM had been mobilised in Britain. In comments before the conference he explained that:

> When I have to talk to the parents of Jermaine Baker (shot dead by police in December 2015), and Pam Duggan, the mother of Mark Duggan and explain to them why they can't get justice and why our young people are more interested in what is happening in America, than England, it irks me.[1]

These words highlight the dwindling community support that movements for justice for Black people killed by the police in Britain have been receiving. The police in Britain do not routinely carry guns, so in comparison to America there are very few police killings. But the problem with the police is exactly the same and I have never met anyone who doubts that if all police were armed then the streets and social media feeds in Britain would be equally stained with Black blood. But aside from the killing of Mark Duggan, which sparked protests in 2011, there has not been the same reaction as to police brutality in America in recent years.

The Black Lives Matter protest in Birmingham, which I referred to in the introduction, drew thousands people onto the streets in solidarity with America. It was planned on the same day as a march to put pressure on the authorities over the death of a local man, Kingsley Burrell, in custody. But the Kingsley Burrell march drew a fraction of the numbers of the BLM protest, and though the two eventually connected, it was not until a large proportion of the BLM protesters had gone home. It is easy to understand the frustrations of campaigners who have been fighting for justice for families, sometimes for decades, and do not feel the support of the community. Scott is also right when he argues that 'when you cannot get justice for people that look like you in your own country, you ain't got no chance for people that might look like you somewhere else'. In fairness to him, he has also been positive about the numbers on the street and has supported BLM demonstrations. However, the comments raise an important limitation on much of Black political thought in that it gets trapped within the boundaries of the nation state.

Political movements that focus their attention solely on local or national problems, accepting the enforced separation of American, British or other issues, fall outside a radical analysis. The vicious system of racial oppression causes impacts at the ground level that must be addressed. Poverty, unemployment, police brutality, mass incarceration, and the list goes on. But we cannot be so focused on the symptoms of racism that we ignore the systemic problem. The issues that we see on the streets on a daily basis are caused by the same system of racism wherever we are located in the Diaspora. There is no 'British' problem that is not an American, Caribbean or African one. BLM protesters in Britain are not being seduced by the romanticism of America, they are responding to the same racism that impacts their lives here. Perhaps the majority of Black politics have not been driven by this global concern and any discussion of Black radicalism has to begin with a separation of the concept from various Black Nationalist traditions.

Black Nationalism has become wrongly conflated with Black radicalism, and Black Nationalism itself is mostly misunderstood. The collective memory has created a set of 'Black nationalist tropes of violence and ultra-sexuality' to represent the tradition,[2] rather than focusing on the revolutionary and liberatory forms of nationalism. In these tropes Black nationalists are portrayed as 'divisive, fanatical, dangerous, unprincipled, racist, delusional and even mad';[3] or 'demonized as the civil rights movement's "evil twin" and stereotyped as a politics of rage practiced by gun toting' and 'men'.[4] The tropes are then used to discredit not only

Black Nationalism but also the distinct yet conflated forms of Black radicalism.

Complicating the effort to decouple the two concepts is that Black radicals have often embraced the rhetoric of nationalism. Malcolm X declared he was a 'Black nationalist freedom fighter'[5] and the call for Black nationhood is essential to the radical tradition. However, revolutionary forms of nationalism must be distinguished from a variety of narrow calls for nationhood that do not seek to radically transform the system.

The nation within a nation

It is wrong to speak of Black Nationalism as singular political philosophy. The label Black Nationalism has been applied to so many different contexts that Hill Collins argues we should now see it as a 'system of meaning' rather than a cohesive set of ideas.[6] Key to this system of meaning is the belief that the Black community needs to unite and work together in order to move forward. The looseness of this idea has brought something of a banality to the term, where anything remotely pro-Black can be included as nationalist. Justice Clarence Thomas, the right-wing ideologue, has been described as Black Nationalist because he 'suggested that black middle and high schools "can function as the center and symbol of black communities, and provide examples of independent black leadership, success, and achievement"'.[7] In one of the more surreal discussions of Black politics, Michael Jackson's *They Don't Care About Us* is said to be 'Black nationalist in temperament' because he talks of an 'us'.[8] As testament to the negative view of Black Nationalism, the apparently anti-Semitic use of the word 'kike' in the song is part of this 'temperament'. When Black Nationalism is used to describe figures as diverse and incompatible as Malcolm X, Clarence Thomas and Michael Jackson, there is certainly a need for a much better understanding of the concept.

Part of the reason for the wide application of Black Nationalism is that one of its common forms is what Shelby terms 'weak Black Nationalism: the political program of black solidarity and group self'. The connection here is so weak that 'it could mean working to create a racially integrated society or even a "post racial" polity, a political order where "race" has no social or political meaning'.[9] This form of nationalism has also been described as 'community nationalism' which 'seeks black self-determination within existing social and political arrangements'.[10] These forms of nationalism are distinguished from the 'strong'[11] or 'separatist'[12] nationalisms, which aim to provide a separate nation outside of the current nation state arrangement. Black Nationalism without a call for an actual nation has a long tradition, particularly in the United States.

W.E.B. Du Bois, who early in his career was a staunch integrationist, argued that,

> With the use of their political powers, power as consumers, and their brain power, added to that a chance of personal appeal which proximity and neighbourhood always give to human beings, Negroes can develop in the United States an economic nation within a nation, able

to work through inner cooperation, to found its own institutions ... it must happen in our case or there is no hope for the Negro in America.[13]

The nation within a nation thesis laid the theoretical foundation for weak Black Nationalism. The pooling of resources in order to improve the conditions for Black communities within the American system is the basis for campaigns we see in Britain to support Black business, and 'keep the Black pound circulating in the community'. This kind of Black Nationalism is not radical, it is simply rational. As a minority group, Black communities cannot rely on the wider society to support us. Any successful minority group, even White ones, have had to rely on community nationalism in order to have success in society. Little Italy in New York stands as testimony to this. When Italian Americans first settled in America, they faced discrimination and built a large community in New York full of Italian business using community support to create an economic base as a platform for success in society. Since the community has raised economic, social and cultural capital, Italians have integrated into mainstream American society and Little Italy is today a couple of streets with a lot of history. Carmichael and Hamilton captured this idea in their book *Black Power*:

> *Before a group can enter the open society, it must first close ranks.* By this we mean that group solidarity is necessary before a group can operate effectively from a bargaining position of strength in a pluralist society ... By building

Irish Power, Italian Power, Polish Power or Jewish Power these groups got themselves together and operated from positions of strength.[14]

Trying to decouple more liberal forms of nationalism from the radical ones is complicated because Black radicalism has argued for and mobilised community nationalism. Malcolm X explained that 'the economic philosophy of Black Nationalism only means that we should own and operate and control the economy of our community'.[15] Quotes like this support the ideas of Black capitalism and pooling resources in order to have a slice of the American Dream for Black communities. However, as will be explored in Chapter 3, Malcolm is invoking community nationalism as part of a radical strategy of liberation. He famously denounced capitalists as 'bloodsuckers',[16] and wanted no part of integration into the 'American nightmare'.[17] For those who embrace community nationalism, building a power base within the existing nation state is the end in itself. Black economic development is key to solving the problems in African American communities. Kunjufu argues that there is a need to increase the number of Black businesses; to convince the 'talented tenth' to invest in those enterprises; and to encourage children to go into business. He even goes so far as to argue that 'we need African American institutions to emphasize economic *over* political development'.[18] Even in his calls for reparatory justice he would use the capital to invest in 'college scholarships, business loans and land';[19] in other words, to achieve success for Black people within the American system.

Weak nationalism within the nation state is clearly not radical because it does not aim to overthrow the existing social system and is therefore perfectly compatible with liberal ideals.[20] The malleability of Black Nationalism is similar to the way that the slogan 'Black Power' can be used to various political ends:

> For some the phrase became shorthand to articulate a critique of the middle class focus of civil rights. For others, 'Black Power' was a catchphrase pushing black America to get its fair share of American capitalism. And still others saw in the phrase a call for African Americans to celebrate themselves as beautiful and their culture as significant.[21]

In his book *Dark Days, Bright Nights*, Joseph attempts to link Black Power politics to the emergence of Barack Obama. There is a passage where he connects the battle for Black Studies, trade union organising, Black feminism, the Black Arts movement and prison reform into a backdrop that led to 'hundreds of thousands of ordinary local people' backing a 'new generation of Black politicians and successfully electing them as mayors of a range of urban cities in the 1960s and 1970s'.[22] Although he is right that this history paved the way for Obama's election, it was also composed of a disparate range of movements and ideologies which are only weakly connected on the basis of Blackness. One of Joseph's arguments is that these movements transformed American democracy enough to allow Obama to be elected president.

However, while they certainly made his presidency possible, neither they, nor his election, fundamentally changed the American system. Black faces on university campuses, in unions or the mayor's office do not alter the function of those spaces. Institutional racism means that no matter the amount of Black presence, if the structure is racist, so too will be the outcomes.

Obama certainly owes a debt to the array of Black social movements that came before him, but counter to the faith held by 69% of African Americans on his election, his presidency was not 'the fulfilment of Martin Luther King's dream'.[23] The structural position of African Americans actually declined under the eight years of Obama's presidency, with a higher proportion in poverty and four million more people in Black communities dependent on food aid.[24] Weak Black Nationalism has rallied African Americans to support a growing political class that has demonstrated a total 'inability to alter the poverty, unemployment, and housing and food insecurity their Black constituents face'.[25] Even though there have been few tangible results from the incorporation of Black faces into the mainstream political machine, Taylor argues that Black communities hold out hope because the 'potential for Black political and economic development was a welcome alternative to decades of neglect and disinvestment'.[26]

The pull of weak Black Nationalism, even when it is irrational, can be seen in the widespread support for Obama's presidency, even within so-called radical organisations. The New Black Panther Party (NBP), which claims to be more radical than the original Panthers, rhetorically rejects the

American system and therefore the legitimacy of a president of any colour. However, it supported Obama based on the weak nationalist logic that 'every President has been a white man, now the Black man must have his time to rule'.[27] The NBP is problematic for far more reasons than this (covered in Chapter 4) but it speaks to the banality of the idea of Black Nationalism when it is reduced to simply supporting anyone who is Black, in whatever endeavour, even if it goes against the core beliefs of your stated politics.

Arguments for creating a Black nation within a nation are not confined to America, with one of the best examples being in South Africa. One of the mechanisms used to manage the country by apartheid governments was to give a measure of self-rule to the African population. Bantustans, or homelands, for specific African ethnic groups were established in 1951, with the move to provide Black people political rights only in their designated 'homelands' completed in 1971.[28] This was not a new idea. The British had created 'reserves' to keep the African population segregated from Whites in the nineteenth century, codified in the 1913 Native Land Act.[29] Bantustans were a form of control used to exclude Africans from the national government of South Africa. Anxiety over the results of the 1970 census, which showed Black people significantly outnumbering Whites, led to calls to strengthen the 'homelands' and ensure that a greater proportion of the Black population was housed in them.[30] Even given their complicity in the apartheid state there remained African leaders who supported the Bantustans as a legitimate means for Black progress.

A good example of collusion with this idea of the Bantu nation within the White nation is Chief Buthelezi, who was appointed head of the Kwa Zulu Natal homeland by the authorities. He created the Inkatha Freedom Party in 1975 as a vehicle to drive Zulu nationalism within the apartheid state.[31] In defence of his political project he argued:

> Zulu nationalism is a real factor in the context of South African politics. Nationalism is nothing to be ashamed of in a situation of cultural and linguistic heterogeneity. Therefore the emergence of Zulu self-consciousness in our attempts to develop inner directedness is inevitable in the circumstances in which fate has placed us.[32]

The problem with his narrow conception of Zulu nationalism is that it was entirely predicated on the apartheid state, in the same way that his authority was. His rise to prominence was facilitated by apartheid leaders, who promoted pliant chiefs who would do their bidding. The combination of his royal Zulu heritage and the platform given by the state led him to be seen as 'a leader worthy of national and international recognition *and* as a bridge between black and white' in South Africa.[33] Buthelezi often posed as a supporter of the anti-apartheid struggle, but was supported by Nixon and Reagan, gave his support to regressive regimes in countries like Mozambique and carried out apartheid policy in Kwazulu Natal.[34] No doubt his aim was to create a Zulu nation free from the rest of South Africa if apartheid did end. The quest for Zulu nationalism as opposed to joining forces with the rest of South Africa led to

conflict with the African National Congress (ANC). From at
least 1985 up until the elections in 1994 (and beyond) sectarian
violence killed thousands of people in the Kwa Zulu Natal
region.[35] This conflict was complex, as are the claims in general
for Zulu nationalism. However, the creation of a narrow Zulu
nationalism, in violent opposition to other Black freedom
movements, was facilitated by the apartheid state. As much as
Mandela can be criticised for selling out the freedom movement
in South Africa and beyond, his decision to make peace with the
apartheid rulers was certainly influenced by violent confrontation with Inkatha.[36] Confronting the forces of White supremacy
was difficult enough, without the internal battle with the Zulus.
Narrow nationalisms can never be the solution to the problem
of Black freedom, because they create divisions that prevent the
unity that is essential for overthrowing the existing social order.

From a radical perspective, the fundamental problem
with the idea of the nation within a nation is that it leaves the
regressive structure of the nation state intact. The goal is to
improve our standing with the national setting rather than
to transform what the nation represents. Better integrating
Black communities into oppressive Western nations, or
former colonies, is not a radical challenge; but there are more
seemingly critical approaches to Black nationhood which
remain outside of the radical tradition.

A nation outside the nation

The Nation of Islam (NOI) is perhaps the most notorious Black Nationalist organisation, whose leader Elijah

Muhammad appealed for a separate portion of land where a Black nation could be founded: 'Come and let us unite under the crescent and do something for ourselves in the way of supporting our own needs. Go after some of this earth for our nation of 22 million here in North America.'[37] The NOI was by no means the first group to advocate for a separate nation, with calls to leave America tracing back at least to emancipation. Perhaps unsurprisingly, after being granted so-called freedom, 'there is little evidence that for Blacks in general, being American was considered desirable, even if attainable, until well into the nineteenth century'.[38] Figures such as Martin Delaney and Hubert Harrison argued that the only solution to African Americans' problems was to leave America and create a new nation.[39] Desire for separation has typically been seen as the radical alternative to integration into the existing society. However, advocating emigration from a Western nation state is not necessarily radical, because it does not always involve an overturning of the existing social order.

Delaney has been dubbed the 'father' of Black Nationalism, being one of the first to articulate the call for Black emigration and laying the foundation for later appeals from groups like the NOI.[40] While this move would require a strong form of nationalism, in a commitment from Black people to build a nation, his was not a radical call. Delaney planned for a carefully selected African American vanguard to establish social and industrial settlements in Africa, with the purpose of instituting the pursuits of 'modern civilised life'.[41] This is just a more advanced version of the Black capitalist logic, which runs through the nation within a national position. America itself is not the problem here; the issue is that because of prejudice Black people will never be accepted. Therefore it becomes necessary to leave America and replicate 'modern civilised life' but with Black faces. The structure of the existing society is maintained, but Black people are given the chance to replicate its success, just elsewhere. It is for this reason that emigration was a popular solution of White politicians to the problem caused by emancipation.

The great Abraham Lincoln saw it as moral duty for African Americans to found a new society on the African continent. In 1862 he informed a group of free Black people that while they may want to live in America, the mere thought of doing so was 'an extremely selfish view of the case'.[42] Key figures like Thomas Jefferson, James Madison and Andrew Jackson all supported African Americans leaving the United States. The American Colonization Society (ACS) was formed in 1816 and attempted to establish settlements in Liberia before emancipation, and afterwards in Haiti, in 1867.[43] The motivation behind this colonisation movement was to maintain the American system by keeping it White. There was no fear that the Black nations they were attempting to create would pose any threat to the social order. In fact, the paternalistic relationship that was at the core of White abolitionism meant that these colonies would always be defined by their relationship to the United States. It is no coincidence that the word colony was used; they were attempting to create a colonial relationship such as existed with European countries and their territories. The call from

African Americans both during and after emancipation, including from Delaney, are bound up in this colonisation discourse. The aim was not to overturn the social order, but to create a co-existing society led by Black faces in another geographical area. Rather than challenging White domination, the creation of such apparently independent states would actually reinforce it.

The idea of excluding Black people from the nation state also has a powerful history in Britain. Enoch Powell's infamous 'Rivers of Blood' speech, delivered in 1968, has been remembered because of its prediction of chaos caused by allowing mass immigration of the dark peoples of the world into the country. However, an often overlooked argument in his speech is not simply that immigration has to stop, but that Britain needed to reverse the movement of people that had already taken place:

> I turn to re-emigration. If all immigration ended tomorrow, the rate of growth of the immigrant and immigrant-descended population would be substantially reduced, but the prospective size of this element in the population would still leave the basic character of the national danger unaffected. This can only be tackled while a considerable proportion of the total still comprises persons who entered this country during the last ten years or so.[44]

Repatriation was a common call from the far right who wanted to 'keep Britain White', who were perfectly happy for Black people to 'go home', to our 'own countries', as long as we no longer polluted Whiteness in Britain. Again, there was never any fear that the nations of the Caribbean or Africa would rise up and challenge the dominance of the Britain, because of the colonial relationship that makes the idea of 'independence' a hollow fantasy. Therefore no call to Black nationhood can be radical if it leaves the existing system intact and is welcomed by Whiteness.

A halfway house between the weak Black Nationalism to connect us to the nation and the strong version that seeks to repatriate Black people to other lands is the call for separation within the geographic area of the existing nation state. The NOI appealed for a 'portion of land' in the South to be given over to African Americans to develop separately from the nation. This idea also spread in the 'Black belt thesis', which emerged from Black communists in the 1920s and held that the South was home to such a large Black population that part of it could secede from the union.[45] But the dangers of segregation led by the White power structure were obvious in America.

The doctrine of 'separate but equal' became enshrined in American race relations with the *Plessy vs Ferguson* decision in 1896.[46] Segregation was deemed legal as long as the facilities provided for both Black and White were equal. This was a key ruling that provided the basis for Jim Crow, the system of segregation in the South, which remained intact until the civil rights movement bought about desegregation and voting reforms in the 1960s. The problem with the concept is that while there was segregation, there was no equality, with African Americans not only being denied access to equivalent services, but also being second class citizens with restricted voting rights. Segregation was used as a tool to disempower and oppress African Americans, providing a glimpse into the problems any Black nation would experience in dealing with an unreformed America. Advocates of a Black nation just outside the nation were keenly aware of the problems with segregation.

While still a member of the NOI, Malcolm X outlined the position on separation in the organisation. He was keen to stress that 'we don't want to be segregated *by* the white man. We don't want to be integrated *with* the white man. We want to be separated *from* the white man'.[47] The distinction between separation and segregation was an attempt to deal with the criticisms that they would simply rectify the oppression of Jim Crow. Malcolm actually argues that reparatory justice is key to this call for separation in that it would be unjust to expect African Americans to flourish in their new land without compensation for the exploitation they had endured:

> the government, again, should supply us with the machinery and the tools necessary to establish our own independent society and our own independent country and in this way it will be creating a solution that the Black man himself, our people ourselves, can bring about if we have that capability.[48]

The separation into a new nation for African Americans was seen as the solution to the limitation of segregation in the

United States. By providing the resources and also the possibility for African Americans to develop their own society, it was hoped that the equality that was denied in America could be achieved.

In the same way that calls for colonisation had support from the far right, so too did the NOI's ambitions for a separate Black nation. Due to their programmes of racial separation the Ku Klux Klan (KKK) and the NOI became curious bedfellows. According to Malcolm, the Klan was supportive of the NOI's goals for national liberation and he negotiated a pact between the two groups to support each other's agendas. As well as dealing with the KKK, the Nation formed alliances with the equally anti-Semitic American Nazi Party, members of which would actually turn up to NOI rallies in their uniforms.[49] At the 1996 National African American Leadership Summit that brought together a range of Black organisations, Farrakhan, leader of the NOI, caused a fist fight to break out when he invited Lyndon La Rouche to speak. La Rouche's participation was so troubling because he was a high-profile far right activist, who supported apartheid and had historic links to the KKK. The NOI's appeal to the far right did not stop at the American border:

> By the early 1980s, Farrakhan's activities and speeches had come to the attention of British fascists, who quickly embraced the black Muslim's programme of racial separatism. The far-right, racist National Front praised Farrakhan as 'God-sent' and subsequently distributed leaflets defending the Nation of Islam's positions.[50]

The political programme of the NOI should never be confused with, or even discussed in the same vein as, a radical politics. However, the aim for a separate Black nation in America was taken up by more progressive forces.

After Malcolm's death, his calls for a Black nation were picked up by the Republic of New Afrika (RNA), founded at the Black Government Conference in 1968. The aim of the movement was to set up a new republic in the Black Belt, which consisted of Alabama, Georgia, Louisiana, Mississippi and South Carolina. In its 1972 Anti-Depression programme, the Republic demanded from America the territory, a vote for Black people on independence and $300 billion in reparations payments to establish the Black nation.[51] The RNA rejected ideas of Western capitalism in how the state should be organised, proposing a form of African socialism, where the wealth was distributed equitably. It also aimed to build international links to protect the new republic by having the new nation recognised by the United Nations. The RNA featured high-profile membership, becoming a standard bearer for Black critical thought in the late 1960s and 1970s. Members included Robert Williams, Queen Mother Audely Moore, Amiri Baraka, Betty Shabazz and Assata Shakur. Given its aims, its roots in Malcolm's ideas and its cast of supporters, the RNA on the surface would seem a logical contribution to Black radicalism. However, complete separation in this manner, even if calls for reparatory justice were fulfilled, still would not lead to the transformation necessary for Black radicalism.

For one thing, the same criticism that was applied to the idea of repatriation still applies. The most likely scenario for the new Black nation in the South would be to fall into a colonial relationship with America. Even if we take Malcolm's call for reparatory justice, America would only agree to a sum that would not cripple it, and to receive support for twenty-five years meant that the system would need to stay intact. It also stands to reason that for America to pay the $300 billion, it would need to be able to do so. In order to be radical, the solutions sought must overturn the system of oppression. America itself is the oppressor, and therefore radical politics must seek to overcome it. Simply leaving, and remaining next door, will not end racism, it will just change the way that it manifests. In many ways, this argument is similar to the ideas of the American Colonization Society, just within the geographic area of America. It is here that we can see another fundamental limitation of its radicalism.

Muhammed specifically calls for a land for 'the 22 million here in North America', while the RNA aims to give a place for African Americans to find sanctuary from racism. This restrictive call entirely ignores the African Diaspora to provide a distinctively American response. It is a call that still clearly fits within the model of 'separate but equal' by not going beyond the boundaries of the nation state. Racism is a global system and therefore Black radicalism must be truly international in how it is conceived. Even if separation would solve the problems for African Americans, it would leave them intact for the rest of the Diaspora. The RNA attempted to add a dimension of internationalism by making connections through the United Nations to other oppressed nations. This approach is problematic because it displays too

much faith in the UN as a body able to equalise power relations between richer and poorer nations. The RNA adopted
this miscalculation from Malcolm, who put a lot of stock
in taking 'Uncle Sam to the world court'.[52] As history has
demonstrated, petitioning the UN has been fruitless for Black
freedom movements, because the institution is controlled by
Western powers.[53] More problematically, the RNA attempted
to add an international element to a fundamentally isolationist
and narrow nationalism. Separation for African Americans,
depending on the support of the American government, is not
at its heart a radical project. It is one that seeks refuge for part
of the Diaspora at the ultimate expense of the rest.

The best example of the limits of the nation outside the
nation may be, ironically, the most successful Black revolution
in history. In 1804 Haiti declared its independence, completing
the rebellion that had started over a decade before. The revolution sent shockwaves around the world, proving that the
might of Europe could be challenged and defeated by enslaved
Africans. One of the impacts of the revolution was the Abolition of the British Slave Trade Act passed in 1807, in large part
because the British were terrified of the African-born enslaved
who were so central to the revolution. Haiti's particular brand of
slavery meant that people were often worked to death and they
would simply restock with fresh African flesh, meaning most of
the population was African-born.[54] Slaving nations were also
terrified that the contagion of revolution would spread across
the Americas and the system would be overturned. This was
particularly the case in the Dominican Republic, which shared
the island with the newly independent Haiti. Upon achieving

freedom Haiti declared itself a sanctuary for those escaping slavery and repelled numerous attempts at European invasions to recapture the island. Haiti is still used as a symbol of resistance across the globe, with figures like Toussain't L'Overture immortalised in the Black imagination. But though they were unable to retake Haiti, Western powers actually achieved a much bigger success with the newly liberated nation.

In 1825 France threatened the young nation with its warships and demanded the equivalent of billions of dollars in compensation for the loss of the colony. In return France would recognise Haitian sovereignty.[55] It took until 1947 for Haiti to make the payment, crippling the country's economy during that time and since. The price paid for Haitain nationhood was not just symbolic; the problems Haiti has faced since its liberation is that it is surrounded by the hostile enemies of Black freedom. Haiti was effectively cut off from the rest of the world and never allowed to be a successful state. The result was internal chaos driven by the poverty that the West created. An American occupation of Haiti in 1915 further destabilised the country and it should come as no surprise that François Duvalier, also known as Papa Doc, was able to come to power in the 1950s and install a violent dictatorship over the island. Haiti remains one of the poorest nations in the world with no route to meaningful change. If ever there was a warning that a Black nation outside the West can succeed without the overthrow of the global system of oppression, it is the story of Haiti.

In the case of Black populations in Western nation states, nationalism is a theoretical discussion, but post-independence there are now numerous former colonies in Africa and the Caribbean that are officially nation states. The search for racial equality in the nation states of the former colonies is even more problematic. At least in America or Britain, there is a faint hope, however illusory, that Black people will be fully integrated into the system and enjoy equal spoils from the nation. Given the neo-colonial relationship that exists with the former colonies, there is almost total futility in seeking a national response to the issues the countries face.

Colonial nationalism

The idea of Jamaican nationalism is a perfect example of the limits of national approaches to freedom. Jamaican nationalism began to emerge as a political project in 1938, with the founding of the People's National Party (PNP) under Norman Manley, and the Jamaican Labour Party, led by his cousin Alexander Bustamate.[56] Importantly, this nationalism was supported and nurtured by the British colonial government which had already cultivated an elite class to help govern the island. Britain designed the transition towards Jamaican independence to be a national system dominated by the two original parties, governed by leaders educated in and produced by the British system. This is the same relationship that exists to this day and should come as no surprise given that the Jamaican nation state is fundamentally a British creation.

'Out of Many, One People' is the national mantra of Jamaica, a creation myth meant to tie the population into a national and multi-racial project. An editorial in the *Jamaican Observer* explained the motto's creation:

> The leadership of the new independent Jamaica and colonialists happily vacating the country wanted to first, assure the wealthy and potential foreign investors that they had no need to fear the desperately poor black masses. Second, it sought to convince the poor black people that those with wealth were their genuine brothers and sisters.[57]

Jamaican nationalism may have succeeded in its first aim of suppressing the masses, which is a key part of any Western nation state project.[58] However, the current state of the nation should make it evident that the second is entirely untrue and has been since before the nation was founded.

Prior to Western interference, Jamaica and the rest of the Caribbean were islands sparsely populated by native Amerindians. Columbus' so-called 'discovery' of the region in 1492 led to European expansion and the genocide of 80% of the native population of the Americas as a whole.[59] The slaughter of the natives meant that Europeans enslaved Africans in order to do the labour necessary to create the industrial revolution in Europe.[60] The majority of the Jamaican population is only Black because of the countless Africans taken there in chains by Europeans. The common conception of Jamaica as 'home' for those who have left the island brings to mind Malcolm's chastisement of African Americans who acted as though they arrived voluntarily on the ship *Mayflower*, with

European pilgrims.[61] The island of Jamaica was a key part of the British Empire, for centuries raising huge revenues from enslaving and killing Black people. There is no way to understand Jamaica and Britain as separate entities, because the entire colony was designed, built and run to enrich Britain. Up until so-called independence in 1962, people born in Jamaica were British subjects, ruled by the crown, paying taxes and living life in service to the mother country. After the Second World War, those born in Jamaica were even invited to work to rebuild Britain, leading to the substantial Jamaican community. This voluntary migration from the Caribbean to Britain is often seen as creating a different relationship between African Caribbeans in Britain and African Americans in the United States.

It is important to recognise that this migration was only voluntary in a very limited view of the term. There are stark similarities in the relationship between the Caribbean and Britain, with the American South and the North. Africans were brought in chains to both the Caribbean and the South, and because they had been enslaved they could only voluntarily migrate after emancipation. During the period of mass migration after the Second World War, Jamaica was British soil, so even though people needed to cross an ocean, this was still internal migration within the British Empire. After independence in 1962 it is not as though the colonial relationship between Jamaica and Britain ceased to exist. It is also no coincidence that independence was granted in the same year that Britain started to limit the migration of Black and Asian people from the colonies by passing the Commonwealth

Immigration Act. Therefore, the illusion of nationhood for Jamaica was primarily granted to limit the number of Black people entering the mother country. The continued migration after 1962 should still be seen in the same way as international migration in America.

Up until 1962, the British Caribbean was essentially the British version of the American South: the former slaveholding part of the British nation, which produced an agrarian economy with a lack of opportunities and jobs, leading to migration to the industrial heartlands. One of the most important myths to dispel is that countries like Jamaica are self-functioning, independent nations. Jamaica has had a measure of political independence since 1962 but its economy is entirely controlled from the outside and is the perfect example of neo-colonial economics.

During the 1970s the Jamaican government under Michael Manley attempted to introduce social democracy to more evenly distribute the wealth and close the gaping inequalities. But the lack of control the island has over its economy became apparent in the response from the international community. The global economic crisis in the 1970s meant that the experiment was blamed for the worsening economy and abandoned in the 1980s. At this point the Jamaican government looked to the International Monetary Fund for loans to support the economy. The problem with these loans is that, like any deal with the devil, there are debilitating strings attached. In order to access the money, nations have to agree to structural adjustments to their economy. These adjustments typically, and certainly in the case of Jamaica, include opening up trade and imports to foreign markets, slashing spending on welfare programmes and ending government subsidies to key industries like food production.[62] The impact of these policies on Jamaica was devastating to the poor, with cuts to provision, and also collapsed agricultural production by flooding the market with foreign produce. In addition to increasing inequality and reducing the limited economic independence of the island, the series of loans from apparently benevolent Western institutions has led to Jamaica having one of the highest debt burdens in the world, currently at around 120% of Gross Domestic Product (GDP).[63] As a result Jamaica spends 'twice as much on debt repayments as it does on education and health combined'.[64] The economic policy of Jamaica is largely dictated by external forces due to these loans, but the economic picture is even bleaker.

In Jamaica the biggest industry by far is tourism, which accounts for 30% of GDP, and employs almost a quarter of the total workforce.[65] An overreliance on tourism is problematic due to the extent to which it makes a country dependent on outside forces. For example, the majority of investment in infrastructure in Jamaica is spent on the tourism trade, building hotels and facilities for visitors. A major road-building project was recently completed on the north coast, to connect the tourist side of the island to the airport. But this kind of investment neglects the less tourist-friendly parts of the island, creating further exclusions. The other major problem with the tourist industry is that it is largely foreign owned, meaning that anywhere between 30% and 80% of the money spent in the industry 'leaks' out of Jamaica.[66] The same is true for other exports, like the diminishing mineral deposits of bauxite.

Foreign ownership of the key parts of the economy means that the biggest source of income for Jamaica is from remittances, which account for 30% of GDP.[67] These are payments made by family members in the Jamaican Diaspora and also pensions to those who have retired to the island after working in the West. Therefore the Jamaican economy is being kept afloat by those who have migrated and kept economic ties. Importantly, this continued relationship depends on the countries to which migration has occurred continuing to welcome Jamaican migrants. In the case of the two primary countries for Jamaican migration, America and Britain, exactly the opposite trend is dominant in immigration policy. As fewer people migrate out, and the previous generations of migrants pass away, this vital source of income for the economy will decline. It is almost unimaginable to think what the impact of a growing population twinned with a steep decline in income will have on the island.

Jamaica's economic future is bleak, and the embrace of colonial nationalism has led to policies and ideas that are the definition of a cul-de-sac. One of the more depressing approaches to this nationalism is the pretence that the economy can become self-sufficient by streamlining and embracing neo-liberal austerity agendas. For example, Andre Haughton, an economics lecturer at the University of the West Indies, opined in his column in the *Gleaner* that 'this year alone, the Government increased spending on social safety net projects to US$14.5 million; a fraction of this could be used to facilitate the establishment of social enterprises to produce niche goods and services for export'.[68] Advocating that one of the most unequal countries in the world should cut back on its paltry welfare spending is problematic enough. Arguing that the money would be better spent in developing exportable commodities in a nation that is in a neo-colonial dependency relationship with the rest of the world takes a special kind of short-sightedness. Jamaica, and the Caribbean as a whole, are net importers of fish.[69] If an island nation cannot even control its waters then it is madness to expect it to be able to gain anything but oppression from the global economy. This is the problem with colonial nationalism; it creates the pretence that Jamaica can possibly be a self-functioning economy that can prosper on the global stage, even though all the evidence is to the contrary.

Perhaps the best example of colonial nationalism is Jamaica's National Diaspora policy. The basis of the policy is to ensure that 'national identity, pride and cultural affinity with "Brand Jamaica" are tenets which will be embraced by all Jamaicans, at home and abroad, and future generations'.[70] The government has recognised that migration from Jamaica has kept the country afloat and is now making strengthening 'national' ties to those who have left a priority.

Remittances are highlighted as an important aspect of Diaspora contributions, with the aim to develop the 'legal and institutional mechanisms implemented to support the[ir] transmission, regulation, measurement'.[71] However, the document also displays the government's problems with individual remittances on a family or personal basis, and the damage that this can do to the nation-building project. In the particularly short section on remittances, given their centrality to the economy, the focus shifts to the 'management' of these payments and exploring 'options for using a portion of remittances for investments created through partnerships with the government and financial institutions in Jamaica'.[72] In the document there is an effort to shift the economic contribution away from an individual connection and towards a national idea of Jamaica, and using social 'remittances, tourism and philanthropic engagements primarily in the sectors of health and education'.[73]

In order to create a sustainable contribution from the Jamaican Diaspora, the policy also recognises the importance of 'engendering national identity and cultural affinity among Jamaican descendants in the second generation and beyond, particularly the youth'.[74] By creating this national affinity with Jamaica the aim is to encourage investment, philanthropy and partnership that will assure the country can succeed. At least the government is acknowledging that the survival of the island requires thinking beyond nation state boundaries. However, it is still based on a narrow conception of the nation. The entire basis of this project is the idea of 'brand Jamaica', and national unity as the mechanism for bringing in the Diaspora. The evidence of remittances is that the Diaspora, in particular the second generation, is personal, with money being sent to family members or in pension payments. There is no reason to assume that Black people born in Britain would have or want a national connection to Jamaica. Nations are always, in part, built on common culture and imagined bonds, but they are solidified by concrete realities of nationhood. The allure of nationhood is never enough, particularly when the second and third generations are often fighting for national status within the countries where they were born. If the fate of Jamaica lies with those born off the island embracing 'brand Jamaica' then the future is very bleak indeed. Even if it were possible to get this national buy-in from the Diaspora, it would remain a very limited and narrow form of colonial nationalism.

One of the reasons the policy highlights that those outside of Jamaica are important is because 'Diaspora capital markets can contribute significantly to national development by mobilizing savings for investments and providing long-term alternatives to facilitate wealth creation'.[75] This is a recognition that out-migration has taken place to developed countries where there are more resources and the aim is to use the Diaspora to utilise access to this wealth to benefit Jamaica. The assumption appears to be that the Jamaican Diaspora has access to this capital, and has ignored the reality that Black people in places like Britain suffer severe forms of economic discrimination. If we cannot mobilise the resources of Britain for those of us in the country, there is little hope of us being able to spread their benefits to Jamaica.

More importantly, what this idea entirely neglects is that the wealth that the Diaspora has access to is derived from the West exploiting countries like Jamaica through neo-colonial trade practices, effectively meaning that this is a policy of supporting the same system that impoverishes Jamaica, in an effort to enrich it. The same applies for all the areas of development in this policy, including remittances, tourism and philanthropy. The entire conception of Jamaica as a nation state, with its own Diaspora that can help better integrate the island into the global economic system is a form of neo-colonialism. Jamaica is a creation of the Western imperial order, and therefore it cannot be the vehicle for its overthrow.

Black Nationalism has all too often been conflated with Black radicalism, making it essential we began the book by drawing clear distinctions. The various forms of Black Nationalism are usually based on narrow concepts of the nation, which mean they do challenge the global social order. From the conservative idea of the 'nation within a nation' to the more militant arguments for land for African Americans, these politics can be accommodated within the status quo. Narrow forms of nationalism across the Diaspora and on the African continent present some of the most short-sighted and dangerous politics that promise to further embed Black people in the global system of racial oppression. Black radicalism must be based on a much broader idea of the nation, one that transcends the limits of the Western idea of the nation state, and unites Africa and its Diaspora to liberate all Black people across the globe.

Chapter 2

Pan-Africanism

One of the most important books for introducing me to the politics of Black radicalism was Stokely Carmichael's (he became Kwame Ture), *Stokely Speaks*. Up to this point I had avoided the vast array of Black political books commanding my parents' bookshelf. I only picked up *Stokely Speaks* because the cover was so unintentionally funny. It had a red background with Stokely holding a shotgun over his head with both hands, complete with Afro and sunglasses. My teenage self was amused and started reading, expecting to find the content as ridiculous as the cover. Instead, the saying about books and their covers has never been truer and I was captivated from beginning to end. Over thirty years after it was published, thousands of miles away, its analysis rang out as though he was speaking to me about the day's events from my living room setee. What really impressed was how the book outlined a politics of liberation that made practical sense. The subtitle of the work is *From Black Power to Pan Africanism* and he argued that the only logical conclusion of Black Power politics in the West was Pan-Africanism. Some of the most powerful words I recall from reading the book that first time are 'a true revolutionary must provide an alternative, not just rhetoric condemning the existing system'.[1]

He outlines Pan-Africanism as an alternative, predicated on a land base and the ability to create a different political and economic system on the continent. Africa has been savaged by both the West and the East because of its wealth of resources, and in Stokely's argument it is this wealth that made the continent uniquely placed to build a different model of society. Pan-Africanism was synonymous with Black radical politics, providing the substance behind the rhetoric.

Pan-Africanism as the mode of the Black revolution has dominated my experience of activist circles since my first reading of *Stokely Speaks.* The Pan-African Congress Movement in Britain has been the standard bearer for work on the liberation of Africa. The fifth Pan-African Congress (PAC) in Manchester in 1945 has been elevated to an almost mythic status for its role in spurring liberation movements across the African continent. The recent commemorations of the seventieth anniversary re-lit this meeting in the radical imaginary and I got caught up in the hype, writing that 'we need to revive the revolutionary spirit of the Pan-African Congress'.[2] It is not difficult to see how the rhetoric of Pan-Africanism would be viewed as being at the forefront of the global movement against imperialism.

Centred on a critique of European colonialism, the Pan-African movement certainly was at the heart of many of the African struggles for independence from colonialism. Shirley Graham DuBois summed up the Pan-African sentiment towards the European colonisers when she argued: 'They love our African sunshine, our beautiful broad rivers, our bright gold, sparkling diamonds, copper, magnesia, bauxite and oil. They do not love Africans or the Children of Africa – wherever they may be'.[3] In his founding of the Organization of Afro-American Unity (OAAU) in 1964, Malcolm X proclaimed that 'Africa will not go forward any faster than we [the Diaspora] will and we will not go forward any faster than Africa will. We have one destiny'.[4] Pan-Africanism was seen to represent the revolutionary overthrow of imperialism on the African continent. Pan-Africanism has become synonymous with movements such as Garveyism, which spread across the globe in the early twentieth century aiming to liberate 'Africa for the Africans'.[5]

Pan-Africanism, however, has a far more complicated history than being the revolutionary antidote to global racism.[6] In much of the literature on the topic the consensus is that, rather than representing a clear set of politics, the movement has 'no founder, or particular set of political tenets' and so 'almost defies definition'.[7] So broad is the realm of the Pan-African that it has been defined as including 'the liberation of Africa; the economic, social and cultural regeneration of Africa; and the promotion of African unity and of African influence in world affairs'.[8] These may all seem like worthwhile goals but Fanon warned that the main problem facing Africa in regard to independence was the lack of a coherent ideology.[9] It is not enough to want to liberate Africa, the question is how we go about doing so. In order to begin to distinguish between the varying forms, Shepperson marked the difference between capital and small 'p' Africanism.[10] Pan-Africanism with a capital letter marks the series of conferences and congresses that were started in London in 1900, while pan-Africanism captures the array of political movements that have put the unity of Africa and the Diaspora at their core.

We must reject this orthodoxy of seeing Pan-Africanism as a wide range of different viewpoints and competing ideas. One of the most infuriating things about the way Black intellectual and political thought is understood is that we lump everything together as though it were one united history. The differences in how Africa is placed at the heart of Black politics are so diverse and contradictory it is an insult to think of them as being part of a whole. Instead, we should view Pan-Africanism *only* as the formal movement that may have had its roots before the first conference in 1900, but was launched at that point. Other traditions have different names, ideas and political bases. Importantly, to separate out the movement in this way is to trace a different reality than the one that has such a hold on the Black radical imaginary.

Far from resulting in revolutionary politics in Africa, the legacy of Pan-Africanism is the Organisation of African Unity (OAU) and after its demise the African Union (AU). Quite rightly, both of these institutions have been heavily criticised for cementing imperialism on the African continent.[11] It is not that Pan-Africanism has been too loosely defined so that it has been 'co-opted and used by the enemies of the African Revolution',[12] but that the movement has from its outset been one that has further embedded Africa into the system of oppression.

Pan-Africanism as imperialism

Britain has been an important site for the formal movement of Pan-Africanism. The first Pan-African Conference and the second congress were convened in London, and perhaps the most influential meeting took place in Manchester in 1945.[13] Britain as the location of the birthplace of organised Pan-Africanism is not a coincidence. Not only was the congress held in Britain, the seat of imperial power, it actually took place in the Palace of Westminster. This is not mere symbolism, but testament to the fact that the movement's origins were not in direct conflict with the colonial administration. In many ways the forerunner to organised Pan-Africanism was not the politics of resistance embedded in slave revolts and anti-imperialism. Instead, it was in the imperial movement to resettle the formerly enslaved in the West back on the African continent. As explained in the previous chapter, efforts to 'save' Africa with enlightened African Americans were conceived as a solution to the supposed race problem in the nineteenth century. Far from representing a rejection of colonialism, these efforts were a collusion in the imperial project and essential to understanding the emergence of Pan-Africanism.

The first Pan-African Conference was organised in Britain in 1900 and spearheaded by the barrister Henry Sylvester Williams.[14] Though the aims of the conference included African unity and improving the conditions of those on the continent and in the Diaspora, the routes to achieving these lie more in the colonisation movement from America than in any radical politics of liberation. Williams saw one of the goals of Pan-Africanism as being to improve the relations between Europeans and Africans, not to overturn the oppressive relationship. He also wanted 'to start a movement looking forward to securing all African races living in *civilized countries* their full rights and to promote their business interests'.[15] Pan-Africanism was founded as a bourgeois project to bring modernisation to the African continent, within the framework of imperialism. There were subsequently Pan-African congresses held in London, Paris and New York. It was not until the fifth of these, in Manchester in 1945, that the delegates called for independence on the African continent. Up until this point they had argued for a form of trusteeship over the colonies, which would still be ruled by European powers. This was the liberal, gradualist, reformist approach of the civil rights movement being enacted on the world stage.

Parallel to the emergence of Pan-Africanism there was a far more radical alternative that called for immediate independence and claimed 'Africa for the Africans, at home and abroad'.[16] The Garvey movement built the Universal Negro Improvement Association (UNIA) into a global organisation with over five million members across the African Diaspora, at its peak.[17] Garvey's message was similar to Pan-Africanism in that he planned for a physical return to the African continent, but not under the auspices of the colonial powers. Central to Garvey's appeal was the rejection of the Westphalian notion of the nation state.[18] Garvey aimed to create a global Black nation with Africa at its centre and a key part of this endeavour was the great conventions, which were held in New York from the 1920s.[19] Unlike the smaller Pan-African congresses with their invited delegates from the limited bourgeois class of Black folk, these were mass events that drew thousands of people. The contrast here is vital to understanding the politics of Pan-Africanism. Due to Garvey's embrace of Africa he is often incorrectly seen as a founder of Pan-Africanism. In fact, while Pan-Africanism developed at the time he was active, during the formative stages of the movement it rejected both him and his more radical ideas of Black sovereignty. The intellectual figure at the heart of Pan-Africanism was W.E.B. Dubois, who was vehemently anti-Garvey, leading to a bitter personal rivalry.

Garvey was an admirer of DuBois, who was actually part of the group that welcomed the American scholar on his visit to Jamaica in 1915.[20] When Garvey moved to Harlem he sought out Dubois in his offices at the *Crisis* magazine in order to see how the two could work together. His experience there was instructive to the differences between the two. Garvey was struck by the lack of Black people employed by the magazine, and Dubois was not keen to embrace Garvey.[21] In fact, Dubois became one of Garvey's fiercest critics, not only attacking his politics but also calling him stupid, ugly and black, in reference to his dark skin tone.[22] This personal attack demonstrates some of the very limited racial politics of DuBois. Hallmarking his early (and continued to some extent later) work is the idea that:

The Negro race, like all races, is going to be saved by its exceptional men. The problem of education, then, among

Negroes must first of all deal with the Talented Tenth; it is the problem of developing the Best of this race that they may guide the Mass away from the contamination and death of the Worst, in their own and other races.[23]

This notion of the 'Best of the race' elevating the masses is the kind of bourgeois sentiment that is the antithesis of Garveyism. Even more problematically, when civilisation is defined as proximity to Whiteness, these ideas also become entangled in the notion of colourism, where being pheno-typically closer to Whiteness also becomes marked as a sign of advancement.[24] Unfortunately, these sentiments are embedded within the early forms of Pan-Africanism, which involved bringing together these upright men to imagine the future for the African continent and Diaspora. While for Pan-Africanism, colourism may not play as central a role, the plan to colonise Africa with the more civilised Black people who had benefited from the West is at the core foundation of the movement. For all the problems of Garveyism, the movement always insisted on being rooted in mass appeal. Pan-Africanism has never achieved this, being mainly coordi-nated between the 'Best of the race' in formal settings.

Britain as a location for the emergence of Pan-Africanism also speaks to the limitations of the movement. As one of the major imperial powers, Britain's influence spreads across the African Diaspora. When Pan-Africanism emerged in 1900, Britain was not limited to the shores of the British Isles. Large parts of Africa and the Caribbean were a part of Britain's imperial project. Henry Sylvester Williams, born in Trinidad, was a barrister in South Africa and founded the first congress in London,[25] and did all of this in Britain. It is not happenstance that London was the site for the first conference; given its status as the metropolis for the colonial outposts it was the logical venue.

As the seat of British imperial power, London also had a central role in reproducing empire. Colonialism could only be carried out with the help of a native bourgeois class that would impart Western wisdom in the colonies. The civil servants and future leaders of Africa and the Caribbean were trained and educated in the West, with Britain being a key landing point. The Pan-African congresses in Europe were therefore mostly made up of this class, the appointed colonial elite. Even some of the more celebrated anti-colonial leaders like Jomo Kenyatta received their education in Britain.[26] Attempts to hold the congresses on African soil were stopped by the imperial powers, worried that ideas of African unity were too dangerous on the continent itself.[27] Separated from the masses, the congresses were free to develop along lines compatible with imperialism.

Dubois himself admitted his earlier problematic view of the African continent. Writing towards the end of his life in 1959 he explained that: 'Once I thought of you Africans as children, whom we educated African Americans would lead to liberty. I was wrong. We could not even lead ourselves, much less you. Today I see you rising under your own leadership, guided by your own brains.'[28] The fact that this realisation had to come to Dubois should be telling. Interestingly, Kwame Nkrumah, the first president of Ghana and a close friend of DuBois, saw his politics as representing 'bourgeois Negro reformism'.[29] In his celebration of DuBois at the sixth Pan-African Congress, Julius Nyerere, president of Tanzania, pointed out that he was not a 'mass or popular leader' and limited his achievements to 'the advances towards human dignity which black people have recorded'.[30] This is one of the greatest limitations of DuBois; from the beginning his work aimed to prove that Black people were equal to, and deserving of, the same treatment as Whites. He was not interested in overthrowing the system of imperialism; he was fundamentally committed to carving out a space of equality for Black people within it. We can see this in his final vision of Pan-Africanism, where he calls for a re-engagement with the congress movement,

> The new series of Pan African congresses would seek common aims of progress for Black Africa, including types of political control, economic cooperation, cultural development, universal education and freedom from religious dogma. The consequent Pan Africa, working together as independent units should seek to develop a new African economy and cultural center standing between Europe and Asia, taking from and contributing to both.[31]

For Dubois, Africa cannot stand on its own feet, and needs to find support from either the West or the East. He even talks of having to 'starve a while longer' in order to extract the best deal.[32] This is not a vision of overturning the system of imperialism, but rather one where Africa can pull itself up to the level where it can fully integrate into the global order. The goal is a form of equality and not a politics of liberation. It is for this reason that 'DuBois's pan-Africanist activities fit squarely within the realm of classical liberal thought',[33] and has contributed to the development of a Pan-African movement that never challenged imperialism. To fully understand the limits of Pan-Africanism it is necessary to examine the role of the nation state in the movement.

Colonial nation state

At the momentous fifth Pan-African Congress in Manchester in 1945 the tenor of the movement changes. There is a declaration that independence is needed for Africa and many of the delegates, including Nkrumah, Nyerere, Kenyatta and Hastings Banda from Malawi, went on to lead their countries to independence.[34] Though there was only one more recognised congress, in Tanzania in 1974, the movement continued through the legacy of formal Pan-African organisation on the continent after independence. The preceding Pan-African congresses laid the foundation for a politics where Africans 'entrusted their new found independence in the colonial state, despite the fact that none of these states had any existence prior to their invention by colonial regimes'.[35]

The container within which independence was allowed to develop in Africa was the colonial nation state. While there were a number of liberation struggles, Europeans were often happy to turn over the running of African nations to the natives.[36] The limits of the nation state set enough boundaries to control against revolutionary notions of African unity. The impact of accepting nation state boundaries was to balkanise the continent, allowing imperial powers to control small territories with limited power. It also solidified national boundaries as artificial divides pitting the proliferation of nations against one another. Pan-African leaders at the time, such as Nyerere, insisted that 'the African national State is an instrument for the unification of Africa, and not for dividing Africa'.[37] The stated aim was to use the development of national movements to independence as a platform for developing a more fundamental African nationalism, which would permeate the colonial borders. However, in much the same way as communist revolutions tend to get stuck in the dictatorship of the proletariat, Pan-Africanism remained firmly rooted in the colonial nation state. As Diop noted, 'for all the fine public statements, multifarious individual and general interests are at work to make people cling to the established frontiers of the various territories'.[38]

From the outset of Pan-Africanism on the continent there were competing nations and groups. The most notable split was between what came to be known as the Monrovia and Casablanca groups of countries. The Casablanca bloc met in Morocco in 1961 and included nations such as Ghana, Egypt and Guinea whose leaders were open to a more fundamental cooperation of African states, under a federal system. Meanwhile, a group of nations met in Monrovia, also in 1961, composed of Nigeria and much of Francophone Africa.[39] The setting of Liberia is more than symbolic given that the country had been the site for one of the largest settlements in the drive to colonise Africa with formerly enslaved Africans from America. This group was steadfastly opposed to the federal approach and insisted on maintaining nation state boundaries and sovereignty.

Founded in 1962, the Organisation of African Unity (OAU) officially brought together the disparate Casablanca and Monrovia groups. This formal commitment was seen by many as a radical step towards unity. Malcolm X took inspiration, explaining that the 'organisation consists of all independent African states who reached the agreement to submerge all differences and combine their efforts toward eliminating from the continent of Africa colonialism and all vestiges of oppression and exploitation being suffered by African people'.[40] So impressed was Malcolm with the OAU that he named his organisation to bring radical change in the West the Organization of Afro-American Unity. Malcolm's optimism, however, proved to be misplaced. This is one of the few miscalculations that Malcolm made in his analysis of the system of racial oppression, but is connected to his other misstep of having too much faith in the United Nations.

By no means was Malcolm alone in putting stock in the promises enshrined in the Atlantic Charter of the UN. Liberal and more radical movements across the globe saw the body, with its one member, one vote system, as a vehicle for holding the West to account.[41] Given the location of the headquarters in New York, the UN became a focal point for Black political movements in America. Malcolm spoke of taking America to the 'world court',[42] and after the assassination of Patrice Lumumba in 1961 there was a protest inside the UN building involving high-profile Black activists including Maya Angelou. It is true, and remains so, that in the General Assembly it is one nation, one vote and the West is outnumbered by the rest of the nations in the world.

In the areas where the General Assembly has control there have been limited benefits to the global majority. For instance, a UN Decade for People of African Descent was declared from 2015. Part of the remit is to call governments to recognise the impacts of their enslavement of African people and to consider paying reparations. However, the existence of the decade is also a reminder of the limits of the UN. There is no money to support these endeavours and no obligation on member states to do anything for the decade, much less consider reparatory justice. The decade is just a rhetorical tool, something that may make us feel empowered but does nothing to empower us. The power in the UN does not lie in the General Assembly. There is no chance that the West would hand over control of world affairs to an actual majority vote. Real decision-making power in global affairs lies in the Security Council and specifically in the hands of the five permanent members: the United States, Russia, France, China and the United Kingdom. While there are ten other member states that are elected to two-year terms, the permanent members all have the power of veto over globally important resolutions that the rest of the UN must adhere to.

The permanent members are a snapshot in time of the bridge from the old colonial order dominated by Britain and France to the emergence of the neo-colonial empire led by America. It also shows the cold war compromises that were struck between East and West, capitalism and communism. In the 1960s, with the battle for the economic future of the globe taking place, this compromise may have represented a victory in itself, especially given the faith that Black radical movements placed in communist countries. However, with communism effectively finished and China and Russia folding into the neo-colonial global order it is now clear that the Security Council members have no interest in the liberation of Africa. Even if the UN did decide to act as a control on the neo-colonial adventures of member states, it has proven itself to be completely incapable. Without the support of a UN resolution America led the invasion of Iraq in 2003, which was effectively illegal. As much hand-wringing as there was from the international community, nothing was done and no one has been charged despite the chaos unleashed. There is no salvation to be found in any international body led by the West.

As fundamental to the issue of power within the UN is the problem that it is based entirely on the Western model of the nation state. Particularly on the African continent this means cementing one of the most serious hurdles to radical political action. The prospect of mathematical superiority in the General Assembly actually led some in the movements for African liberation to celebrate the balkanisation of the continent.[43] The more countries Africa was divided into the more votes it had at the UN. It should be a stark warning sign that the UN incentivised the break-up of Africa under the illusion of global influence.

The UN works because it guarantees nation state sovereignty to each member, and nations are seeking protection for this statehood. In order for the OAU to bring the newly independent African nations together it also had to deal with the issue of sovereignty. The way this was achieved was to insert into the constitution of the OAU the principle of 'non-interference in the internal affairs of individual states'.[44] This nation state compromise blunted the radicalism of the OAU by promoting colonial state nationhood. As Adoghame argued, 'the dilemma of African post-colonial states is that they have not really abandoned the colonial logic of oppression and domination ... One major obstacle to African integration is the fear of losing state sovereignty'.[45]

As much as is made of the Monrovia group leading the charge towards neo-colonial statehood, the Casablanca group was just as complicit. If the principle of African nationalism beyond the nation state was so important, it would not have ceded to the demands of the Monrovia group. So fundamental is the issue of sovereignty that basing unity on the premise of individual nation states undermines any point of having a collective. Even the preferred creation of a federation of states by the Casablanca group would have maintained colonial borders. They may have had less meaning but it is instructive that they would still have been the vehicle for African nationalism. The uncomfortable truth is that most of the leaders who attended the much heralded fifth Pan-African Congress did not strive for African nationalism and revolutionary change, but became heads of African colonial nation states and remained in power well beyond any reasonable period of time. The only leader to whom this does not apply is Nkrumah, who remained a stalwart for revolutionary nationalism until he was overthrown in a coup. Unsurprisingly, it appears as though accepting the limits of colonial nation statehood was a prerequisite for maintaining power in Africa.

Rather than representing a revolutionary body on the African continent the OAU played a role in facilitating the continued grip of imperialism. Malcolm recognised that many of the key players were 'considered Uncle Toms',[46] with a number being complicit in the assassination of the revolutionary leader of Congo, Patrice Lumumba.[47] He had hoped that uniting the continent would lead to differences being erased in the fight against colonialism. It is interesting that, looking at the case of Africa, Malcolm becomes accepting to the notion of compromising ideology. Just a few months earlier he had celebrated China as one 'of the toughest, roughest, most feared countries on this earth'. The reason he gave for this was that there were 'no more Toms in China', because they had been wiped out in the revolution.[48] On founding the OAAU, however, the idea of sitting down with reactionary, traitorous leaders becomes 'maturity'. The OAU could serve as a case study in how unity is not worth sacrificing to ideology.

The failure of the OAU to challenge imperialism is not simply down to a compromise between competing ideas in order to promote unity. The problem is that the ideology of Pan-Africanism was always suited to maintain and not challenge the imperial social order. Given its historical roots, ideas and the leadership of African countries there was little hope of revolutionary nationalism being embraced in the movement. Even at the most radical of the congresses, held in Tanzania in 1974, the ideological limitations of Pan-Africanism were apparent.

Held at a time of armed struggle in Angola and Mozambique, the sixth PAC was the largest of the congresses, drawing in over 1400 delegates from the African continent, South America, Europe, the Caribbean and the United States. The congress came out in support of the armed struggle and also professed a commitment to ideas of socialism.[49] However, for all the rhetoric of liberation that came from the congress it did not practically offer support to revolutionary movements. If anything it was hallmarked by the differences and disunity that have been features of Pan-Africanism in general. There was little agreement amongst the delegates and the African American delegation came in for particular criticism for being too large and disorganised.[50] The sixth PAC also marked the last time an agreed congress took place. After this, formalised Pan-Africanism became crystallised in the OAU and later its successor the African Union.

As with many progressive Black movements, Pan-Africanism became obsessed with Marxism, which will be explored in more detail in Chapter 6 when we discuss the concept of African socialism. The infatuation with socialism in Pan-Africanism also had implications for questions of how race and racism were understood within the movement. Pan-Africanism developed alongside and was partly shaped by its relationship to Garveyism. While the movement was led in the West, with a heavy influence from African American academics like DuBois, 'Garveyism was an embarrassment to it'; but when it moved to the African continent Garvey became 'almost an essential element'.[51] Garvey's influence on the African continent cannot be overstated, with the red, black and green that appears in flags across the continent being a testament to this. Garvey's politics of race were uncompromising and always at odds with a Marxist analysis. For Garvey it was *race first*, and he saw Black people coming together on the continent to liberate themselves.[52] This has put him at odds with Marxists in early Pan-Africanism such as George Padmore, and Garvey's stance on race was also heavily criticised.

Garvey's view of race was controversial because he appears to reify the European conceptions of racial difference. He was vehemently against race mixing so as not to dilute the Blackness of the Diaspora. His belief in this was so strong that he even met with the Ku Klux Klan in America to discuss their similarities on the issue.[53] This problematic view of race led to accusations of racialism, that he reinforced the prejudices of the oppressor and that his politics were therefore ultimately regressive.[54] As revered as Garvey became in Pan-Africanism once the movement shifted to the African continent, there are clear denunciations of unity around race.

Two of the main speeches at the sixth PAC were given by Nyerere and Sekou Toure, president of Guinea. Nyerere makes direct reference to fighting against ideas of 'racialism' in his explanation that the congress had 'non-black participants, and has to concern itself with oppression affecting any man, of any color'.[55] Toure railed against Leopold Senghor's concept of negritude when he argued that 'the racists of Southern Africa and the poets of Negritude all drink from the same fountain of racial prejudice and serve the same cause'.[56] Though he does not mention Garvey, this is clearly logic used to critique his ideas of race and unity.

The embrace of socialism should be seen in the context of rearticulating a rejection of Garveyism within Pan-Africanism. Marxism provided a theoretical basis for the renunciation of Garvey, as he prioritised race over class. The American delegation's dogmatic insistence on scientific socialism at the sixth PAC is emblematic of this reaction.[57] The rejection of Garveyism and the importance of Blackness had important consequences for Pan-Africanism.

The Third World movement offered a promise of a unified resistance to imperialism from the darker parts of the globe.[58] Pan-African leaders embraced this promise as early as the Bandung Afro-Asian conference in 1954,[59] and continued to do so in aligning with communism. As previously explained, this faith was ill-conceived and led to a path of further exploitation. By not rooting the politics around Blackness, the movement never safeguarded the interests of the Black people on the continent or in the Diaspora.

The overt rejection of racialism is also one of the reasons why the movement became trapped in the colonial nation state. As we will discuss in the next chapter, for all of Garvey's flaws, once you view the Black nation as consisting of '400,000,000 men and women with warm blood coursing through their veins' it becomes impossible to be contained by the nation state.[60] The irony is that in the desire to avoid racialism, embrace Marxism and make links to the Third World, Pan-Africanism needlessly rejected the one concept that could have provided the revolutionary glue to the project. Rather than redefining sovereignty, Pan-Africanism developed into one of the most frustrating movements centred on narrow nationalism.

Pan-Africanism as neo-colonialism

The African Union was launched in 2002, after the failure of the OAU to deal with the issues on the continent. The elusive search for African unity was spearheaded by Gadhafi in Libya, but carried over all the problems of its predecessor. The AU continued to enshrine colonial nation statehood as the vehicle for unity and if anything further embraced the logic of Western imperialism. The OAU arose at a time of global revolution, with armed struggle taking place on the African continent. There was real hope for an overturning of the capitalist world order, and though the OAU did nothing to aid in this endeavour it had to give a nod to more radical ideas. In contrast, the AU formed at a time of complete Western domination, after the collapse of not only the revolutionary struggles in Africa, but the fall of the Soviet Union and China's wholehearted embrace of the Western economic and colonial model. All the dissenting voices to the tide of capitalism had at this point been assassinated or run out of office in Western-backed coups. The AU never had to present a façade of revolutionary politics and quickly set about fully integrating the future of the continent into the global system of oppression.

Prior to the founding of the AU, President Thabo Mbeki of South Africa was devising a new way forward for Africa's development, creating a Millennium Action Plan in 2001. Demonstrating the fatal flaw in Mbeki's efforts was that he was attempting to create a strategy that 'both George Bush and Robert Mugabe would sign up to'.[61] He had to appease the dominant Western power on the one hand, and on the other the demagogic leader who seized power in the Zimbabwean liberation struggle only after the revolutionary leaders had been killed. There is perhaps no better metaphor for the limits of Pan-Africanism. This plan was endorsed by the OAU before its demise, being fully adopted by the AU and launched as the New Plan for African Development (NEPAD); it became fully integrated into the structures of the Union in 2010.

To understand the limits of NEPAD we need only listen to Olusegun Obasanjo, former president of Nigeria, who praised the programme for focusing on the key issues of 'bad governance, democracy deficit, corruption, lack of transparency and poor leadership'.[62] His analysis of the problems facing the continent entirely adopted the Western paradigm of development. In this model, Africa is poor because it is backwards and has not gone through the necessary industrial, scientific and political revolutions that have made the West exceptional. This is the classic logic from the Enlightenment, which promotes the idea that knowledge is produced in Europe by the great dead White men and spread out to the less advanced, savage parts of the world. In order to succeed, therefore, Africa needs to learn the lessons from the West and accept its benevolent helping hand.

A doctrine called modernisation theory has come to dominate how we understand international development, which was developed by Rostow in the 1960s. The key tenets of the theory are that backwards countries need to move from their position as 'traditional societies' through a 'drive to maturity', eventually arriving at the 'age of high mass consumption'.[63] Just in case it is not clear that this is very much a hierarchical process, the transition is depicted as an 'evolutionary ladder' that the savages must scale. It is quite literally social Darwinism on a global level. Importantly, the essential element to so-called development is that the West has to come in and provide the necessary industrial and financial aid to set the conditions for economic development. As much work on development theory has evolved since Rostow, it is indisputable that this basic premise still drives the development industry. Whether it is on the nation state, not-for-profit or transnational level, aid is dispensed on the premise that the West knows best. The International Monetary Fund (IMF) and the World Bank have built a formidable reputation for dictating economic policy to developing nations in return for assistance in the form of loans. This advice always looks the same: liberalise the economy by removing trade barriers and state assistance; open up to foreign imports; remove what little state support existed by enforcing extreme austerity measures; and foster 'democratic' models of governance. The technical term for this package of aid has been dubbed the 'Washington consensus', named because it is the proscription of the DC-based IMF, World Bank and the American treasury.

Of course, this entire paradigm is utter nonsense and ignores the role that the West has played in the impoverishment of Africa. The continent is not poor because of corruption, but due to rampant colonial and neo-colonial economics that have destroyed any possibility of prosperity. The current existence of Africa is one entirely manufactured in order to promote the development of Western imperialism. Science and industry may have been central to the emergence of the West, but they were both built on the three pillars of genocide, slavery and colonialism: genocide of the natives of the Americas, where 80% of the population was erased to make way for Western expansion;[64] the transatlantic slave trade, which for three centuries enriched the West on the backs of African flesh to unparalleled levels of wealth;[65] and colonialism, which provided the markets, labour and resources necessary to feed the insatiable hunger of capitalism. The West was built and is maintained on the oppression of the African continent, under-developed by design to provide sustenance to global capital.[66]

It would also be wrong to see these horrors as acts restricted to the distant past. For one thing they continue to shape the world today. Africa would not exist in its current form were it not for borders imposed by European powers, and also would not be the most underpopulated continent without transatlantic slavery killing or forcibly removing countless millions. The wealth extracted from the continent during slavery and colonialism did not just disappear; it is the founda-tion of the current inequalities. Africa was purposefully held back from developing, with the only infrastructure designed to take wealth out of the continent. Even if formal indepen-dence actually marked a removal of Western domination from Africa, the damage caused by slavery and colonialism still has far-reaching consequences today. But the end of Empire and direct rule did not signal the death of Western oppression in Africa. Domination continued, in a different form known as neo-colonialism. Africa is still under the control of the West, both economically and politically.

Rather than providing a helping hand for poorer countries, the development initiatives are actually neo-colonial tools to further embed systems of oppression across the globe. Ghana, covered in the introduction, would be a case in point. The country went to the global institutions looking for money to develop its rice production and the opening up of the markets to American rice ended up destroying the industry, further developing only the nation's dependency on the West. Ghana ended up owing the institutions crippling debts in return for destroying its rice industry.

Ghana is far from the only case of the destruction on the continent by the IMF and the World Bank; we could pick out almost any developing country as an example. After independence in 1980 Zimbabwe managed to halve infant mortality, preside over a growing economy and had no problems with food security during the 1980s.[67] The economy of Zimbabwe was by no means perfect, but it went to the IMF and the Word Bank for a loan after sluggish growth. The country received the money with all the strings that are usually attached. Amongst other things Zimbabwe had to open up to foreign trade, abolish subsidies for key industries like farming and cut government spending. Just some of the results of this action were to drastically reduce healthcare and education spending, cut a quarter of public sector jobs and collapse wages across the country. With reduced public spending the number of women

dying in childbirth doubled from 1990 to 1993, life expec-
tancy fell from sixty-one to forty-eight and the vast majority of
children did not attend secondary school because of the introduction of fees. To make matters worse, all of this social pain
did not result in any economic gain. After the loans Zimbabwe
fell into recession, manufacturing and farming declined and
even foreign direct investment declined during the 1990s. On
top of all of this, Zimbabwe was left with crippling debts from
taking out loans that significantly damaged the economy and
the life chances of the population. It is easy to blame Mugabe
for hyperinflation after he kicked out the White farmers, but
that disaster had been years in the making due to the neo-
colonial claws that are so deeply embedded in Zimbabwe.

When Malcolm stopped condemning individual White
people as devils he could easily have reserved the term for the
IMF and the World Bank. These two institutions have deci-
mated the developing world, allowing corporations to exploit
resources and markets while trapping poor countries into
unsustainable debt. But when you make a deal with the devil
the only thing you can be assured of is pain and suffering.

The very concept of African nations owing any debt to
the West is absurd. The West enriched itself through exploitation and Africa is clearly owed sizeable reparations for the
exploitation of labour and resources and the damage caused to
the continent. But reality is not shaped by what is just, rather
simply by what is. Once we accept that Africa is poor *because*
the West is rich then it is entirely impossible to conceive of
any action the West would take to transform the situation on
the continent. Liberation can only come at the expense of the

prosperity of the West. In academic discussions much is made of the shift from production to consumption in Western economies. However, neither is possible without resources, and Africa remains the continent richest in mineral wealth. None of the technology that the West is so proud of could be produced without the wealth literally stolen from the ground in Africa. If the West had to pay a fair price for these resources then the entire edifice of Western capitalism would crumble.

In order to maintain control of Africa the West has used direct tactics such as the assassination of revolutionary leaders like Patrice Lumumba in the Congo or supporting coups like that which deposed Nkrumah in Ghana. However, political violence has not been the preferred or necessary method for reproducing neo-colonial leadership. Any radical analysis must completely do away with any notion of Western-led development, which is why one of the most insidious features of neo-colonialism is the continued training of future African leaders in Western countries.

The entire structure of Western education is designed to maintain and reproduce the oppressions upon which the system is based. Students from Africa come with good intentions to learn about systems of governance and development that can improve conditions at home. However, they leave poisoned with economic and political ideas created to continue the oppression of the continent. In fact the roots of neo-colonial education are so deep that they have probably already been trained into these ways of thinking in Africa before entering Western universities. White rule is not necessary when the mechanisms of knowledge production are so tightly controlled that the system can reproduce itself through the very population that is trying to overcome its oppression. There is nothing worse that the future leaders of Africa could fill their head with than the propaganda which disguises itself as international development.

Given the Duboisian and colonisation roots of Pan-Africanism, the embrace of Western ideas of development in the AU should come as no surprise. In researching this book I came across an edited collection, *Pan-Africanism Reconsidered*, which draws together papers from a Pan-African conference hosted by the American Society of African Culture in the 1960s. Not only were some of the contributors quoting Rostow but the man himself actually presented a paper. It was called 'Some History Lessons for Africa', and he argued the need on the continent for 'men and women trained appropriately and motivated to operate a modern society'.[68] Obviously, not all of the movement embraced his ideas, but the fact that he could even be entertained at such an event points to the extreme limits of Pan-Africanism.

The AU is effectively based on a model of nation state cooperation, which aims to fully integrate into the global economy. The key word in NEPAD is the partnerships that lie at the core of the supposedly new strategy for development. The agency is meant to be an African initiative but the partnerships it is seeking to form are with the G8, Western developed countries whose resources are seen as necessary to drive economic growth. Before he was deposed Gadhafi registered a defiant tone for NEPAD, proclaiming that Africa would 'accept help, but we refuse conditions. We are not beggars'.[69] Rhetorically, NEPAD is meant to represent a break with the neo-colonial relationship, where Africa decided the projects and engaged in meaningful partnerships with the West to deliver them. Any real hopes that this would happen were dashed very quickly when the G8 refused to back specific projects, like a hydroelectric dam in the Congo, in favour of more vague and general commitments to aid. They insisted on conditions for their funding, including only supporting countries with a track record of 'good governance and economic performance'.[70] The G8 was also keen to emphasise the role of good governance and security on the continent and gloss over the need for infrastructure development, food security and schools and hospitals. The fundamental problem with NEPAD is that rather than recasting the relationship with the West it is ultimately a continuation of the imperial legacy of Pan-Africanism. It is a strategy of going cap in hand to the West for billions of dollars of investment, while accepting all of the neo-colonial conditions which have so disabled African progress.[71] NEPAD's complete adoption of the neo-colonial framework of African development is the logical conclusion of Pan-Africanism: a bourgeois, colonial nation state-led enterprise that looks to further integrate into the oppressive world system, rather than to overturn it.

Part of the reason that Pan-Africanism has been embraced as radicalism is because of the assumption that embracing Africa must represent a radical politics. We all too often act as though African unity in and of itself must lead to revolutionary politics. This was one of the few limitations of Malcolm X's work and why he was more optimistic about the OAU than he should have been. Africa is a place, it is not a politics. If we only focus on unity then it is easy to develop a politics like Pan-Africanism, which compromises any radical analysis to keep the 'uncle Toms' at the table. It is certainly true that in order to rule the continent Western powers have used strategies to divide and conquer, but simply coming together does not represent revolutionary change. National unity within the colonial nation state was used to control the independence process in the same way that Pan-African unity has been used to bring the continent into the global system of oppression. Unity is not enough; we need clear politics and ideology if a movement is to produce radical change.

As dispiriting as this journey from the Pan-African Conference in London to the formation of the AU and NEPAD has been, it is an essential step to charting a truly radical politics of Blackness. Too often we look for the positives in our history and find salvation in the rhetoric rather than the reality. There is not a number of different Pan-Africanisms, there is a clear history, tradition and doctrine that explains the current neo-colonial version of unity. There have certainly been competing ideas and politics for African unity and revolution, but to cast them all in the same mould as Pan-Africanism actually does them a disservice. Pan-Africanism may not be the radical programme it is heralded as being, but there are movements which have radically redefined sovereignty that form the basis for a Black radical approach to nationhood and the liberation of Africa and its Diaspora.

Chapter 3

Black is a Country

'That's offensive, you can't say that' came the interruption from the man in the front row who was so angry it looked as though he only came to the talk to tell me I was wrong. 'There are too many countries in Africa alone to say that "Black is a Country", that is what the Europeans think that we are all the same.' At this point I hadn't even started the talk, which was being held in Harriet Tubman bookshop in Handsworth, Birmingham. The angry audience member was from Zimbabwe and his frustration demonstrated the extent to which the nation state is such a powerful force in how we understand the world. 'Country' is taken to mean the nation state, best summarised by Smith's five components: 'an historic territory or homeland; common myths and historical memories; a common, mass public culture; common legal rights and duties for all members; and a common economy with territorial mobility for members'.[1] For the man who challenged me on the title of the talk, to say that Black was a country erased the 'national' standing that we have all become so invested in. There is no passport, no currency, no elections for the nation of Black, nothing that we are trained to cherish and obey in the nation state framework, so the idea seems foreign to us. In the previous chapter we explored how the trappings of the colonial nation state were a key tool used to entice African leaders into maintaining the neo-colonial oppression. The same is true for the masses, which are sold the idea of a national belonging that separates them from the rest of the continent and the Diaspora. We take for granted the reality of the nation state and believe, because we are told, that the millionaire bankers in the south of Britain are connected to the poor migrant workers picking cockles on the beaches in the north. To question the reality of the nation is to challenge some of the basic assumptions about how we understand the world. But as ingrained as these ideas have become, it does not take too much to unravel them. As I got into the talk and explained the argument and the weak foundation upon which our ideas of nation are built, I could see my accuser's body language change. By the time I had come to the end of the talk he was interrupting me again, this time to tell me that we experienced the same issues across the Diaspora because 'Black *is* a country'. In this chapter we will explore the idea of the global Black nation, an alternative construction of nationhood that is absolutely essential to the politics of Black radicalism.[2]

Empires not nations

One of the greatest myths at the heart of Western knowledge is that the treaty of Westphalia, signed in 1648, brought in the era of sovereign, separate nation states which became the driving force of the modern world.[3] The emergence of the great nations give immense pride to those embedded in nationalist projects in the present day. According to former

British Prime Minister David Cameron, Britain is the country that 'launched the Enlightenment, that abolished slavery, that drove the industrial revolution, that defeated fascism'.[4] The dangers of the nation state go much further than promoting such misty-eyed, rose-tinted reminiscences.

We have fallen into the trap of 'methodological nationalism', in which we 'equate society with nation-state, and see states and their governments as the cornerstones of analysis'.[5] But there are a number of problems with treating the nation state as though it is a natural site for analysis, which must be viewed as a social construction. What becomes key to a discussion about the concept of nation is how 'particular definition[s] often favour one group (in terms of interests and identities) at the expense of the claims of another'.[6] It turns out that the cultural and linguistic sameness central to classic understandings of nation exist in less than 10% of countries recognised by the United Nations. In order to understand this, the role of Western imperialism must be acknowledged. While promoting an ideal form of the culturally unified nation, Western powers enforced artificial national boundaries on continents like Africa, as we explored in the previous chapter. In fact, during the root period of the Western mythic nation, the colonial era, there were in truth very few nations.[7] Most Western states were in reality empires, which do not adhere to any of Smith's mythic five components, with the colonies being subjected to entirely different forms of national belonging than the metropolis.

Once we understand the nation state as a controlling idea, rather than a reality; an ideology, not a natural creation, then we can begin to undo the dominance it has on how we understand the world. The hallmark of Western imperialism is a system of cooperation between so-called nation states in the service of White domination. On the surface it may seem as though there has been conflict between the nations of West, but these have been wars for the resources taken from the collective system of Western oppression. For instance, Britain and France battled for supremacy over the seas and colonies in the seventeenth and eighteenth centuries. The two nations' slave colonies were in direct competition in producing commodities for the world market, and the threat of one nation invading the other's territories always had to be accounted for. But despite all of this, over half of the enslaved Africans in French colonies were taken there by British ships, meaning French slavery could not have survived without the support of Britain.[8] The transatlantic slave trade was a system collectively maintained so that Western powers could engorge themselves. Even countries that were not directly involved in the trade in African flesh enriched themselves off the profits from the system.

We often talk about globalisation as if the interconnectedness of the world today is something new, but 'what is more global than a few European countries colonising almost all of Africa, Asia, Australia and the Americas and organising them into a hierarchical world system of nation-states?'[9] The IMF and the World Bank may be the most blatant collective tools of Western oppression, but they are following in a long tradition.

After the First World War, in the 'scramble for Africa', victorious European powers doled out German-owned territory. The treatment of Germany after the First World War was a major component in stoking the German nationalism that resulted in the barbarous Nazi Party. Again, though, we should not pretend that the Nazis, and their brutal final solution, were unique to the German national ideology. Racial science, a subject that was accepted across Western universities as valid, lay at the heart of the persecution of the Jews. Eugenicists, like Francis Galton at Britain's University College London, were key to developing the logic that led to the extermination of six million Jews. Concentration camps had been developed by the British during the Boer War in South Africa, and lest we forget that genocide is at the foundation of the Western project. The holocaust is an expression of the logic of Western imperialism, the collective system that created race in order to facilitate conquest.[10]

One of the most patronising and dishonest parts of British nationalism is the erasure of the colonies' contribution to both world wars. The sentiment in the period after the war that servicemen were losing out to the foreigners in terms of housing sums up the national ignorance on this issue. Troops from the Empire fought and died in both world wars as well as fully contributing to the war efforts. This should come as no surprise given that the colonies were a part of Britain, and designed to support crown and country. After Britain needed to be rebuilt it again turned to the colonies for the necessary labour, inviting workers into the mother country in large numbers for the first time. The NHS is the perfect example of a so-called British staple that could not exist without support from the Empire. A significant proportion of doctors and nurses are still born in the former colonies, matching a trend that goes back to its founding. Black nurses have historically made a huge contribution to the NHS, so to pretend it is a story of the British Isles alone is a complete fantasy of Whiteness.

The British Isles itself is a contested site of the nation. Scotland may be on the brink of leaving the union; Northern Ireland has always been controversial; and even Wales has its own parliament. The contestation over who is British has created a hiding place for some from the evils committed in the name of the nation. If we see Britain as an empire then it is possible to view Scotland, Wales and Northern Ireland as victims of English colonialism. While constructing the nation of Britain has certainly involved conflict and conquest, to do so would be to get lost in the fantasy of nostalgia. Nation building is always a contested project, and often involves one region subsuming others. The question is not whether there was any force used in creating a nation, but in building the state how regions were incorporated. It would be madness to suggest that the incorporation of the rest of the British Isles into the British nation state was on the same terms as the colonies. Northern Island would have the most compelling case given the terrible history of Britain in relation to Ireland. But so-called Irish slavery was actually indentured labour, which may not have been pleasant but was not equivalent to chattel slavery. As many problems as the Irish have had in Britain it would be difficult to make a case that they remain disadvantaged today. Around 10% of the British population is of Irish descent and they have better than average success in most major economic and social categories. Irish migrants have also made a major contribution to America, becoming White by, amongst other things, racially abusing and lynching

African Americans. The traditions of the New York Police Department are as steeped in memories of Ireland as they are in the blood and bruises of Black people.

For the Scots and the Welsh to claim affinity with the colonies really does display the levels to which the 'psychosis of Whiteness' prevents rational thought.[11] Both parts of the British nation state hugely benefited from slavery and colonialism. It is no coincidence that my surname is Andrews, taken from the Scottish slaver who owned my ancestors in Jamaica. Cities like Glasgow and Edinburgh are knee-deep in money from the slave trade. Wales is no different, and there are still Welsh speakers in Argentina where a colony was formed in Patagonia in 1865. All of the countries of the British Isles benefited from the system of slavery and colonialism, and continue to do so to this day. Rethinking the concept of nation does not include revisiting the status of the component parts of so-called Great Britain. It does however change how we see the place of minorities within Western nation states.

Ghetto as an internal colony

In America, high residential segregation has created large inner city areas where the vast majority of the population is Black and which are hallmarked by high unemployment, poverty and violence. This experience has led to a 180-year tradition of viewing the ghetto as an internal colony.[12]

Carmichael and Hamilton accept that the analogy of the colony is not perfect because in the ghetto there is no appropriation of land or exploitation of raw materials that are then sold back to the population.[13] Although with commodification of Black cultural forms you could argue that the process continues of exploiting raw materials (this time cultural) to be sold back to Black communities. Though the classical relationship of colonialism may not apply, they argue that the 'white power structure is as monolithic as Europe's colonial offices have been to African and Asian colonies'.[14] This can be seen through the political, social and economic domination of Black America by the mainstream.

In terms of political domination, Carmichael and Hamilton argue that the ghetto is controlled by a system of indirect rule, with the people elected to represent the ghetto serving as puppets for the mainstream political parties. As they explain, Black politicians have to 'put loyalty to their political party over loyalty to their constituents and thus nullify any bargaining power the black community might develop ... Colonial politics causes the subject to muffle his voice while participating in the councils of the white power structure'.[15] Within this system Black people strive for political representation in order to get power, without realising that once in elected post their role is to keep the people in check. This dimension of political domination by Black faces, with strings pulled from the outside, is key to the internal colony argument.[16] It is also important to note that this indirect rule is often carried out by the Black people fortunate enough to raise themselves out of the condition of ghettos.

Allen explains how the civil rights gains led to the expansion of a Black middle class that could gain access to mainstream America.[17] In keeping with classic colonialism, this class served to divide and conquer the Black colony and acted as a buffer between the Black masses and the White power structure. Following on from Malcolm X's House versus Field Negro split,[18] it is this class of 'Uncle Toms' that is appointed to manage and suppress revolt in the ghetto.

That the classical colonial economic relationship is not present in the American ghetto has been used to diminish the internal colony argument even by those who mobilise it. Blauner rejects the term colonialism but instead argues that African Americans experience a colonisation complex.[19] This experience is deemed to be similar in many respects to those in the former colonies in terms of being forced into the system; the destruction of culture; being managed by the colonisers; and racism. Blauner's utilisation of the internal colony argument is helpful in better understanding the experience of oppression of African Americans, but it does not see the ghetto as a real colony, subject to economic subordination. Such a lack of economic elaboration is taken by Marxists to be the fundamental flaw with the concept.

In keeping with a Marxist analysis, Burawoy argues that Blacks in America should be 'looked upon as an exploited but nevertheless integral part of capitalist societies',[20] unlike the colonies that are seen as separate entities to the metropolis. However, capitalism is not merely a process of economic development that emerges in Europe and then exploits less developed countries. The colonies are, and always have been, an 'integral part of capitalist societies'. Far from lacking an economic analysis, as Burawoy claims, the internal colony argument is based on an understanding of both the ghetto and the external colonies being economically exploited units within the system of Western imperialism.

The economic exploitation of the internal colony can be traced back to the surplus value extracted during the slave trade.[21] Abolition of slavery was a strategy by the North to control the industrial economy of the South, and the Jim Crow laws further cemented the Black colonial economic exploitation. Post-segregation, economic stagnation and a lack of capital for business start-ups meant that African Americans were dependent for income and products from outside the ghetto, trapped in a colonial relationship.

Alongside the political and economic domination of the ghetto, the internal colony argument also features social and psychological colonialism. The ideas of Black inferiority and imprints of the dominant culture are institutionalised into the ways of life that Black people must depend on in the internal colony. School plays a foundational role in this process, as Tabb explains:

> ghetto schools traditionally teach the history of the 'Mother Country' as if blacks had no part in its development, as if blacks had no identity of their own, no culture, no origins worthy of mention in the chronicles of the world's great nations and peoples. The dominant culture is constantly held up as good, desirable, worthy of emulation. The destruction of the [Black] culture is an important weapon in creating dependence and reinforcing control.[22]

The internal colony argument presents the case that African Americans are controlled through political domination, economic dependency and cultural imperialism through institutionalised practice. However, due to the particular conditions of the American experience, namely slavery within the nation state and high residential segregation, there is a question as to whether this can be applied across Black populations in the West.

In Britain, for instance, though minority groups are concentrated in particular urban centres there is not the high level of residential segregation that is seen in the United States.[23] A key ingredient for an internal colony is therefore missing. However, Tabb argues that 'the spatial separation of colony and colonial power is secondary to the existence of control of the ghetto from the outside through political and economic domination by white society'.[24] Political domination by indirect rule can certainly be applied to the limited Black political class; economic dependency as seen in the United States is an insidious feature of the Black British experience;[25] and cultural imperialism embodied through institutions such as schools has been consistently argued in the British context.[26]

In the traditional nation state view, African Caribbeans and African Americans are invited not to make allies across the Atlantic, but to create movements for equality within their respective nation states. In Britain this manifests itself in embracing 'political blackness', which is the unity of 'African, African-Caribbean, Asian and other visible minority ethnic communities who are oppressed by racism',[27] while in America it is argued that 'people of colour' must build an 'epistemic coalition' to battle against racial injustice.[28] Although there is certainly a place for and a long history of activism in both nation states, such politics is limited by methodological nationalism. It is assumed in the strategic essentialism of people of colour that all those who are not White in a nation state are tied together by their experience of racism. However, this ignores the reality that racial inequality works in far more nuanced ways.

Any analysis of racism in Britain shows that different minority groups experience different levels of success in British society. For example, educational attainment at sixteen (a key measure for success), shows Indian and Chinese students over-performing compared to the White average and Pakistani, Bangladeshi, African and African-Caribbean students traditionally under-performing. Different groups have different levels of access to success in British society, which should not be a surprise given the different histories and experiences of colonialism across the former colonies.

Similar dynamics are true of minority groups in America. A good example of this would be in the Latino community; although they are viewed as people of colour, almost half of them identify as White.[29] There is a history in the United States of Latinos claiming Whiteness, for example Mexican Americans attempting to assimilate in the 1950s as 'whites of a different colour'.[30] There remain issues that African Americans and Latinos should unite on, but it is also increasingly the case that 'as Latinos become more Americanized it is likely that more among them will become white, and we will see an ever-growing distancing from Blackness'.[31]

Political blackness traps us in a regressive nation state logic of race relations. Black radicalism is based on a radical politics that necessitates an analysis of racism that transcends nation state boundaries. Members of African Diasporas separated by thousands of miles are subject to processes of racial oppression that are more similar than those experienced by their allies 'of colour' in the adjacent neighbourhood. To illustrate this connection, the example of African Caribbeans in Britain and African Americans is instructive.

Underlying the history of Black people in the West is the original sin of enslavement. It can be argued that the slave experience of Black people in America is markedly different because the plantations were not on the British Isles. But as we discussed in Chapter 1, we need to conceive of Britain as an empire, not a nation state. The Caribbean was Britain's version of the American South. The migration from the slave-holding South to the free North, and from the Caribbean to enlightened Britain is remarkably similar.

The size of America shielded much of the North from the realities of enslavement, but more importantly from the associated guilt, with it being seen very much as a Southern issue.[32] In a very real way Northerners take responsibility for ending enslavement, but not the system itself. It was the South that had the plantations and the North that fought for the freedom of its African American citizenry. For an example of this, see none other than the romanticism surrounding New York. This was the same New York that was founded by one of the most vicious corporations in history, the Dutch West India Company, and was originally built by slave labour.[33]

British notions of freedom and progressivism are also built on myths surrounding the slave trade. Britain is only ever actively conceived of being engaged in the ending of, and not participation in, enslavement, because the plantations were outside of its borders. Abolitionist heroes like William Wilberforce are elevated in the historical record to obscure the insidious history in which Britain took such a leading role.[34] Largely ignored is the role which British cities played in the slave trade, Liverpool and Bristol in particular, having been built almost entirely off the back of enslavement. What is clearly set up on both sides of the Atlantic is an enlightened part of society that ended enslavement and embraced the Black population, which lies at the heart of the liberal myth of progressivism in both countries.

Black people in both America and the Caribbean found themselves in a post-enslavement society where they remained firmly at the bottom. Both groups had little choice with unemployment but to migrate to the urban centres of their respective saviours. When they arrived in these 'progressive' countries they encountered the same forms of racism. For African Caribbeans in Britain and African Americans in Northern cities of America the stereotype of the aggressive, over-sexualised savage that was key to enslavement formed the basis of relations with the majority population. It should come as no surprise then that in terms of discrimination the experience of African Caribbeans and African Americans (regardless of which part of the country) are mirror images. Education is very good example of this, where both groups are associated with lower educational attainment. If we look more closely at schooling, the arguments about the hidden curriculum, devaluation of Black cultural forms, treatment of Black vernacular language and teacher expectations have been argued to apply equally to both settings.[35] The *nature* of the racism along with the *formation* of racial characterisations facing African Caribbeans in Britain is identical to that faced by African Americans.

In Britain there is no internal colony akin to the expansive American ghetto because the descendants of the enslaved live in the Caribbean, not on the island. So the colonies are the Caribbean islands, or the African nations where migrant families arrived from, but relations on the British Isles remain defined by the colonial relationship. We have to go beyond a national analysis so as not to be blinded to this fundamental point, and when Black people are viewed as a colonised minority it necessitates a transformation, rather than reform, of the societies in which we reside.

Perhaps the most serious issue the internal colony argument has to overcome is that of independence. In the former colonies battles for economic and political independence, though difficult, are conceivable because they exist outside of the physical encompass of the West. The question is how to disentangle the mechanisms of control that the West uses to dictate from afar. Residing in Western nation states means that however much community control can be gained there can never be full independence for the Black population. The advancement of Black people in the West is therefore inextricably linked to the success of the Western nation states in which people reside. For those in the former colonies the relationship is inverse, as Western power and success is generated from neo-colonial exploitation.[36] This relationship would appear not only to undermine the internal colony argument but also to set Black people in the West in opposition to those in the former colonies. This can only be resolved by embracing Black radical positions that are grounded in global understandings, which transcend national boundaries.

For Black radicals, America, Britain or any other Western nation state are not places which we should be seeking to integrate into but rather empires that we need to 'oppose – not beloved communities of shared tradition and aspirations but coercive states to be overthrown'.[37] Black radicalism sees the Black population in the West as cells of displaced Africans who must play their part in the overthrow of the Western empire, as we will explore further in Chapter 8.

Redefining sovereignty

Nation states in the Caribbean and Africa did not exist before European intervention; they are creations of imperialism. Supposed Caribbean nation states are even more so, because the people who inhabit the islands were taken there in chains on European slave ships. The Europeans erased the natives, created plantation societies from stolen Africans, ruled over the colonies and then freed them into separate nation states. Seeing the Caribbean as constituent parts of European nations also means that we have to do away with ideas of colonial nation state sovereignty.

For instance, I often ask audiences who the most influential Black Briton is. When you confine yourselves to the British Isles the answers are uninspiring, which should not be surprising because there have not been that many of us on the island for all that long. Once we open up the nation to include the Empire the answer quickly becomes apparent: Marcus Mosiah Garvey. Garvey was born a subject of the British crown on the island of Jamaica long before the pretence of independence was bestowed. After his incarceration in America he was deported to London, because the authorities feared his influence on the Jamaican colony. They were only able to do this because of his nationality. He died in London in 1940, never having experienced the Jamaican so-called nation state. Garvey is as British as a cup of tea, or going to eat at an Indian restaurant on a weekend. This will sound like heresy to those committed to the Jamaican national project, but it should also point to the limitations of that venture. Garvey understood that he was rejecting the product of an oppressive world system that needed to be overturned and he put no faith in the Jamaican national state. He saw the solution as the physical return of Black people to the African continent, and in doing so entirely redefined claims of national sovereignty.

Ethiopia's place in the Bible meant that it had particular significance to Black movements in the West and also in Africa. 'Princes shall come out of Egypt; Ethiopia shall soon stretch out her hands unto God' (Psalms 68:31 KJB) was used a rallying cry for various movements that sought to connect to Africa. Figures like Blyden and Delaney in the colonisation movement used the passage as a signal to their civilising mission on the continent; while Garvey embraced it as evidence of the need for African self-rule.

The Bible has had so much importance historically because of the role of Christianity in Western imperialism. As Jomo Kenyatta, the first president of Kenya, explained: 'When the missionaries arrived, the Africans had the land and the missionaries had the Bible. They taught us to pray with our eyes closed. When we opened them, they had our land and we had the Bible'.[38] The same verse of the Bible that inspired Black people to self-rule was also used to justify civilising the African savage, stretching out their hands for help from enlightened Christians who could save their heathen souls. Colonialism was not only done by force but by implanting a Western religion with the aim to pacify and control the natives. Missionary education was the dominant form of schooling, teaching not only European languages but the codes of behaviour and values expected of the colonised.

For those who were enslaved, Christianity also was used to attempt this pacifying role, and to de-Africanise the beasts of burden made to toil on the plantations. Reading was forbidden, with the only teaching permitted being from the Bible. A few of the enslaved were allowed to learn to read the Bible in order to teach the word and obedience to the rest of their kin. The result of this history is the embeddedness of Christianity across the Black world. Black participation in churches in the West, the Caribbean and Africa are now outstripping that of White people, with the Anglican Church facing a shift of power away from the mother country. It should come as no surprise that the Bible had such an impact with regard to understandings of Blackness. But as regressive as the history of Christianity and Black people is, they were never able to remove the spirit of resistance from how we interpreted it. There is not a single part of our history where we simply passively accepted what was passed down to us.

Many of the revolts during slavery were led by preachers on the plantations, by figures such as Sam Sharpe in Jamaica and Nat Turner in America. Far from being disabled by the Bible they were spurred on by it, reading it not as a text of submission but as a liberation theology. With the greater freedom to travel around the plantations to spread the word they were also in a unique position to bring together slave revolts. Preacher as slave revolt leader is not our typical association but we need to reform our imaginations. Given the dominance of the church in Black communities, they are perhaps the only independent, well-funded institutions that regularly bring the masses of Black people together, even today. The Black church would do well to remember its roots of resistance.

The spiritual connection to Ethiopia was transformed into a radical redefinition of sovereignty by the invasion of Ethiopia by the Italians. Ethiopia was one of the few parts of Africa untouched by European colonialism at the end of the nineteenth century, but the Italians wanted to expand their colonial territory, which included Eritrea and part of Somalia. In 1896 at the Battle of Adwa the Ethiopians won a decisive victory over colonialism that is still celebrated today. This was an immense source of pride across the Diaspora and galvanised the movement for Ethiopianism. When Ras Tafari

Makonnen Woldemikae was crowned emperor of Ethiopia in 1930, he assumed the name Haile Selassie I, and Western dignitaries came to celebrate his coronation. A picture of Queen Mary bowing to the emperor during the celebrations was extremely powerful at a time when Europe dominated the world. Another image with his foot on an unexploded bomb gave him an almost supernatural aura of power. Selassie became seen as not only the emperor of Ethiopia but of the entire global Black nation.[39] When Italy again launched a colonial invasion under Mussolini in 1934, the global Black nation rallied to protect Ethiopia. In the war that followed, Black people in South Africa and America were stopped by their respective nation states from going to join the battle for Ethiopia. Narrow conceptions of nationalism were torn apart by the desire for Black liberation.

A connection to Ethiopia also birthed the influential Rastafari movement, which remains active today. The movement takes its name from Selassie's title 'Ras' and name 'Tafari' before he became emperor. Rastafari was hugely influential in changing the terms of the debate on racism in West, critiquing the 'Babylon system' as corrupt. Rastas rejected the ways of the 'crazy baldheads' who integrated themselves into the system of colonialism, and they embraced the rural poor of Jamaica, aiming to create a political re-education of the masses. The message has been popularised in reggae music, but it is more than just a cultural movement. Rasta ideology changes how we see the world, presenting a radical critique of the system that oppresses Black people by design. Rastafari has been hugely influential in the West, particularly in Britain, and today represents one of the truly independent and radical critiques in the way that it aims to create new forms of liberatory knowledge.[40] Rastafari also calls for a physical return to the African continent, pledging absolutely no allegiance to colonial nation statehood. In 1948 Selassie gave a portion of land in Ethiopia called Shashamane for Rastas to repatriate back to the continent. Though diminished in size, the settlement remains to this day.

As much as both Ethiopianism and Rastafari redefined sovereignty, embracing the global Black nation, they were both limited in their radical scope by their roots in religion. Ethiopianism never really overcame its foundation in the Black Christian civilising mission of the colonisation movement. Rastafari has developed more along religious lines, making links to the Ethiopian Coptic Church, rather than strengthening its commitment to the revolutionary struggle. Given the religious basis of the connection, both movements have been hurt by their loyalty to Selassie as the vessel. The problem is that the Selassie of myth and divinity in no way matched the real-life figure. Selassie was a staunch ally of the West, a strong defender of colonial nationalism on the continent, and also had his own imperial agenda over Eritrea, which still has implications today.[41] His vision for Pan-Africanism was for a limited set of African institutions, even more watered down than the Monrovia group's plans. Rastafari will be further explored in Chapter 8, but for all its limitations it helped to develop the platform for the global Black nation.

Garveyism

Rastafari's roots are as much in Garveyism as in Ethiopianism, explaining its radical take on sovereignty. Garvey's appeal to the Rastas was his focus on the rural poor and devotion to Africa, and he remains revered in the movement. Garvey's legacy is complicated and Garveyism has significant limitations, by no means representing the perfect ideology of liberation. Garvey's was not a revolutionary economic analysis; in many ways his vision was to create a capitalist Africa that could take its place in the existing economic system. It would be tempting to see Garveyism in the same light as the American Colonization Society, a bourgeois Westernised project wanting to 'modernise' the continent. However, this would be an unfair caricature and ignores the importance of Garveyism's redefinition of nationhood as a revolutionary concept.

The inspiration for Garvey's Universal Negro Improvement Association was his travels around the Caribbean, South America and the United States. He recognised that the plight of the formerly enslaved was the same in each location; that there was a common problem for all to oppose.[42] From its conception Garveyism transcended the nation state, arguing that 'Black is a country', which includes all Africans and their descendants.[43] At the root of his analysis is the conclusion that the West can never provide freedom for Black people, and therefore there is a need to liberate the African continent and for the physical return by those descendants in the Diaspora. The UNIA set about selling shares in order to purchase steamships for the Black Star Line, which would transport those in the West back to the African continent. Garvey was trying to secure land in Liberia in order to resettle the Black population in exile. This is completely different to the colonisation movement in that it was neither sanctioned nor controlled by the imperial powers. Garvey was arguing for the complete liberation and independence from imperialism in Africa, and building a mass organisation, owned by the people, in order to do so.

It is true that Garvey's position from outside the continent is effectively one of Black capitalism. He had a lot of reverence for the West and what he saw as the great achievements it had built. In a speech praising capitalism in general, and J.D. Rockefeller in particular, he explained that White people had nothing to fear from the Garvey movement. He argued that the UNIA was striving for 'progress of and among' Black people that would 'advance them in the respect and appreciation of their fellows'.[44] By their fellows he meant the White world that held Black people in such low esteem. In this respect Garvey's self-help mission is similar to that of Booker T. Washington, who thought that Black people needed to 'pull themselves up by their bootstraps', and make no excuses for the state in which they found themselves.[45] This conservative version of Black self-help still has resonance as it can easily be read as absolving White racism of all responsibility. But Garvey was making no simple appeal to hard work; the reason he advocated the physical return to Africa was that he recognised that due to the structures of racism, no amount of toil in the West could produce Black liberation. Garveyism did not extend to radically transforming the economic system but his reliance on capitalism has been overstated for a number of reasons.

Firstly, because of imperial control Garvey was never able to visit Africa and he was also prevented by federal authorities in America from continuing the work of building the Black Star Line. This is important because political ideas adapt when they are enacted. Had the prospect of nation building been allowed to develop it is very possible that Garvey's economic analysis would have changed. He was not raised to believe that the West could never provide for Black people, but came to this conclusion through experience. The practicalities of establishing a liberated Africa would have necessitated a radical rethink of the economy, given how embedded capitalism is in the system that impoverishes the continent.

Second and relatedly, unlike Pan-Africanism, the UNIA was a mass movement, which meant that the people themselves shaped and influenced the politics and economic ideas. Once you base your politics on the concept of the global Black nation, it necessitates building an analysis that can provide for the masses. Capitalism and imperialism can never provide for all of us, so through the process of doing the work the movement would *have* to have oriented away from capitalism. This is where we need to separate out the radicalism of Garveyism from the limitations of the man himself. The power of Garveyism is creating a movement that both redefined the idea of sovereignty and was led by the masses, both central ingredients to Black radicalism.

The UNIA was an achievement unmatched by any Black social movement before or since. The organisation spread across the Americas, the Caribbean, Europe and onto the African continent between 1915 and into the 1920s, a time before the internet, social media or even widespread use of the telephone. So successful was the UNIA that it was given observer status at the League of Nations in the 1920s. Garveyism was seen as an enemy to the British Empire with its focus on overturning colonialism, and the *Negro World*, the official publication of the organisation, was banned across the colonies because it was deemed to be a seditious paper. Nevertheless the UNIA was so effective at organising Jamaican (meaning British) migrant workers in Haiti that the colonial authorities seriously considered officially recognising the organisation.[46]

Garveyism was full of pageantry and parades and he saw the UNIA as the bedrock of the new global Black nation. He even appointed ambassadors and handed out titles to those across the Black world who were seen as deserving. There was no room for colonial nation statehood in Garvey's analysis or politics, which was a key reason for the success of the organisation. Even though he never set foot on African soil, Garveyism had a massive impact on the continent. During the Kenyan battle for independence people would go from village to village reading out the *Negro World* in their native tongues.[47] As explained in the previous chapter, Garvey was one of the most influential thinkers for Pan-African leaders as his message captured the spirit of liberation. These notions were not alien concepts from a foreign elite: 'Africans in Africa agreed to adopt the theories given birth by Africans in exile, because of the truth these theories embrace'.[48] By no means does Garveyism provide a fully formed radical politics. However, it does include some of the key ingredients, including building a mass movement and being rooted in the revolutionary concept of the global Black nation. Malcolm X later developed these threads into the most complete under-standing of revolutionary Black Nationalism.

Revolutionary Black Nationalism

Malcolm X defined himself as a 'Black nationalist freedom fighter' all the way up until his assassination in 1965.[49] This is important because in the narratives that aim to redeem Malcolm from his days in the Nation of Islam he is often said to have abandoned his Black Nationalism in favour of a more civil rights type of approach to Black politics.[50] This mythical convergence between Malcolm and Martin Luther King never actually took place. Malcolm never stopped embracing Black Nationalism; in fact he best articulates the radical nature of the global Black nation in his redefinition of the idea of being American. Five days before he died, Malcolm explained:

> When I speak of the Afro-American, I'm not speaking of just the 22 million of us who are here in the United States. But the Afro-American is that large number of people in the Western Hemisphere, from the southernmost tip of South America to the northernmost tip of North America, all of whom have a common heritage and have a common origin when you go back to the roots of these people.[51]

Malcolm was always destined to leave the Nation of Islam (NOI) because his politics was far more radical than its narrow nationalism. Throughout his time in the NOI he met with global revolutionary figures, most famously talking to Fidel Castro during his visit to New York. By the time he split with the NOI in 1963 his politics had fully integrated into the revolutionary struggles taking place on the African continent, and this global outlook put him at odds with the organisation that had raised him.

In many ways Malcolm's 'basic ideology was Garveyism'.[52] His father was murdered for being a Garveyite preacher and Malcolm was nurtured by the NOI, which was heavily influenced by the Garvey movement.[53] Malcolm's analysis also located racism as the fundamental site of oppression, but he evolved from a narrower view of race to progress some of the more regressive positions of Garvey and the NOI. For instance, Malcolm abandoned the NOI's blanket indictment of all White people as devils and began to indict Whiteness as a system of control. Prefiguring much of the literature on critical Whiteness, he distinguished White being used as an adjective, as he had heard on his trip through the Muslim world, from what White meant in America: 'When he says he's white, he means something else. You can listen to the sound of his voice – when he says he's white, he means he's a boss. That's right. That's what "white" means in this language'.[54]

After leaving the NOI Malcolm also moved away from Black capitalist ideas of advancement to considering the global battle against imperialism. This meant engaging with, though not wholeheartedly embracing, Marxism, and it was at the Militant Labor Forum in 1965 that he declared: 'it is impossible for this system; this economic system; this political system; this social system; this system, period. It is impossible for it as it stands to produce freedom right now [for Afro-Americans] … in the same way it is impossible for a chicken to produce a duck egg'.[55]

One of Malcolm's strongest criticisms of the civil rights movement was that 'whenever you are in a civil rights struggle, whether you know it or not, you are confining yourself to the jurisdiction of Uncle Sam'.[56] If the goal is to get rights within the nation state, then the message will have to be accepted by the powers that be in order to make the necessary reforms to society. This means having to keep powerful people and the society at large on board. Here we find one of the most fundamental differences between the philosophies of Malcolm and Martin Luther King. King firmly believed that America could be reformed and that activists needed to get powerful people to listen. So he made allies of presidents, politicians and high-profile White people who could help spread the message to turn public opinion. The best example of this would be the 1963 March on Washington, a multi-racial march that ended with a photo opportunity in the White House with Kennedy.

Malcolm slammed the march, condemning it as the 'farce on Washington … a circus, a performance that beat anything Hollywood could ever do'.[57] Malcolm's frustration was that he saw the march as having been taken over by the civil rights leaders who wanted to contain and control the anger of the people. The march was originally a grassroots idea that had arisen out of frustration at the lack of progress on racial issues.

The original protesters were going to march on the Congress, and 'tie it up, bring it to a halt; not let the government proceed. They even said they was going out to the airport and lay down on the runway'; this is what Malcolm saw as the 'the Black revolution'.[58] After the civil rights leaders got involved, they sanitised the march by bringing to bear the weight of their organisations. The organic grassroots movement became tightly organised and controlled, with approved speakers, march route and timings, and they only allowed official placards to be displayed.[59] Malcolm was furious that the march had been infiltrated and integrated, asking 'who ever heard of angry revolutionists swinging their bare feet together with their oppressor in lily-pad park pools, with gospels and guitars and "I Have a Dream" speeches?'[60]

Contrary to the historical memory of Malcolm, his outright rejection of the march had nothing to do with its peaceful nature, or because he hated White people. Rather, the march was the opposite of his politics of liberation. Being limited to nation state boundaries, the civil rights leaders had to control the march, put on a good public face and keep the president happy. This put obvious limits around the appeals and demands that could be made. Malcolm was looking beyond the American nation state and therefore his audience was not the politicians or White society, but solely the Black masses. Only once you have given up on reforming the system can you articulate a politics of liberation, and this means going beyond the limits of the nation state.

Methodological nationalism prevents the struggles in the Diaspora being systematically linked. When Garvey went to

America he faced significant hostility to his politics, partly on the basis that he was from the Caribbean. His ultimate goal of a physical return to Africa was rejected by the Black intelligentsia at the time, who were committed to integrating into the nation state. Dubois dismissed Garvey because he did not understand that 'the American Negro problem is very different from ... the problem of the Negro in the West Indies'.[61] This idea of American exceptionalism is something that has hallmarked much of Black political thought in the nation. By focusing only on African Americans, even the stronger forms of Black Nationalism have forgone a radical analysis. Racism is a global system and therefore any politics that offers a national solution can never be radical, because it will never overturn the existing system.

Malcolm was able to develop and remove some of the serious limitations of Garveyism before he died, but he is indebted to the movement for his political ideology. This is clearest in the formation of the Organization of Afro-American Unity (OAAU). Focusing on his violent rhetoric and anti-White sentiment, the Malcolm of the popular imaginary is a fiery demagogue with no practical programme. In truth when Malcolm died he was building the OAAU as the vehicle for revolutionary change and left a detailed blueprint for his vision in the organisation's constitution.[62] The OAAU insisted on mass membership and was organised around departments on issues such as education, health and defence. The idea was that different locations in the Diaspora would develop their own strategies for combating the key issues that faced them, funded by money from within the community.

The different chapters would then form to make one cohesive organisation built for radical change. Key to this was that the OAAU was made to be an organisation for the Western Hemisphere, taking no regard for nation state boundaries. If this plan were to be fulfilled, the OAAU would have effectively created a government for the African Diaspora in the West, developed from the grassroots level into a global organisation. This may sound unlikely, but it is a model taken directly from the UNIA. If the OAAU were expanded to include the African continent, the blueprint would allow for the creation of a mass movement, rooted in local concerns replacing any idea of the colonial nation state. We explore the OAAU further and this practical programme in Chapter 8.

A key ingredient of Black radicalism is the redefinition of national sovereignty. Radical politics must always reject and dismantle the central pillars of the status quo and there is none more pivotal to Western imperialism than the idea of the nation state. There can be no room in Black radicalism for the narrow nationalisms, in any of their varied forms, which have defined so many Black political movements. Revolutionary Black Nationalism transforms not only how we analyse the problem of racism, but more importantly how we solve it.

Chapter 4

Cultural Nationalism

On 17 January 1969 a meeting took place at the University of California, Los Angeles to discuss the leadership of the Afro-American centre at the college. It was a small meeting with around fifteen people attending but the tension behind the gathering far outstripped the numbers present. The Black Panther Party for Self-Defense and the US Organisation had been fighting over control of not just the centre, but of the Black community in Los Angeles. At the end of the meeting a fight broke out between the groups and two Panthers, Alprentice 'Bunchy' Carter and John Huggins, were shot dead. The killings marked the lowest point of the struggle between the two groups and destabilised both organisations in the aftermath.[1]

Many factors led to the rivalry between the two Black Power groups turning so destructive. Both groups recruited heavily from the 'bad niggers off the block',[2] meaning the politics of the street often collided with revolutionary ideals. The competition for recruitment to an extent aligned along gang lines in LA, with the requisite territorial disputes. One of the main criticisms of the Panthers has been how they did not reform the streets but became trapped in the negative aspects of masculinity and violence.[3] As well as importing gang culture into the politics, the White power structure also played a role in the conflict that led to the shootings. Sowing seeds of division both within and between Black Power groups was one of the major strategies of the Federal Bureau of Investigation's infamous counterintelligence programme (COINTELPRO). The FBI specifically disrupted any alliances between the Panthers and the US Organisation by planting agent provocateurs and fabricating insulting messages in the name of each organisation.[4] As much as it would be reassuring to believe that it was the state that caused the unrest between the two groups, they only added fuel to a much larger fire of division. The Panthers and the US Organisation were destined to conflict, not because of gangs or the feds but due to them embracing entirely different sets of political beliefs, one radical and the other reactionary.

As we will cover in Chapter 6, the Panthers are firmly within the tradition of Black radicalism, with their global politics of liberation. The US Organisation, however, was based on cultural nationalism, which substitutes revolutionary change of the system for the internal mission of saving the self spiritually, by connecting with Africa. The Panthers referred to the US Organisation as 'pork chop nationalists',[5] who obsessed over culture at the expense of revolution. It is no coincidence that US was founded by Malauna Karenga, who lies at the foundation of the regressive politics of cultural nationalism. If the Panthers were the children of Malcolm, then Karenga was his illegitimate child with no rightful claim to his legacy. Karenga has had a major influence on Black politics, with his influence reaching across the Diaspora. The problem is that the regressive politics of cultural nationalism have become conflated with Black radicalism in the popular imaginary. This chapter will present a detailed critique of cultural nationalism, making clear the distinction between its regressive ideals and the politics of Black radicalism. Before doing this, though, we need to consider what makes cultural nationalism so popular.

We are a broken people

It is indisputable that the destruction of African culture was a primary process in maintaining slavery. Europeans did not just enslave us; they sought to break us in order to control us. Central to being able to do so was to create what the late Cedric Robinson called 'the Negro ... who had no civilisation, no cultures, no religions, no history, no place, and finally no humanity that might command consideration'.[6] The Negro was the beast of burden who had no more rights than cattle under the law. The Negro could be traded, abused, raped and worked to death. It was not enough that the enslavers saw us in this way; to prevent revolt they needed us to internalise the nature of the Negro. Therefore, from the very beginning of enslavement everything possible was done to break connections to the African continent. Different tribes were purposefully separated and mixed up on the slave ships to limit communication. African names were replaced with European ones, and we were given the surnames of the masters. African languages and religions were banned, and Christianity was enforced on the plantations. We were taught to loathe Africa, its backwardness and evil black magic. We were taught to fear the remnants of Africa that made it to the New World in the maroon communities that had escaped enslavement, which we will discuss in more depth in Chapter 7. In Jamaica, for example, the maroons were led in the early eighteenth century by Nanny and her brother Cudjoe, who had been Asante leaders in Ghana. In order to scare the enslaved away from attempting to escape to join them, Nanny was painted as an evil witch, with dark and supernatural powers. The idea of traditional African religion as evil and wicked, the voodoo from the horror movies, comes from trying to instil fear in the enslaved. These messages were so powerful they still have purchase; the mysticism surrounding Maroon Town in Jamaica leaves many afraid to stay beyond nightfall even today. As explained in Chapter 3, one of the main motivations for stopping the trade in Africans was because of fear of the influence of those who were African born, who still had connections to their roots.

There was of course resistance, and the connection to Africa remains in the cultural forms that emerged out of enslavement. The widespread celebration of carnival across the Caribbean is a testament to the undying connection to Africa. On the solitary day of the year the enslaved were allowed to celebrate, they used the time to recuperate their African-ness. Carnival is not just culture, it is politics; a statement of never being cowed, of maintaining the links that were supposed to have been extinguished. But the separation of families, the widespread rape of men, women and children, and the unceasing brutality severely damaged the social lives of the enslaved.

Cultural genocide against Black populations did not stop with the end of chattel slavery, nor was it confined to the process of enslavement. Images of the lazy coon, thieving nigger and salacious Black vixen have dominated popular culture for centuries. Blackface in Britain has been a consistent feature since the sixteenth century. Do not believe those who peddle the myth that Blackface is a harmless pastime from the days of mining; the practice far outdates the industry. Blackface comes from the early encounters in Europe with the African Moors who ruled Spain for 800 years from 711 AD. The Blackamoor and 'Ethiop' became features of English popular culture. Donning Blackface was done to signify either evil (the Black threat) or foolishness (the coon). The tradition of Blackface in Morris dancing not only includes the fool sooting up their face but also donning a frizzy wig, wearing coconuts and being called King Coffee, Old Sooty Face or Dirty Bet.[7] Shakespeare's character of Othello was an outlier in that he was seen to be a forthright, commanding and noble presence. That is until he caught the White woman disease and descended into madness, demonstrating the fragility of Blackness. From books, to film, to theatre and the arts, the cultural genocide of Blackness has continued to the present day.

Representations of Black as evil, dirty and inferior have real-world implications. Studies going back as far as 1940 have consistently shown that Black children prefer to play with White dolls from a young age.[8] Results such as these are said to prove the low self-esteem of Black children, poisoned as a result of the legacy of 'four centuries of white supremacist beliefs' being programmed into them.[9] Post-traumatic slave syndrome attempts to explain the devastating legacy that not only enslavement, but the lack of reparations after so-called emancipation had taken place.[10] It is as impossible to truly account for the cost of the dehumanisation of Black people during enslavement as it is to ignore it. In a sense, then, we are seen as a broken people, who have fallen into destructive cultures of being that must be remedied. Healing plays an important role in Black politics, given this history of abuse. Even Kwame Ture (formerly Stokely Carmichael), who denounced cultural nationalism, argued that

> [the] cultural personality of the Black community must be preserved ... integrity includes a pride – in the sense of self-acceptance, not chauvinism – in being Black, in the historical attainment and contributions of Black people. No person can be healthy, complete and mature if he must deny a part of himself.[11]

Cultural 'revolution'

Cultural nationalism emerged to fill this void, the absence of African culture in Black life. In order to become whole again Afrocentrism is the most developed and popular paradigm. Pioneered by Molefi Asante, a professor at Temple University, the discipline aims to restore us to our cultural heritage. As he explains, 'culture is at the base of all values ... a people without an appreciation of the value of historical experiences will always create chaos'.[12] Reclaiming Africa is said to allow for not only a fuller appreciation of the African self but also to restore African knowledge in the 'global village'.[13] This basic premise of centring Black life around a cultural and spiritual return to Africa has been very popular and cemented itself into American academic life and even onto high school curricula.[14]

Afrocentrism owes its intellectual heritage to Maulana Karenga's influence. Karenga laid the foundation for the academic flourishing of cultural nationalism, and is currently a professor at California State University. The founder of US thought that the first stage for Black liberation must be a cultural revolution. One of his lasting achievements was the creation of the celebration Kwanzaa, meaning 'first fruits', which starts on Boxing Day and lasts seven days. The festival is based on seven Afrocentric principles known as the Nguzo Saba, and drapes itself in Garvey's colours, using the Swahili language to draw on for its legitimacy. Rhetorically, Kwanzaa hits all the right notes with its calls for *kujichakalia* (self-determination), *umoja* (unity) and *uhuru* (freedom). Kwanzaa is now very popular across the Diaspora, including in Britain, and is used as a tool to bring Black communities together. On the fiftieth anniversary of the celebration in 2016, Karenga reaffirmed how essential the celebration is to his politics,

It is an act of freedom in its recovery and reconstruction of African culture, our return to its best values and practices and our resistance to the imposition of Eurocentric ways of understanding and engaging the world. Kwanzaa was also conceived as an instrument of struggle, to raise and

cultivate the consciousness of the people, to unite them
around principles that anchored and elevated their lives
and involve them in the struggle to be themselves and free
themselves and build the just and good world we all want,
work for and deserve.[15]

With the history of enslavement and psychological assault
on the formerly enslaved, the appeal of Afrocentrism and
a festival like Kwanzaa is easy to understand. Everything,
including our names, was taken from us, meaning that we still
bear the mark of the master even within our identities. One
of the most fascinating clips to watch of Malcolm X is of an
interview he did on Chicago's news show 'City Desk' on 17
March 1963. Members of the Nation of Islam dropped their
last name and replaced it with an X to remove the slave name
that had been handed down from the plantation. The interviewer pushed Malcolm to reveal his 'real' or 'legal' name and
he steadfastly refused to speak it. When the interviewer asked
him his father's last name he responded 'my father didn't
know his last name. He got it from his grandfather, who got
it from his grandfather, who got it from the slave master'.
Malcolm also stressed the importance of connecting back
to African history and at times spoke of a 'cultural return'.[16]
There is no doubt that restoring a connection to Africa has to
be a part of any progressive Black political movement in the
Diaspora. As Garvey said, 'take the kinks out of your minds,
instead of your hair'.[17]

Cultural nationalism also has a history and a role in
Africa. Until so-called independence Africa was directly

controlled by European powers, meaning Africans had the same colonial education as those in the Diaspora. The majority of these nations retain the school systems of their former mother countries and, as we explored in Chapter 3, one of the key neo-colonial mechanisms is the training of the African political and economic class in Western universities. Africa has not been spared the cultural genocide, with high levels of skin bleaching being a testament to the depth of hatred of Blackness that has taken root. Leopold Senghor was the first president of independent Senegal, taking power in 1960. As well as being a politician he was also a poet who helped mould the negritude movement in the French-speaking colonies. Negritude was founded by the Martiniquean poet Aimé Césaire and focused on centring Blackness and Africa in cultural life, in order to overcome the whitewashing that was so endemic. Césaire's impact was electrifying, creating a 'delirium' in the Caribbean and across the Diaspora.[18] Fanon, never a fan of cultural nationalism, explained the importance of Black people being represented for the first time in cultural terms. He explained that 'before Césaire ... the West Indian identified himself with the white man's attitude, "was a white man"' and that negritude helped to bring a 'new generation into being'.[19] French colonialism always put a particular emphasis on the devastation of other cultures because to be 'French' means to submit to the country's cultural values. This holds true today, with the republic adopting a policy of assimilation towards its minority groups. France does not even keep records of its ethnic population and therefore cannot measure discrimination, because it refuses to formally recognise that there are differences. To be French is to be one, the same, the unified body. Deviations from this cannot be acknowledged, much less tolerated. That is why the ban on face coverings in public was made law, in the name of protecting the sameness of the republic, not of course to penalise the un-French religion of Islam. It should come as no shock that France faces such a serious problem with terrorists bred in the country. The totalitarian approach to French culture and identity means it is impossible for the nation to come to terms with its horrendous slave and colonial history or its legacy. The *banlieues* are filled with the descendants of the French empire, who remain locked out from success in the nation, with far more reasons to hate France than to embrace its whitewashed identity.

France's cultural impact was no less great in its African colonies, with Blackness being just as erased. Therefore, Senghor's influence on Senegal and the African continent was keenly felt. As president he argued for the role of negritude in fully liberating the people. The problem with negritude, or Afrocentrism, is not the idea of reclaiming African culture, which is clearly important given the extent of cultural genocide. The problem is that it presents reclaiming our culture as an end point to liberation itself. Asante would have us believe that 'Malcolm's philosophy generated a thousand ways to fight for liberation',[20] but this is untrue. Culture was one small part of Malcolm's political philosophy of Black radicalism. To take that alone, or apart from political liberation, is to create a hollow and regressive form of politics.

Civic religion

The problems facing Black people worldwide are not in our minds. They are in our streets, the schools, and the political and economic system. There is no way to think, teach or drum our way to freedom. Senghor's version of Pan-Africanism has been severely critiqued, where he reduced the connection of the Diaspora to the 'realm of ideas and aesthetics rather than political activism'.[21] Rather than embrace a revolutionary concept of Black Nationalism, Senghor relied on the poetics of Blackness and in fact was a keen advocate for keeping Senegal within the French system. He argued for the creation of a French commonwealth, explaining that 'in Africa, when children have grown up, they leave their parents' hut, and build a hut of their own by its side. Believe me, we don't want to leave the French compound. We have grown up in it, and it is good to be alive in it. We simply want to build our own huts'.[22]

On achieving independence Senegal maintained close ties to France, retaining the language and also French control of the currency. For all his rhetoric of negritude, Senghor was to all intents and purposes a French man. As president he married a White Frenchwoman; on leaving office he became the first African elected to the Académie Française, the key authority on the French language, and he died in 2001 in his spiritual homeland, France. Senghor's version of Pan-Africanism was clearly a 'reactionary and dangerous concept advocated to retard the African Revolution'.[23] Senghor's politics were all about integrating into France, the imperial infrastructure, and there was no contradiction between this and his cultural nationalism.

To understand the reactionary politics of cultural nationalism we need to view it as a 'civic religion' rather than a political ideology.[24] Hill Collins explains that the movements are based on symbols, dress and other cultural codes. Though the rhetoric may be about freedom, the reality is that cultural nationalism prepares for internal rather than societal transformation. Ras Makonnen spoke of the need for 'Pan-Africanism from within' in order to liberate our minds.[25] Karenga described the Black nation as 'injured physicians who have it within themselves to heal, repair, re-new and remake themselves'.[26] Asante ends his book detailing how Afrocentrism can be used for social change by declaring 'let the artist imagine, let the scientists expand, let the priests see visions, let the writers be free to create, and let an Afrocentric revolution be born!'[27] The whole metric for salvation is based on the cultural system: dressing correctly, using the right language and praying to the correct gods. Mazama, one of the key disciples of Asante, acknowledges as much when she explains that African spirituality is essential for Afrocentrism and that being in tune with 'African metaphysics' is necessary to produce liberatory practice.[28] A version of history is presented where radical figures such as Nat Turner, who used the Bible as his motivation, embraced African spirituality as a starting point for liberatory practice.

Afrocentrism is popular because of the historical attack on Blackness, but Asante's attempts to make it the basis for social change border on the absurd. His practical uses of the concept are limited to a number of different ways to 'help others to take control of their minds and bodies through an Afrocentric lifestyle'.[29] These include avoiding deviations from African symbols and imagining greatness, and he actually argues that progress has been made because we now have salad dressings that are not just named after European countries. Apparently mental liberation includes such revolutionary practices as when flying in an aeroplane thoughtfully considering 'how you would design it Afrocentrically'.[30] Perhaps, the revolution will be televised on the back seat of the headrests at 30,000 feet, and there will be no Eurocentric commercials.

It should come as no surprise that the largest section of Asante's book on applying the lessons of Afrocentrism is focused on the church as these are the biggest Black-owned, Black-led institutions in the Diaspora. Thousands of people flock to Sunday services, and it is one of the few places you can see hundreds of Black people gathering that do not revolve around music and dancing (though even in the church this is a major part of the appeal). Focusing on spiritual salvation over trying to solve the problems facing people in their real lives has been a perpetual issue for the Black church. Once you gear your life towards eternal salvation, it can make the routine struggles seem mundane, even secondary. As Bob Marley famously sang, 'some people think great god will come from the sky, take away everything and make everybody feel high'.[31]

Asante wants an Afrocentric revolution in the Black church, to remove the symbols of Whiteness and recommit the congregation to the Black community. Again, here Asante is drawing some inspiration from Malcolm X, who criticised churches that prayed to a 'white Jesus and a white Mary and some white angels', explaining that those churches were 'preaching white nationalism'.[32] While Malcolm recommends people support those churches that promote Black Nationalism, Asante misses the point. Malcolm is not making a special case for the church; he is telling the world that Black radicals will work with anyone, and explicitly pointing out that religion should not be used to drive the cause. His message in that same speech is 'to leave your religion home ... keep it between you and your god', because it will only get in the way. Malcolm was not against any form of religion as long as it did not detract from the Black revolution, and he did not see an overhaul of the church as an essential or necessary step to revolution. This is one of the most fundamental changes to Malcolm's philosophy after leaving the Nation of Islam.

The NOI is one of the best examples of a civic religion, stressing as it does religious authority and using this as a basis of community action. According to the NOI, Whites were bred by the evil Dr Yacub in order to 'trick and rob and rule the earth'.[33] They are literally devils on earth, whose purpose is to destroy Black people. The leader of the NOI when Malcolm was recruited, Elijah Mohammed, prophesied that the White man's time on the earth had been preordained and that they would soon be wiped out in an Armageddon.[34] Therefore, there could be no solution found to the problems of Black people in politics or revolution. The choice was simple: we could either 'integrate into this wicked race' and 'be destroyed along with them' or separate and inherit the earth.[35] So the NOI focused on building its own way of life; supporting itself through collective economics and; reclaiming minds by connecting to the original nature of the Black man. Importantly, because it was waiting for salvation the NOI did not want to cause too much tension with the state. Malcolm's departure from the group occurred after he learnt that far from practising what he was preaching, Muhammad was committing adultery and had fathered a number of children with his young secretaries. But his split was inevitable on political grounds. Prior to his leaving he had been suspended for speaking his mind on the Kennedy assassination. His explanation that it was simply 'chickens come home to roost' angered Muhammad, who did not want to upset the country at such a tragic time. Malcolm had also been barred from engaging with the civil rights struggle. In 1965 he sent a telegram to George Lincoln Rockwell, the leader of the American Nazi Party, that he was 'no longer held in check' and that 'you and your Ku Klux Klan friends will be met with maximum physical retaliation from those of us who are not hand-cuffed by the disarming philosophy of nonviolence'. For all its blood and damnation rhetoric towards White people, the reality is that the NOI has a history of collaborating with police and state forces to keep order in Black communities. There is a reason why Malcolm was assassinated, while Farrakhan is allowed to retain his pulpit even today. Once we accept religion as *the* solution to the problem of racism we have lost the battle.

Rastafari has been a standard bearer for radical politics, producing the culture and soundtrack for the revolution. In Britain, in particular, the impact of Rasta was profound, with its calls to reject the evils of the 'Babylon system' and presenting a liberation psychology.[36] To be a 'dread' came to be symbolised both by the community and the police as being a rebel, someone who resisted the system. Cloaked in the red, black, green and gold and the politics of Garvey, Rasta has been at the forefront of the rebellions and political movements of Blackness in Britain.

As real as the radical roots of Rastafari are, there has been an ascendency of cultural nationalist themes.[37] Authors such as Nettleford and Owens have highlighted the mysticism and religious sect-like qualities of Rastafari.[38] Campbell argues against this characterisation, but recognises a shift in Rastafari, with the doctrine becoming increasingly religious and more interested in maintaining cultural distinctions than being involved in liberatory politics. He explains how the Jamaican state was involved in strengthening the religious aspects of the Rastafari, by taking action such as officially recognising the Ethiopian Coptic Church.[39] Visions of Selassie as a Christ-like figure emerge later on in Rastafari with this religious turn to the movement. While once Rastafari was shunned and demonised by the national apparatus, the dreaded figure, singing reggae and smoking a spliff, has become an integral part of brand Jamaica. All of this is made possible by the retreat to cultural nationalism that presents no threat to the neo-colonial status quo on the island.

Cultural nationalism is a way of making ourselves feel better without challenging the system. We can find salvation in our African spirituality, or our reasonings where we condemn the Babylon system. We can feel superior to the crazy baldheads and sell-outs who have not come to their true nature. We can fill ourselves with spiritual joy on a Sunday, feeling confident in navigating our lives as we walk with Christ. We can do any of these without having to address the structural causes that so harm us. There is no healing for a broken people while the system that breaks us is left intact.

None of this is a critique of any religion or culture. There are many different routes to Blackness, to the politics of liberation. Islam, Christianity, Afrocentricity and Rastafari can all lead to and play in a part in Black radical becoming. But they should never be confused with Black radicalism itself. Religious people have a role in the Black revolution, but there is no religious solution to our problems, and certainly none that could ever be radical. Once we start to view cultural nationalism as another religious system of belief, we can allocate its place in the revolutionary struggle. As Warren succinctly explains, 'Kwanzaa might liberate the mind but it does little to eliminate economic and political oppression … Culture is crucial to revolution, but it is not revolution'.[40]

Cultural nation within a nation

Cultural nationalism is at its most dangerous when it prevents radical action by masquerading as a politics of liberation. The main way it does this is by providing an alternative way of living that appears to take the followers out of the mainstream system. The NOI was the model for Karenga's US Organisation in the sense that it involved a 'complete acceptance of an alternative lifestyle … dress, mannerism and an entire social life'.[41] Members were given new names and had to submit to the principles of the Kawaida. This kind of wholesale devotion to a way of life can unsurprisingly have a profound impact on the individual, but it has little effect on wider society.

The US Organisation was originally founded by Karenga and Hakim Jamal, who was a close friend of Malcolm X. One of their first activities was to found a newspaper, *Message to the Grassroots*, and to take up Malcolm's political programme. However Jamal quickly left because he saw 'little value in US's use of African rituals and languages' and was dismayed by the cult of personality growing around Karenga.[42] Maulana means 'master teacher' in Swahili, a title Karenga anointed himself with. He was the unquestioned head of the organisation and members had to pledge 'loyalty to Maulana Ron Karenga who believed in us and accepted us before we believed in or accepted ourselves, or him, who found in all our weaknesses a hidden strength who gave us more than we asked from us that something of value which no one can take'.[43]

The new identity, lifestyle and value system showed a devotion to a Karenga that reached 'mystical proportions'.[44] The US Organisation was not only a form of cultural nationalism, but an actual cult. This brand of cult-ural nationalism even included the kind of violence and control we would expect from a sect. Karenga was jailed from 1971 to 1974 for torturing and imprisoning a female US member because he believed she was a traitor. Before those of you who believe in conspiracy theories protest, it should be noted that his own wife testified against him.[45] US was clearly a regressive, cult-like organisation, whose leader's idea of a cultural return was of no revolutionary value. Given this, it is somewhat astounding that Karenga's legacy has been so long-lasting and pervasive. He is the definition of the fruit of the poisonous tree that invalidates Afrocentrism in particular, and post-NOI Black cultural nationalism in general.

Amiri Baraka represents the best attempt, and also the severe limits, of applying cultural nationalism to the social world. Baraka also took his lead from Karenga, and faced the same accusations that his work amounts to 'telling Black people what Blackness is'.[46] He was an integral member of Karenga's US and later founded the Committee for Unified Newark (CFUN). One of the regular events it ran were Soul Sessions, a mixture of dancing, cultural and political talks. One of the attendees at a Soul Session remarked of a Baraka speech, 'I will never forget it. It was dealing with morality, like cleaning up your lifestyle – like drinking smoking, this kind of stuff. The new man, and alternative system'.[47] This kind of transformative appeal is key to the popularity of cultural nationalism, and also its inherently conservative nature.

The Nation of Islam has probably been the most successful organisation at changing the lives of ex-convicts. It recruits heavily in prisons and aims to provide a new social and moral system for those who have been caught up crime. The NOI preaches moral responsibility, clean living, smart dress and discipline. Malcolm always wore a suit, even after he had left the NOI. He spent the first couple of minutes of one of his last speeches apologising because of his attire. His house had been firebombed, ruining his clothes, and he felt he had to give an explanation for his appearance.[48] The sense of belonging and new structure provided to NOI members helps to keep them away from their former lives and from re-offending. But as we have already explained, the NOI does not change the situation for those outside its reach, simply creating a cocoon which members can be a part of. The result is that the politics of clean living becomes *the* solution to the problem, perfectly fitting into right-wing rhetoric about responsibility and family, affirming the 'Black cultural pathology paradigm'.[49]

The high point of Farrakhan's leadership of the Nation of Islam was the Million Man March in 1995. The march saw hundreds of thousands of African Americans march on Washington in order to 'atone to God for our failure as men to be the providers, the protectors, the defenders of our women and children'.[50] We will address the regressive gender politics of this idea later, but it is striking how over forty years after the march for jobs and freedom the rhetoric had changed to atonement for our failures. As much as Malcolm savaged the 1963 march, at least it was trying to address the issue of racism. Malcolm critiqued the alliances with liberal Whites, so it is not difficult to imagine how much scorn he would have poured over the Million Man March's 'political cooperation with white conservatives'.[51] Marching to Washington for atonement almost entirely removes any societal responsibility for the issues that are present in Black communities. Farrakhan and the NOI have always played off being able to reform the inner city, which is seen as 'crime driven, drug crazed, and over-run with immorality'.[52] Having designed a programme of self-repair, they can then stand as the moral guardians, the ones who have cleaned up and offer a model for others to follow. This is why the NOI was praised by Republican vice-presidential candidate Jack Kemp, in 1996, for its 'emphasis on personal responsibility, Black self-sufficiency and morality'.[53] When you focus on the cultural as political, you end up supporting the status quo, because the cultural nation *has* to fit into the existing one.

In fairness to Baraka, he makes the best attempt to deal with the political conservativism at the core of cultural nationalism. He argued that it was not enough to produce revolutionary rhetoric and that the 'most revolutionary Africans as far as the community are concerned, are those who can deliver goods and services'.[54] In the 1960s and 1970s Baraka became one of the key figures of the Modern Black Convention Movement, which organised mass meetings of Black politicians and activists to try to create a Black political alliance. By 1972, at the Black Political Convention in Gary, Indiana Baraka was the de facto leader of the move to create a distinctive Black political agenda. The convention drew in over 10,000 delegates and Baraka's fingerprints are all over the declaration from the convention, which called on the Black nation to stop relying on Democrats and Republicans, and seek to represent ourselves. It declared that the time had come to 'consolidate and organize our own Black role as the vanguard in the struggle for a new society. To accept that challenge is to move into independent Black politics'.[55] Creating the Black nation as a political force within America was seen as vital to success.

Baraka's work in Newark stuck to these narrow nationalist lines. He aimed to create a model for Black Power in practice, developing a 'liberated zone' for African Americans.[56] In order to do this CFUN, along with Karenga's United Brothers, campaigned successfully for Black representation on the city council. In 1974, both Mayor Kenneth Gibson and the head of the city council, Earl Harris, were Black and owed their success to Black cultural nationalist support. In fact, Harris was a former member of United Brothers. With this representation at the political level Baraka pushed forward two urban development projects. The first was Kawaida Towers, a 210-plot development to provide decent housing and a community hub for Black residents. The second was a more expansive vision called the New Ark, which would include affordable quality housing; communal cooking facilities; a multi-purpose community centre; a communications centre to produce television and radio; as well as a medical centre. Both were designed by Black architects and aimed to enhance community life, based as they were on Afrocentric principles.

In order to get this plan approved and funded Baraka had to work closely with federal, state and local officials. To get the dig started on the Kawaida Towers project he even compromised on Afrocentric principles, hiring an Italian building firm as the main contractor and ensuring the building site had White as well as Black labour. He negotiated a minefield of local politics and mob justice to get the project ready to go. However, on the opening of the building site the web he had managed to weave quickly started to unravel. The site for Kawaida Towers was in an Italian neighbourhood, rather than one that housed predominantly African Americans, which caused uproar in the local community. A picket line formed around the dig, the same White politicians who had supported the project in secret openly challenged it in court and violence erupted to stop Black labourers entering the site. The project was held up in the courts and eventually ended when the city council removed its support in the form of a tax break. The collapse of Kawaida Towers also spelled the end of the New Ark project and Baraka's vision of cultural nationalism in practice.

That the project fell apart should come as no surprise given the history of racism and housing in America. White Americans have fought extremely hard to ensure that Black people stay in their place, in substandard housing and away from White neighbourhoods. The limits of any politics that works within the system always end up being the system itself. The idea that Baraka could create a liberation zone within a hostile and racist America speaks volumes to the problems of narrow nationalism. The best that could be hoped for is a much smaller version of the issues we discussed in Chapter 1 in regard to so-called independent former colonies, or Haiti after it won its freedom: a freedom so limited by the surrounding imperialism that it ends up being just another form of subjugation. Even the most progressive form of cultural nationalism cannot ever hope to be radical when it involves working within the system of oppression. The fact that mainstream institutions were keen to work with Baraka is testament enough to his lack of a radical project. What may (or may not) come as more of a surprise though is the role the Black elected officials played in the downfall of the CFUN initiatives.

Within two years of being elected due to CFUN support, Mayor Gibson was already at odds with Baraka, attempting (and failing) to get an opposing slate of candidates elected to the city council. At the outbreak of the hostility over Kawaida Towers the mayor was at first silent, and eventually sided with the White power structure. Council leader Earl Harris was even more brazen in the betrayal of his former backer, at one point declaring him a 'racial extremist', a 'dictator' and declaring that the council would work with anyone else but him.[57] Boiling point was reached when Harris had Karenga and a number of CFUN activists arrested during a council meeting. The strategy of electing Black officials severely backfired on Baraka, to the point that he ended up rejecting integration into the system and advocating a socialist revolution. The problem with cultural nationalism is that it transforms the individual, resurrects and empowers them. As the impact is on the individual then there is nothing that automatically leads to that person using any successes they reap for the benefit of the community. Leaving the structures of power and oppression in place allows for the possibility that these supposedly liberated individuals will fall into the system's ways of working. This is particularly true of politicians, who have routinely showed that they become part of the machine, rather than challenging it.

Lacking a political philosophy, cultural nationalism has also supported the narrow nationalism of Black capitalism. Asante makes it crystal clear that one of the steps to so-called liberation is to 'gain a foothold in every sector of the American economy'.[58] The logic goes that by doing capitalism Afrocentrically we will produce fairer practices. This is the classic liberal argument about representation. The only difference is the idea that we first need to transform into our true African selves in order to deliver the social change. Once we know our history, have pride in self and carry ourselves with an 'erect posture',[59] we will be able to take our rightful seat at the table with the rest of civilised society.

Not only does cultural nationalism embrace the politics of integration, it is also based on claiming 'authenticity' that can be measured by how 'rooted we are in our tradition'.[60] This idea of cultural authenticity is hugely problematic, particularly when it is based on the concept of a return to some mythic, utopian ideal of pre-colonial Africa. The notion that we can look back to a specific point in time where the true African identity can be found is regressive in both theory and practice. There is not one truth of pre-colonial Africa that can be restored, but a number of different interpretations and understandings of that history. What cultural nationalism does is to take a particular view of African history and render it immovable. When we consider who is doing the rendering of history, it becomes clear that a narrow, patriarchal and heteronormative vision of Africa is being created.

Black Power movements in general have been criticised for their gender and sexual politics. Kwame Ture once remarked that the best place for women in the movement was 'prone', meaning on their backs.[61] The Black Panthers had many issues with gender inequality and sexual violence was not uncommon in the party.[62] We tend to deify the great men of history like Malcolm X, Marcus Garvey and Toussaint L'Overture and ignore the women who were integral to those movements. In Chapter 5 we will discuss in more detail the Black radical position on gender, but it is essential to distinguish the politics from cultural nationalism, which is patriarchal and heteronormative at its core.

Building on the success of the Million Man March, Farrakhan took the next logical cultural nationalist step and announced plans to marry 10,000 couples on the fifth anniversary of the march. He explained that he wanted to 'go into the new century and new millennium not black male, black female but as a wholesome family with God at the center'.[63] He also claimed that the march had led to a drop in the crime rate as Black men were 'returning to their families and taking responsibility for their lives'. It is not difficult to see how his ideas have so much support from conservative Whites because it clearly lays the responsibility on the community atoning and recommitting to a more positive and 'wholesome' culture with marriage and stable family at the core. The apparently dysfunctional Black family, with absent fathers and single mothers on welfare, is targeted as the cause of the issues facing Black people.

Before taking these notions apart it is important to acknowledge that the destruction of Black family units has been a consistent feature of racism in the West. When we were kidnapped in chains from Africa this tore apart familial bonds. Systematic efforts were made to split up families on the plantations, breaking apart relationships and removing children from their parents. Constant sexual violence meant that there could be no sanctity of relationships or families. In America enslaved men had no paternal rights, and women were reduced to passing on the inheritance of slavery. After emancipation the conditions for raising a family were far from ideal. Poverty and racial violence made the prospect extremely difficult. We have to consider the impact that thousands of men being lynched would have on the family.

In the British context, the mother country's call for labour after the Second World War was a further assault on the family. The first migration was predominantly male, and people who came to the country started new lives and often families. There is a lot of work to be done on the impact this had on family life, on both the children who stayed in the Caribbean and those who were brought over and had to integrate into new family dynamics. These realities of migration still occur today, presenting the same complex issues.[64] The state has also played a divisive role in Black families, often being far too eager to take children into care because of how they perceive cultural deficits. There have been campaigns both in America and in Britain to keep social workers and the state out of Black families due to this interference.

It is certainly true that Black families in America (and Britain) are more likely to be headed by a single woman. But this should not come as a surprise given the staggeringly high Black male unemployment rate, and the historically unprecedented number who languish in prison every year. We live in a society that has made it extremely difficult for Black men to play a productive role in their families and then wonder why some do not. Western society is certainly geared towards the two-parent nuclear family, and financially it definitely makes sense to have two adults in the house. But there is a much bigger question here as to what is meant by a family.

It is ironic that cultural nationalism puts such emphasis on the nuclear family, when African cultures have been replete with different family forms. 'It takes a village to raise a child' is not just a mantra to keep an eye out for your neighbour's children. It is a recognition that child rearing is a communal activity that stretches beyond the boundaries of the two-parent family. These kinds of practices survived into post-enslavement communities, with grandparents, uncles and aunts (related by blood or otherwise) taking on roles within the family. In Baraka's plans for the New Ark there were to be communal kitchens precisely to acknowledge the role of collective cooking that they did within the organisation. We should be extremely careful about demonising alternative forms of the family just because they do not fit the societal norm.

The Black, or rather the African, family in cultural nationalism is a fixed idea, with specific gender roles. Even when different forms of family are embraced, they remain steeped in patriarchy. The separation of men's and women's roles that exist within the NOI were replicated in groups like the US Organisation. It was the women who did the cooking and served their men. Women were meant to reproduce for the revolution, not actively create it. Karenga made it abundantly clear that the role of a woman was to 'inspire her man, educate her children and participate in social organisation'.[65] Black men were the gods of their household and Karenga even went as far as to say that 'what makes a woman appealing is femininity and she can't be feminine without being submissive'.[66]

I had heard stories from my mother about women having to serve the men in some cultural nationalist movements in the old days. I only half believed them until I witnessed it myself in the twenty-first century. We were at a meeting and food was mentioned; the women around the table just got up, brought out the food and served it up to the hungry warriors. These regressive ideas of family and gender have no place in radical politics; aping the discrimination of mainstream society is not revolutionary.

The narrow ideas of gender also mean that Black women bear the brunt of the blame for dysfunction in the family. By claiming their independence they are seen to be emasculating men and driving them away from their families. The welfare state is said to have destroyed the family by replacing the father with a benefits cheque. By restoring traditional family values, equilibrium can be restored to the family and Black life.

By attempting to restore the traditional family, cultural nationalism logically leaves no room for same-sex relationships. Women's role is to reproduce and men's to plant their seed, so it is unquestioned that the healthy relationship is the heterosexual one. Asante attempts to take a measured tone, arguing that African culture has never persecuted anyone because of their sexuality, but is also sure to mention that it has never been promoted as ideal. He is keen to insist that although he is not 'homophobic', he does not 'support homosexuality as a way of life for black people'.[67] He sees same-sex relationships as a deviation from the African concept of being and therefore 'the optimum relationship, the historical relationship, the biologically natural relationship is between men and women'.[68] Also important in Asante's position on same-sex relationships is what he sees as an agenda that is anti-Black liberation.

One of the reasons he cites for homosexuality being a deviation is that it causes people to place their sexual orientation before their African-ness. He complains that 'black gays are often put in front of white or integrated organizations to show the liberalism of the group', essentially being used as token for another cause. The issue of the gay agenda is one that has a certain amount of purchase in Black communities. As part of the cultural genocide against Black people, the imposition of homosexuality is seen to be one of the tools. The 'feminisation of Black boys' is said to rob them of their manhood and effectively castrate them, so that they are pliable and easy to control.[69] The images of Black homosexuality on television and the idea of teaching about same-sex relationships in schools are seen to be part of this conspiracy. I have had numerous conversations with people who are convinced that there is too much focus on the gay issue, with the aim of blunting Black progress. One of the most uncomfortable moments in my academic career occurred at one of our major Blackness in Britain conferences. A stalwart of the community struggle had been listening to discussions about Blackness and Queerness and snapped. He went on a tirade about the gay agenda, feminisation of Black boys, the spread of HIV and ended with 'I'm sick of all this Battymanism!' As you can probably imagine, the room exploded in outrage and dissent. When confronted with these kinds of attitudes it is easy to dismiss them as outrageous and try to silence them. Unfortunately, they are more commonplace and deep-rooted than we would perhaps like to believe. The idea of the gay agenda can be traced all the way back to enslavement. Rape was not just reserved for women, but was a tool used to 'correct' men who were enslaved, to punish and placate them. The rejection of homosexuality that is seen in Black communities is at least in part attributable to the legacy of such abuses never having been dealt with. None of this is to excuse homophobia, which has some terrible, even deadly consequences. But in order to overcome it we need to understand and trace its roots. The problem with cultural nationalism is that it is based on principles that will never be able to accept same-sex relationships.

If freedom is about finding the authentic self, it means being entirely proscriptive in defining what that self is. There can be no space for deviation from the accepted norm, because to do so ruins the very basis of liberation. Defining the authentic by a mythic conception of Africa compounds the issue by freezing Black identity in the past. It may well be true that polygamy was the basis of tribal life and there was a clear gendered division of labour in pre-colonial Africa. It may also be true that homosexuality was given no space or legitimacy. It is likely that this is not actually the case, but the truth of the matter is irrelevant. Debating the cultural norms of communities centuries past can never lead to any progressive ideals or outcomes. Although Europe interrupted Africa's progress, the idea that hundreds of years ago pre-colonial Africa was some kind of utopia of values is clearly nonsensical.

There was no unified Africa in pre-colonial times. There were different kingdoms, empires and tribes speaking diverse languages with a range of cultural traditions. Attempting to define a restricted African culture is exactly how Europeans treated (and continue to treat) the continent. When Blackness becomes a set of behaviours, ideas and cultural codes then it is easy to conflate the idea with race, a limiting set of attributes to be that should rightfully be rejected. As will be discussed in the next chapter, it is precisely this kind of logic that has led to Blackness and Black politics being so heavily criticised.

Just as importantly, the Sankofa bird of the Ghanaian Adinkrah symbols has two heads, one looking to the past and one to the future. It is not simply fixed on the past as the salvation, but acknowledges that as we develop we adapt and change. The radical nationalism that lies at the heart of Black radicalism cannot be contained in traditions from pre-colonial Africa. In fact, some of those traditions would necessarily need to be transcended. Tribalism is certainly an African tradition but it is the antithesis of the unity needed to create the global Black nation. Even Nkrumah, who used tribalism in order to gain power, understood that it prevented the unification he sought.[70] Rather than being forward looking, however, cultural nationalism stresses tradition, even when it goes against the logic of African unity.

Black or African

A perfect example of the regressive nature of cultural nationalism is the insistence that proclaiming oneself to be African is an essential step to liberation. I have lost count of the number of times I have been challenged on using the word Black by people who insist that referring to yourself as African is an evolution. The logic runs that we used to be Niggers, then Negroes, then Coloured, then Black, then Afro, and finally African. We have now arrived at our rightful designation and 'the use of the term "black" for Africans should be abandoned'.[71] It is probably the question I am most asked about, and when we started the Black Studies degree at Birmingham City University I had to deal with a potential petition that wanted the course renamed because they found the term 'Black' offensive. The 'African or Black' question is a seemingly endless debate rooted in a cultural nationalist perspective that freedom is a mental state rather than a structural one. The fact the question is still raised indicates the limits of cultural nationalism.

The idea of evolution suggests that as we have moved through different stages of identity we have also made social progress. When we were enslaved we were Niggers and now that we can be bankers we are Africans. This demonstrates the conservative nature of the politics. Rather than focus on Black suffering, we should rejoice in the glory of our African-ness. Unfortunately, progress is an illusion. For all the freedoms some of us enjoy, Black people remain locked out of the social system worldwide. The prison industrial complex and mass unemployment in the West; extreme poverty and violence in the Caribbean, Latin America and parts of Africa; and three million children a year dying in East and Southern Africa alone for no good reason. African migrants crossing the Mediterranean Sea are purposely left to drown, their floating bodies used as dead Nigger buoys to warn off other Niggers from attempting to come to Europe. To pretend that we have made any progress in these conditions is to succumb to the delusions of advancement that have kept the West afloat. This brings to mind Tupac Shakur's passionate defence of his use of the word Nigga during a panel discussion:

> I don't care if you're a lawyer, if you're a man, if you're an African American, if you're whatever the fuck you think you are. We're thugs and Niggas to these motherfuckers … How you gonna be a man if you're starving? You know? You could go to four or five different houses and there ain't a man in any one of those motherfuckers. How we gonna be African Americans if we out here dying? We're thugs and we're Niggas until we set this shit straight.[72]

He is literally spitting these words out of his mouth, so frustrated is he by the idea that calling yourself an African is any kind of progress. We can only judge our success by how far we have improved the condition of the Black nation, and we are desperately failing by that metric. Calling yourself an African, wearing Kente cloth and celebrating Kwanzaa is a lifestyle choice and not an achievement. Tupac reminds us of our political commitment to each other over our individual quest for selfhood. His remarks should also challenge the idea that language is all-powerful. Meaning gives language sense rather than the other way round. When Tupac says Nigga, or Malcolm said Black, or Garvey said Negro, they were all drawing on radical conceptions of Black unity. How they used these words is far preferable to how the cultural nationalists mobilise the term African.

Africa is a place, not a politics. As we discovered in the last chapter on Pan-Africanism, neo-colonialism can make just as strong claims to Africa as can radical politics. If being African meant embracing a politics of liberation then there would surely be no problems on the continent itself. Many supposedly authentic African leaders have sold out to Western interests; in fact many have done so in the name of Africanism. If being culturally African is the marker of authenticity then surely the White settler colonialists who have laid down roots and embraced the native culture are now equally African. I have sat in meetings with staunch cultural nationalists who refute the word Black, and when it has come to discussing the politics of the continent they have had to use Black to distinguish between the indigenous and the settlers. I constantly hear that Black is inauthentic because 'they don't use Black in Africa'. For one thing that is not actually true. But more importantly, the politics of Blackness is just as important for those on the continent as it is for the Diaspora.

People who do not like the word Black simply do not understand it. Black is beautiful and Blackness is liberation. The politics of Blackness rejects the faux unity, principles and notions of self that lay at the foundation of cultural nationalism. These are entirely inauthentic visions of an African identity that in truth has never existed. In constructing a narrow, patriarchal and conservative view of African-ness not only is cultural nationalism not radical, it is actually a regressive politics that must be overcome. In the next chapter we will explore the Blackness that is forward-looking, building on what has gone before but laying a foundation for the liberation of Africa and its Diaspora. Blackness is never a complete process, but is essential for the politics of Black radicalism.

Chapter 5

Blackness

Beyoncé's performance during Super Bowl 50 was hailed as a representing 'a new political moment',[1] delivering as she did a 'radical halftime statement'.[2] Clad in black leather and singing about loving her 'Negro nose', she paid homage to the Black Panthers, with raised fists and all. This outpouring of Black pride was one of the most watched spectacles on television and drew praise, including from Black Lives Matter activist Melina Abdullah who was impressed that Beyoncé was using her 'artistry to advance social justice'.[3] The Super Bowl performance in tandem with the video for *Formation*, with its strong anti-police violence message, raised Beyoncé from performer to activist.

For days after the Super Bowl my social media timelines were full of awe for Beyoncé's bravery and apparently revolutionary act in taking Blackness to the half-time show. I was mostly surprised by the response. I had watched the performance live and honestly had not even noticed the supposedly political statement; as far as I could see it was a case of Beyoncé being Beyoncé. There were the customary well-choreographed dance routines, on-point vocals and of course the nod to sexualisation, with her and the dancers wearing fishnet tights, hot pants and garters. We get so used to this commodification of Blackness that I didn't even have a response. Well done to Beyoncé for finding her niche and exploiting it for every penny. But the reaction from Black people across the spectrum was truly troubling. When we are canonising pop artists' performances during the most commercial moment in mainstream culture as revolutionary, then Black politics has reached its low point.

There was nothing brave or activist about Beyoncé's performance, it was well-orchestrated and sanctioned by the mainstream media. She received some criticism from the right-wing press and the police, but all that just played into the marketing campaign. Beyoncé was not risking anything during the performance, unlike when Nina Simone wrote *Mississippi Goddamn*. The civil rights anthem about America's naked racism sparked a major backlash against Simone. The song was banned in several states, significantly damaged her career and she eventually left the country. Simone openly condemned America at a time of extraordinary racial violence, and even her level of stardom could not guarantee her safety. Beyoncé eventually making the choice to sing about being Black, with mild references to her nose and the Jackson 5, once she had attained a level of celebrity that completely incubated her from real-world consequences, pales in comparison. To elevate Beyoncé's performance to the level of activism disrespects the struggles and sacrifices that have gone before.

What really incensed me about the reaction to the performance was the idea that Beyoncé was treading new ground with her ode to the Panthers. In reality she was drawing on the same tropes of Black Nationalism we covered in Chapter

1. The top half of her costume was two ammunition belts, invoking the violent masculinist memory of the Panthers. The bottom half, with fishnets and garters, clearly gives women a particular role in the struggle. The Black Panthers had a uniform, and it did not involve fishnet tights and garters. This sexualised representation of women in the Panthers in the mainstream media is nothing new. Blaxploitation movies in the 1970s were popular precisely because of this patriarchal representation of Black Power politics. Pam Grier's Foxy Brown is the embodiment of this view of Black female supposed liberation. In one movie poster she is described as 'brown sugar and spice, but if you don't treat her nice, she'll put you on ice'. Foxy Brown had two main assets to appeal to mainstream audiences, and neither involved revolutionary politics. Worse still, Beyoncé had already invoked this trope of Blaxploitation when she played the role of Foxxy Cleopatra in *Austin Powers in Goldmember*. Not only was the representation of the Panthers regressive, but we had already seen it from Beyoncé over a decade ago.

After a few days of being deluged by the adulation for the half-time show I penned a piece for the *Independent* explaining why I thought people were getting a bit too caught up in the hype. Of all the things I have written this got the most volume and negative response on social media. The headline that the paper gave the article certainly did not help the reception: 'Beyoncé's "bootylicious" sexualisation of black women isn't inspiring'.[4] My argument that Beyoncé was reproducing sexist tropes of Black women was greeted by a deluge of criticism, including being called an Uncle Tom and being guilty of misogynoir. I well and truly kicked the Beyhive by calling out the sexual politics and lack of revolutionary credentials of Queen Bey. I probably should not have been surprised by the response; the image of a Black man policing the body of a Black woman is one that sparks a lot of emotions and for good reason, as we will explore in this chapter. Something missed in the criticism of my piece is that I have no problem with Beyoncé advancing her career in any way she sees fit. If she wants to shake her booty, try to look as light skinned as possible or pay homage to the Panthers by drawing on regressive tropes, then more power (just not Black power) to her. My problem is with the response to her supposedly radical performance, rather than the spectacle itself, which I honestly had no reaction to at all. To dismiss the critique of her performance because of misogynoir is to divert attention from the point being made. Comments from bell hooks about Beyoncé's *Lemonade* were just as mauled by the Beyhive.[5] These arguments are not about trying to police how people use their bodies, but a critique of the politics that are attached to such performances.

Beyoncé's performance was undeniably a political act, one endorsed by the Columbia Broadcasting Service (CBS), the National Football League (NFL) and a whole host of corporate sponsors. It was not subversive, or remotely radical. Unfortunately, Beyoncé at the Super Bowl managed to draw on the same reductive problematic tropes of Black politics that have so prevented us from having a proper discussion of gender, sexuality and Blackness. Black radicalism has to account for all the varied forms of Blackness and in this chapter we will consider just how the politics has done so.

Black radicalism is anti-misogynoir

In the first four chapters of this book I have dealt in depth with the need to separate out different strands of Black politics. There is no such thing as a unified take on Black Power; there are a variety of different ideas and movements, many of which violently disagree with each other. But the collective memory conflates and confuses these different politics into a mass trope of a movement defined by violence and misogyny. In constructing our understandings of Black Power movements it is as though we have collectively agreed that 'womanhood was not essential to revolution. Or so everyone thought by the end of the 1960s'.[6] Michele Wallace's highly controversial book *Black Macho and the Myth of the Black Superwoman* has been taken as a credible account of Black Power politics, even though she reduces the movement to a quest for 'black manhood, black macho – which could combine the ghetto cunning, cool, and unrestrained sexuality of black survival'.[7] In this reductive account of the movement, Kwame Ture's call for Black Power was nothing more than 'a black man with an erect phallus, and he was pushing it up into the face of America'.[8] Endorsing this reductive view of the movement does a disservice not only to the men, but also to the women involved.

Across a range of Black activist movements there is no denying that there have been issues with sexism and misogyny. For example, the Panthers have faced heavy criticism for the way women were treated in the movement. But there is nothing special about Black Power or Black activism in this regard. For example, the Socialist Workers Party in Britain is in crisis after covering up rapes of women in the organisation. To mark out Black Power as some kind of unique space of misogyny is to do the work of the state in discrediting the politics.

Certainly true is that the 'hetero-patriarchal Black male body' has dominated 'mainstream scholarship'.[9] Not only do we view the history of Black struggle through great Black leaders, most of the writing is done by Black men too. This book is a case in point; a brief scan of the authors cited so far and their subjects demonstrates a male-centric discussion. Much more must be done to bring out the voice of women in this history and scholarship. But we should never confuse the historical record or collective memory with the actual reality of the movements that took place. This is why I have gone to such lengths in the book to distinguish the different traditions of Black politics. Cultural nationalism of groups like US and the Nation of Islam were, and remain, misogynistic at their core. The roles they assign for women are those of the domestic and caregiver, in support of their revolutionary men. But these are not radical movements; in fact they are regressive and can never form a basis for progressive Black politics. It is also in these groups that you find virulently anti-LGBTQ ideas. Much has been made about how efforts to integrate Black communities, such as Dubois' 'nation within a nation', are structurally misogynistic because it means embracing the mainstream idea of a feminine home life and a masculine public sphere.[10] Again these claims to mainstream nation statehood sit well outside of the Black radicalism I am outlining here so cannot be used to discredit the politics. In seeking to overturn the system, Black radicalism must be calling for 'the whole system of colonialism' which produces misogyny to be transformed.[11] Black radicalism is not the politics of Karenga, or Farrakhan, or even Dubois, so to criticise it for their gender biases is unfair.

In the next chapter the Black Panthers will be discussed as a key strand in Black radicalism, but even here we need to distinguish which Panthers we are talking about. When I think Cleaver, I imagine Kathleen and not Eldridge. In the struggle to view Black Power as misogynoir, Eldridge is a key figure, especially because he admitted raping Black women in preparation for committing the crime against White ones.[12] Rather than being spurred to a life of misogynoir action by his book *Soul on Ice*, I had to put it down in disgust before finishing it. If there is any person who is held as an example of Black radicalism but can lay least claim to it, it is probably Eldridge. His entire role in the Panthers seems to have been to destabilise it. He was famous for incendiary comments and for pushing violent confrontations with the police. On 4 April 1968, after the assassination of Martin Luther King, Eldridge led an ambush on a squad of police. This kind of action was the Black Macho in search of his manhood that Michele Wallace so caricatured and that is so present in the memory of the Panthers. The latest documentary, *The Vanguard*, lionises these 'bad niggers off the block' who were ready for action.[13] The unsurprising result was a shootout that led to Eldridge and L'il Bobby Hutton being trapped in a burning building surrounded by the police. Hutton was shot to death but Eldridge survived. He later managed to smuggle himself out of the country and ended up in Algeria.[14] From there he became a vocal critic of the Panthers and their programmes of free food and medical supplies. From the safety of abroad he demanded the party take violent action against the state. Even if Eldridge was not working with the state, he did just as much to undermine the solidity of the Panthers. His conversion to the Republicans in later life only adds fuel to the suspicion that his motives towards the party were never pure. His prominence in the memory of the Panthers and his actual place in their history do not match up. I was surprised when I mentioned Eldridge to my father; his first words were 'we always thought he was planted by the FBI'. I am apparently not the only one who saw through Eldridge.

The Panthers must take responsibility for creating a culture in which Eldridge was ever allowed to be a prominent figure. No doubt, many of the members subscribed to his poisonous views of women. But that doesn't mean we should ignore the totality of the role of women in the party. The Panthers' membership was 60% female and only a small fraction of their work involved armed confrontation. The bulk of the efforts involved producing and distributing the Black Panther newspaper, the free breakfast programme, free health clinics, running liberation schools and giving out free legal advice. Women were active across all areas of the Panthers' work, and though men may have dominated powerful positions in Black politics we should not discount the role of women. As Kathleen Cleaver explained, 'the form of assistance that women give in political movements to men is just as crucial as the leadership that men give to those movements'.[15] In the case of the Panthers, though, Elaine Brown spoke of the discrimination facing women in the party, of which she became chairperson in 1974.[16] This is a testament to the idea that the problem of misogyny within the Panthers was the members, rather than a structural limitation like those that render cultural nationalism inherently regressive.

Garvey's Universal Negro Improvement Association also suffered from similar limitations of leadership. Both of Garvey's wives were hugely influential in the organisation, with Amy Jacques being the de facto second in command and the person who curated the legacy of Garveyism through books like *Garvey and Garveyism* and *The Philosophy and Opinions of Marcus Garvey*. When Garvey was imprisoned in 1925, he entrusted the leadership of the UNIA to Amy Jacques but the men in the organisation rejected female direction, contributing to its downfall. Even though misogyny was certainly present in the UNIA, it did not define it. The organisation took leadership on 'women's issues' from the very beginning because, as Amy Jacques explained, 'if the mothers of men are not treated fairly, men are but limiting their own progress and development'.[17] In 1920, Henrietta Vincent Davis founded the Black Cross Nurses (BCN) as part of the UNIA, set up as a vehicle for women to be involved in nation building. There is certainly something patriarchal in setting up the female work as that involving nursing, nutrition and education. But this was 1920, and an organisation openly discussing and working in women's health, being run and led by women, was far ahead of its time. The role of women was also not limited to the BCN in the Garvey movement. The UNIA was an organisation of over five million members at its peak, so we should de-centre the role of Garvey himself. While he was the founder and inspiration, the organization was successful because of the collective; and if we think of Garveyism as a movement, women were fundamentally involved at all levels. In many ways it is our memory of these movements that is the problem and not their actual structures; somehow 'both historians of the Black movement and women's movement have overlooked the activities of Black women in the most important mass movement in Black history'.[18] We should not be surprised misogyny exists in movements that developed in a misogynistic society; the question is whether the organisation itself allows the limitations of the mainstream to be overcome.

Building the Black nation has been the central concern of Black radical politics in order to overturn the existing political and economic system. The focus on the nation has been used to argue that the movement is misogynistic because of the gendered nature of national formations.[19] This argument misses the point of Black radicalism, which is to shatter the Western nation state in order to rebuild with a revolutionary foundation. Nation takes on an entirely different meaning in this context. The idea that only men have been involved in imagining revolutionary concepts of nationhood is disrespectful to the women who have been central in pushing for a redefinition. It is not just young Black men who obsess over the nation, as someone once disparagingly warned me at a conference. Women like 'Queen Mother' Audley Moore, Grace P. Campbell, Claudia Jones and Sunni Ali all engaged in rethinking the nation. Ironically, marking out the nation as something men think about is precisely the gendering of social thought that mainstream knowledge is based on. The same is true for the issue of violence.

To engage in revolutionary politics means having to consider the question of violence. Not as some kind of psycho-analytic tool for Black manhood, but because the system that needs to be overturned is the most violent that has ever existed. When Malcolm admonished the Civil Rights movement for its 'love thy enemy' approach, he was chiding the naïve belief that non-violence could solve the systemic problems. To see this discussion of violence as inherently male is extraordinarily problematic. To do so again draws on the tropes of the masculine demagogues of Black Power: they *must* have meant men do the violence and women make the home. Though this was definitely true for some regressive figures, we are distorting Malcolm's legacy if we cast him in the same light as someone like Eldridge Cleaver. 'Message to the Grassroots' is Malcolm's most vivid speech on violence, where he consistently talks about 'bloodshed' in the cause of revolution. But the example he uses for revolutionary violence couldn't be further from the caricature of the Black Macho:

> when I was in prison, I read an article in *Life* magazine showing a little Chinese girl, nine years old; her father was on his hands and knees and she was pulling the trigger 'cause he was an Uncle Tom Chinaman. When they had the revolution over there, they took a whole generation of Uncle Toms – just wiped them out. And within ten years that little girl become [sic] a full-grown woman. No more Toms in China.[20]

Not only is his example of revolutionary violence enacted by a little girl, but the traitor, the Tom, is male. Malcolm made it clear that 'you don't have to be a man to fight for freedom',[21] and if we honestly account for the legacy of Black radicalism it should come as no surprise that he would draw on a female figure to represent the use of violence. Contrary to the failures of our collective memory, Black women have been just as involved in political violence as men. Dahir Al Kahina led troops against the Arab invasion into Tunisia in the seventh century, declaring 'Africa for the Africans'.[22] Queen Nzinga in Angola fought on the front lines in the battle against the Portuguese in the sixteenth century, until she was sixty. Queen Nanny of the Maroons in Jamaica led a fearsome guerrilla war against the slaveholders in Jamaica until her death in 1734. Her brother Cudjoe, on the other hand, signed a treaty with the British and colluded in returning enslaved Africans and rebels. During the Haitian revolution Black women were just as involved in revolutionary violence as the men. Mbuya Nehanda fought the British in Zimbabwe and was executed by hanging in 1897. Yaa Asantewaa led a rebellion of the Ashanti tribe against the British in 1900, chastising the men 'if you the men of Ashanti will not go forward, then we will. We the women will. We will fight till the last of us falls in the battlefields'.[23] Whether it was the revolutionary post-war struggles in Guinea, Tanzania, Angola or South Africa, women shed just as much blood as men.

Throughout this book you will hear me draw on Malcolm X more than any other person. This is not because he is a man, but because he provides the fullest account of Black radicalism that can be found. To centre on Malcolm does not mean to belittle the contributions of Black women, because Malcolm is harnessing a tradition that has always had Black women at its core. We absolutely do not need to create 'definitions of Blackness that do not exclude, isolate or stigmatize', because such an understanding is already the basis of Black radicalism.[24]

Blackness is not race

When Malcolm declared that there 'is a new type of Negro, who calls himself Black ... He doesn't make any apology for his Black skin',[25] he ushered in a new type of Black politics. Prior to this, in the English-speaking world we did not refer to ourselves as Black. We were Niggers, Negroes, Coloureds, West Indians, and the list goes on. Malcolm was claiming Blackness as the political basis for revolution. He was also building on historical precedents like the Haitian constitution which declared the nation after the revolution in 1804 as a Negre, or Black, republic.[26] Blackness in Haiti had to be built, and was a not a natural identity before the revolution. In his excellent analysis in *Black Jacobins* C.L.R. James explains in detail how the French built a system designed to fragment the population of African descent in the colony.[27] As well as the enslaved, there was a small number of liberated Africans and also a class of free people whose heritage was mixed with the slave owners. None of the free Black people on the island were quick to join the revolution, which started on the plantations with those at the bottom of the system. The revolution was only successful when all the groups came together as Black and united to defeat the French. Blackness has never been simply about colour, but a commitment to a liberatory politics that our colour ties us into.

Malcolm distinguished between the 'Negro' and 'Black' revolutions to make clear the politics behind Blackness. He dismissed the Negro revolution stating:

> The only revolution based on loving your enemy is the Negro revolution. The only revolution in which the goal is a desegregated lunch counter, a desegregated theater, a desegregated park, and a desegregated public toilet; you can sit down next to white folks on the toilet.[28]

Blackness was a rejection of the politics of civil rights, of trying to gain access to a system that oppresses us. There would be no more patiently waiting, cap in hand, for incremental changes to the system. The Black revolution was 'hostile', knew 'no compromise' and 'overturns and destroys everything in its way'. The key for Malcolm was to eradicate the existing system and build a new nation on a completely different set of principles, and Blackness was central to this goal.

Blackness is a radical concept because it ties the destiny of the Diaspora together. As we discussed in Chapter 3, breaking the conceptual prison of the Western nation state is essential to building a radical project. To claim a connection to all those marked with Black skin means incorporating Fanon's 'wretched of the Earth' into your political programme.[29] The liberal politics of civil rights must be rejected because there is no way to integrate the three million children who die for no good reason in South East Africa every year into the global political social order. Malcolm's embrace of Blackness took the struggle outside of the 'jurisdiction of Uncle Sam',[30] and laid a foundation for connecting the struggles against apartheid in South Africa, Jim Crow in America and colonial rule in the Caribbean.

Given that White supremacy has devastated most of the world, rooting Blackness on the wretched of the earth could lead to the inclusion of more than just the African Diaspora. A child dies every ten seconds because of lack of access to food, and many of those children live in Asia and Latin America. In fact, in the speech quoted above Malcolm says 'when I say Black, I mean non-white', and includes China in the Black revolution sweeping the globe. Malcolm very much believed in the Third World Movement against imperialism, which was hallmarked by meetings such as took place in Bandung between Pan-African and Asian leaders in 1954.[31] But it would be incorrect from this quote to think Malcolm saw Black as equal to non-White. His use of the term more often relates to what he termed the 'so-called Negro' and his Organization of Afro-American Unity, the political organisation he was building when he died, was explicitly targeted to those of African descent. As much as I have used Malcolm as the basis for the arguments in this book, he is also not infallible. Malcolm died before the optimism of the Third World Movement had waned. Not being White did not prevent Arab exploitation of North Africa or China's neo-colonial role on the continent. It is also entirely disempowering to define yourself in relation to White people; it marks Whiteness out as the standard, the norm.[32] The hierarchy of White supremacy creates the Negro at the bottom, as the inhuman beast of burden, cementing our location in the political economy. Blackness is a rejection of the Negro, the reclamation of our link to each other and to Africa. This political statement is an essential component of the Blackness at heart of Black radicalism.

It would be easy to critique Malcolm's expression of Blackness on the basis that he declares the Black subject as male: 'he calls himself Black'. The focus on violence and the nation could be highlighted as the standard male imagining of agency. It would be easy to do so, but also lazy. As explained above, Malcolm imagines the revolutionary subject as female and draws on a tradition where women have been instrumental. Also, Malcolm's OAAU did not have defined roles for men and women. The question is not whether Malcolm used the patriarchal language of the time but whether the idea is structurally exclusive. A slight tweak leads to a new type of Negro who calls *themselves* Black, making no apology for *their* Black skin. It is here that we have the radical platform of Blackness.

Blackness was called into being during the 1960s but the concept pre-dates this. At its root Blackness is the call to unite all those of African descent in order to organise a struggle for liberation. As we discussed in Chapter 3, one of the strongest influences on Malcolm was Marcus Garvey and the Universal Negro Improvement Association. Garvey mobilised around the idea of the Negro, but this was identical to how Malcolm used Black. In fact, Garvey was in Harlem and influential for the new Negro movement, which aimed to challenge the gradualist approach to freedom. Garvey built the UNIA into the most successful global organisation linking the African Diaspora.

To understand the link of Blackness, we must be able to separate out the concept from race, because the two could not be more distinct. Unfortunately, the vast majority of scholarship on Blackness has conflated the two. For example, Michelle Wright argues in her book *Physics of Blackness* that 'Blackness was not a scientific discovery but an economic and political argument first used to justify the slave trade'.[33] That is an excellent description of race, the regressive concept used to slaughter and dominate the globe. However, it is literally the opposite of Blackness, which is first used to resist the work that race was doing. When Europeans loaded Africans onto the slave ships, purposefully mixing up tribes so that they could not communicate, it was the Blackness of the enslaved that brought them together. It was their Blackness that unified them into a force to resist and mutiny. Blackness is relational to Whiteness *only* in that sense; it was the contrast to the racism of Whites that brought together the expression of Blackness in that form. Our understandings of difference and Blackness are not simply to mimic those of White society. They have their own genealogy, and distinct meanings.

In their inability to accept that we have produced our own knowledge and understandings, academia has been quick to distance itself from Blackness. Black liberation movements are patronised for their 'romantic conceptions of "race", "people" and "nation"',[34] and advised to 'consider abandoning' altogether the 'misleading discourse' of unity and nationhood.[35] The inability to distinguish race from

Blackness has led to figures such as Garvey being either demonised or ignored.

Garvey's embrace of race certainly had problematic elements; for instance, he viewed race mixing as a sin that could not stand. His motto was 'race first', and to be a member of the UNIA meant pledging to maintain the purity of the Black race. The extreme end of this logic led him to meet with the Ku Klux Klan in America to discuss how they could work together on their common goal of preventing race mixing.[36] This was actually very similar to Malcolm meeting the KKK during his time in the Nation of Islam and the uncomfortable alliance between the group and the American Nazi Party.[37] Although this is clearly problematic, we have to be more nuanced in our analysis and not condemn him for 'drinking from the same fountain of racial prejudice' as the fascists.[38] Western concepts of race are not only based on supposed genetic differences, but also on a hierarchy with Whiteness established as the pinnacle. Neither of these apply to how Garvey viewed race, or what it mean to be Black.

Even the NOI's view of race, which creates a distinct version of Black supremacy, cannot be simply lumped together with Western notions of race. In the NOI's creation myth White people are literally the devil incarnate. While a member, Malcolm would teach the story of Dr Yacub, an evil scientist who started breeding the light-skinned Black people, then their offspring, and subsequent generations until he had created the 'blonde haired, blue eyed devil'. Once he had bred the White devils, Yacub taught them 'tricknology, which is a science of tricks and lies, and then this weak man' was 'able

to use that science to trick and rob and rule the world'.[39]
White people are inferior in this narrative and there are many
uncomfortable references to the White race being more like
dogs than people. However, this is still clearly distinct from
European ideas of race. The basis of Whites' inferiority is in
some sense genetic, in that they were bred that way by Yacub.
But the reason they are evil is because they were taught tricknology; it is based on their actions in the world rather than
pre-supposed by genetic traits. There are clearly similarities here to race in that these traits become mapped on the
biology of Whites; to be White is to be a devil and there is
no redemption from this. In contrast to race, though, the
role of this story is not to rule and dominate Whites, but as
a tool for Black people to liberate themselves. Whites' reign
on earth was only supposed to last 6000 years, which ran out
in 1914, and it is supposedly only because Black people have
been asleep as to the nature of our divine selves that we have
not yet inherited the earth. The story is told for Black people
to resist racism, separate from White America and start anew
in a land for ourselves.

As flawed and regressive as this story is, it is the basis of a
version of anti-racist politics, and therefore a repudiation, at
least to some extent, of Western notions of race. By subverting
the Western racial hierarchy it aims to deal with the problem
of racism. White supremacy is a fundamental part of race, and
you cannot reify race with claims of Black superiority. As problematic as this notion of Black supremacy is, it can also be a
powerful step towards radical versions of Blackness. Malcolm
was politically raised in the NOI and ended up articulating the

most powerful and radical concept of Blackness. We cannot dismiss the influence of his eleven years in the organisation in a desire to present a sanitised version of Malcolm that the bourgeois and academic can relate to. We like to pretend that once Malcolm left the NOI he transformed, throwing off the shackles that were holding him back, with his visit to Mecca being this transformative part of his journey, his supposed reinvention. Nothing could be further from the truth. There is only one moment of complete transformation for Malcolm and that is from when he was Detroit Red, the hustler, to when, after immersing himself in reading in prison, he joined the NOI and became Malcolm X. He refers to that period as completely altering his way of thinking and entire approach to life, likening it to the suddenness of falling 'snow off a roof'.[40] Malcolm's radical approach to Blackness and the nation was developing during his time in the NOI, with his split being inevitable given his revolutionary politics. His trip to Mecca opened his eyes only to the reality that all White people were not evil and led him to condemn the system of Whiteness, rather than individuals. Malcolm's journey is one of evolution, not transformation, and was the inspiration for one of the most influential psychological models of Black identity.

William Cross developed the 'Nigrescence' model to explain what he called 'Negro to Black conversion experiences'.[41] Heavily influenced by both Malcolm's journey and Kwame Ture's statement that 'every Negro is a potential Black man', Cross tried to explain the stages someone could go through to achieve a radical Black identity. In the first stage they are the Negro, unaware of racism and playing along with their role in White society. For Malcolm this is him as the hustler, the stereotypical Black man for the mainstream to fear (and desire). Then, Cross theorised, came the Encounter, an event that shakes you out of the pretence that your colour is not important. Malcolm's incarceration would serve as quite a vivid encounter with the racism of the criminal injustice system. Cross gives the example of people's reaction to the assassination of Martin Luther King, seeing the non-violent spokesman gunned down woke people to the realities of the system. After the Encounter there would be a period of intense anti-Whiteness, what Cross called Immersion/Emersion. As people threw themselves into learning about racism they could not help being anti-White given all of the horrors and injustices that the West has wrought. This would be Malcolm embracing the NOI and its view of White people as devils. But eventually, as people went through a process of Internalisation of Black consciousness, they would become Committed to the liberation struggle and be the 'new type of Negro', Black, proud and in the struggle. Picture Malcolm after he leaves the NOI and founds the OAAU, pro-Black but no longer defined by Whiteness, whether for or against it. Cross' model oversimplifies the issues here and he updated it in later versions,[42] but the point is that anti-Whiteness can be a part of an oppositional politics and may even be a necessary stage to Black radicalism. To simply see even the most Black supremacist logic of groups like the NOI as the same concept as race is to badly miss the point. This is particularly the case when there are plenty of forms of Blackness that involve no hierarchy at all, such as Garveyism, which has often been dismissed as Black fascism.

Although Garvey was against race mixing and met with the KKK, he was not arguing that White people were inferior or that mixing would ruin the Black racial stock. For Garvey, mixing meant diluting African blood and therefore weakening the connection to Africa, the Diaspora and the politics of liberation. It's worth noting that in Garvey's day the impact of colourism across the Americas was unmistakeable. He would have directly witnessed the privileges afforded to those with lighter skin tones and seen how some had been incorporated into the management of imperialism. Given the colour-coded hierarchy it is not surprising that he would have associated dark skin with the masses and liberation, and light skin with the bourgeois and imperialism. More problematic for Garvey in how he viewed White society was that he was too complimentary to it. Garvey wanted to elevate the Negro world to the level of the White race and can therefore stand accused of capitalism, but not mimicking the fascists.

Garvey consistently mobilises the word 'blood' in talking about the connection of the African Diaspora, and this is a term that Appiah takes issue with in his supposed classic *In My Father's House.* He rails against Dubois' use of the term 'common blood' to speak of the connection of Blackness because he argues that 'dressed with fancy craniometry, a dose of melanin, and some measure for curly hair is what the scientific notion amounts to'.[43] For Appiah, the *only* use of colour, blood or ancestry in identity is rooted in the European concept of race, and he is entirely blinkered to the idea that Blackness is a separate and opposing concept. We need to be much more sophisticated in how we understand 'blood' in the connection of Blackness.

For Garvey, blood is not meant as a genetic marker of attributes and abilities. Blood is the familial, historical connection to Africa. It does not presuppose any genetic traits, and limits the connection to a shared history and experiences of those whose skin in Black. Due to this connection, Garvey effectively argues that the Diaspora has a responsibility to each other, and must unite under a common destiny. Blood is our ancestral connection, the ties that bind us together. To the extent that it is genetic, it is the loose familial bond, that which colours our skin and curls our hair. It is our direct link back to the continent of Africa, the permanent reminder of a shared connection. Blood takes on such importance because due to the horrors of slavery and cultural genocide we have nothing else to connect us. What academics like Appiah are ignorant of is that Blackness is not about the colour, or even the blood, but is founded on what they both represent. We *choose* to see the connection to Africa and the Diaspora as important. This is why it is no way a surprise that, as Appiah admits, 'Dubois managed to maintain Pan-Africanism while officially rejecting talk of race as anything other than a synonym for colour'.[44] It has never been anything more than that, embracing our Blackness as the starting point for understanding our place and struggles in the world.

Wright takes issue with a narrative of Blackness that ties the Diaspora together through the middle passage of slavery.[45] She argues that it is impossible to maintain historical continuity and prioritise the middle passage at the same time as including all parts of the Diaspora. Wright argues that in order to have a more open definition of Blackness we need to use non-linear ideas of time and to de-centre the middle passage. The idea of linear progress may be central to narrow and cultural nationalism, but the same is not true of Black radicalism. To say that we are connected because of our shared history and roots in Africa does not mean this is based on a simple step-by-step link to the past. Wright expends a lot of intellectual energy using the analogy of quantum physics to argue the need to see the past, present and future as fluid in space and time. Rather than mooring her understandings on Eurocentric philosophies of knowledge, Wright would have found that this very concept is alive in African knowledge systems, and is the basis of Black radicalism.

I am usually wary of claiming the idea of African episte-mologies because of the large diversity of thought across the continent and Diaspora. But on the issues of time, specifi-cally linked to death, there is a clear distinction to European thought. Death does not mark the end in African thought, because the ancestors retain a connection to the world.[46] You pray and atone to your ancestors to influence the present and future, and it is this connection to the spirit world that Euro-peans have used to demonise and mock traditional African belief systems. The act of praying to the dead in the present to influence the future transcends any notion of linear time. The Akan Adinkrah symbol of the Sankofa bird, which looks backwards and forwards simultaneously, is the visual repre-sentation of this idea. When Garvey talks of blood, he is making that ancestral connection. Not in a simple linear sense, but viewing the future of Black people through the lens of the past. So the middle passage is not a horror that happened a long time ago and is necessary for a continuity narrative, it is something that we connect to from this moment to understand our place in the world. The same is true of slave rebellions and struggles for resistance across time.

The idea that the middle passage is only important for the narrative of the enslaved Diaspora is extremely problematic. The victims of transatlantic slavery were not just those who boarded slave ships. There was fierce resistance to enslavement on the African continent and countless died fighting Europeans. The impact of transatlantic slavery on the continent was also devastating, removing millions of people, destroying communities and setting back economic and political progress for centuries.[47] Slavery did not just happen to the Diaspora; nor did the middle passage break the link to the African continent. Many rebel leaders like Nanny of the Maroons were African born and drew on these roots for the struggle. Nanny was an Asante leader and used her knowledge of guerrilla warfare to get the best of the British in Jamaica. As discussed in Chapter 1, the presence of so many African-born leaders in Haiti was a key reason for the success of the revolution. Rather than seeing the middle passage as some sort of discontinuity between Africa and the Diaspora we should instead embrace it as the 'unbreakable umbilical cord' between the two.[48] It is entirely incorrect to analyse the situation on the continent of Africa as somehow distinct from the Diaspora, as Appaih does when he argues that 'the "discrimination and insult" Dubois experienced in the ... industrialized world were different in character from that experienced by, say, Kwame Nkrumah in colonized West Africa'.[49] This is a painting by numbers analysis of racism, which has become all too common when theorising Blackness.

The middle passage is perhaps the ultimate example of the creation of the 'Negro'. Stripped, shackled, beaten and packed like cattle with those whose language you cannot speak: this is the definition of the sub-human being with no history or culture; the beast of burden necessary to build the new world. But the Negro is not just essential outside of Africa, but also on the continent; to procure the labour force upon which capitalism is based, but also to control and dominate the continent. The mineral resources from Africa were as important as the labour, and certainly more so today. Negroes do not have claims to land, or need of mineral wealth. They do not have the capacity to rule themselves and it is therefore the 'white man's burden' to do so.[50] King Leopold's Belgium killed up to ten million people in the Congo and maimed countless more. The punishment for not meeting your rubber quota was to lose your hand, even if you were a child.[51] The justification for this genocide is no different than that for transatlantic slavery. White supremacy was, and remains, the same problem on the African continent as it is in the Diaspora. So while Dubois' problems may have manifested differently in America than Nkrumah's in Ghana, the root problem was the same.

One of the most quoted parts of Fanon's work is the story of when he first realised he was a Negro. Growing up in Martinique surrounded by other Black people he had never considered his colour, it was only in France when a young boy shouted 'look mama, the Negro ... I am frightened' that he understood he was Black.[52] Stuart Hall had a similar experience:

> Until I left [Jamaica], though I suppose 98 per cent of the Jamaican population is either Black or colored in one way or another, I had never ever heard anybody either call themselves, or refer to anybody else as 'Black'. Never. I heard a thousand other words. My grandmother could differentiate about fifteen different shades between light brown and dark brown.[53]

I cannot count the number of times I have heard these two accounts, or variations of them, used to distance the experiences in the West from those in the colonies, to argue against the unity of Blackness. The fact that you do not appreciate something does not mean it has not shaped your life. Once we accept that the Negro was created across the continent of Africa and all of the Diaspora, then even though Hall or Fanon did not realise the impact of this it does not mean they did not feel it. Hall's reference to the multitudes of shades his grandmother could differentiate is an indication of the power of colourism in Jamaica. Even today the political world and economic prosperity in the island is colour coded. In fact, issues like skin bleaching, being so disgusted by your Blackness that you burn off the colour, are far more prevalent in Caribbean and African countries than they are in those nations where we are the minority. Fanon was keenly aware of the issues of racism in the Caribbean, arguing that the West Indian identified himself with the White man's attitude, stating that 'the West Indian … is a Negro'.[54] The astronomical murder rate in Jamaica is allowed to continue because the victims are Negroes. Families trying to cross the Mediterranean from Africa in search of a better life are left to drown, because they are Negroes. Three million children die in South East Africa every year because they are Negroes. People do not become Negroes in the West, they just realise it when they see the contrasts to Whiteness.

Wright's other objection to how we understand Blackness is that in trying to find continuity we narrate a narrow story dominated by men as the only way to 'point to the existence and pedigree of Black culture, Black politics, Black music, Black literature'.[55] This is a perfect example of how academic discussions of Blackness have become limited to viewing the concept 'as political expression of racial essentialism'.[56]

Blackness is a political essentialism

Essentialism in the discussion of Blackness means to 'assume the existence of a transhistorical and organic "black essence"' that defines all Black people.[57] It is to reduce us to set ways of being and cultural forms, to make Blackness rigid and inflexible. There are two primary concerns from the academy with essentialism and Blackness. The first is that the 'myth of a black community'[58] *'inadvertently* helps to reproduce some of the thinking and practices that have created black disadvantage in the first place'.[59] In this dubious logic, racist society is based on dealing with Black people as a unit, and we collude in this project by embracing the idea that we are a separate and different community. Basically, this is the latest version of the integration over separation debate. We should have long ago realised that dreaming that we can be an undifferentiated part of the system is a fantasy. Whether we imagine ourselves as equals, or cosmopolitan individuals who transcend the boundaries of race, makes absolutely no impact on the realities of racism. Even the most successful Black people, who have apparently 'made it', have their 'acute moments of disrespect' that Elijah Anderson calls the 'nigger moment'.[60] This whole argument is predicated on the idea that the only way to see Blackness is through the lens of Whiteness as if we have no control over our own meaning. When enslaved Africans during the middle passage united in their Blackness to mutiny, they were hardly supporting the logic that disadvantaged them. Perhaps they should have avoided embracing the myth of Blackness and appealed to the slave ship captains as equal members of the human family.

The more serious critique the idea of essentialism presents for Blackness is the idea that it creates an exclusionary Black subject, which reinforces ideas of patriarchy and anti-LGBTQ narratives. Cultural nationalism, as we discussed in Chapter 4, is most certainly guilty of this error, with clear cultural and behavioural roles for the authentic 'African'. There is no space in this logic for men who are not protectors, women who are not domesticated or anyone who is not straight and reproducing the Black family. It is from these kinds of politics that the obsession over creating a more open Blackness has emerged. Stuart Hall proposed that we need newer, more hybrid forms of identity that open up space for varying forms of identity.[61] bell hooks articulated the need for a 'postmodern Blackness' in order to 'challenge notions of universality and over-determined identity' in movements.[62] In trying to retain some sort of basis of Black politics Paul Gilroy tied himself in theoretical knots arguing for an 'anti-anti-essentialism' to recognise both the lived experience and the limits of cultural authenticity.[63]

Hundreds of thousands of words have been split on trying to retain a form of Blackness that can move beyond the limits of cultural authenticity. But lacking in this myriad of work is a recognition that Blackness is a *political* rather than a cultural essentialism. Blackness is the ultimate rejection of Negro status, the call for unity in order to overturn the system that oppresses Africa and the Diaspora. In this sense it is mediated through the Black body but there is no need for any cultural sameness or hierarchy. We are linked because of politics and not culture, and therefore whatever cultural forms people choose to embrace are unimportant. Authenticity for Black radicalism simply comes down to a commitment to the liberation of the Diaspora. But there is no doubt that authenticity has been generally misread, and more widely misused, even outside of cultural nationalism.

To sell out, be a traitor to the race, has become defined in cultural terms.[64] Having a White partner, dressing a certain way, speaking in a particular manner have all become symbols of 'acting White'.[65] The cultural performance of a so-called authentic Blackness determines who is labelled a 'bounty bar' or a 'coconut' (brown on the outside but white on the inside). Yet it was never meant to be this way.

Malcolm likens the House Negro on the plantation to the middle class Black folk who receive material advantages in capitalist society. He contrasts this to the Field Negro who caught hell on the plantation, in the same way that poor Black folk experience the brutal realities of racism today. Malcolm is saying that the poor Black person is more authentically Black than the middle class, not because of their culture but due to their location in the system of oppression and more importantly their political outlook. The House Negro is duped by the system because they cannot see a reality where they can 'get a better house', 'better clothes' or 'better food' than from the master. So they 'identify with the master more than the master identifies with himself',[66] and refuse to run away from the plantation or separate from White society. Catching hell on the plantation makes the Field Negro much more attuned to the realities of racism. So if 'someone came to the Field Negro and said, "Let's separate, let's run", he didn't say "Where we going?" He'd say, "Any place is better than here"'.[67] The Field Negro is authentic because they embrace the politics of revolution, while the House Negro 'is out of his mind' because they are committed to the system that is oppressing them. Black radical authenticity takes this further and is not based on class distinctions but political ones. To understand this we must distinguish between the House Negro and the Uncle Tom.

For Malcolm, it wasn't just any old middle class Black person supporting a racist system who was an Uncle Tom. They were Kwame Ture's 'potential' Black people who could be awakened to the system. The Uncle Tom was a specific role where the system 'takes a so-called Negro, and makes him prominent, builds him up, publicizes him, makes him a celebrity. And then he becomes a spokesman for Negroes'.[68] Tomming means to pretend to be speaking on behalf of Black liberation while being an agent of the system, a tool used to slow down progress. It is easy to point out the well-educated, middle class, government-appointed Uncle Toms like Supreme Court Justice Clarence Thomas in America, or former head of the Commission for Racial Equality Trevor Phillips in Britain. But we miss the point if we conflate Tomming with the culture of the middle class.[69] A good example of the modern-day Uncle Tom would be a rapper like L'il Wayne who clothes himself in the culture of street to appeal the masses, but writes lyrics such as 'I whip it like a slave'. By removing the cultural basis from authenticity we have a solid platform for the political nature of Black radical solidarity.

Securing Black authenticity within this political framework is seen as problematic because of the lens though which Black radical history is viewed. Viewing Black politics as a history of misogyny means Blackness is seen to exclude those identities that do not fit, for example 'LGBTTQ Blacks during decolonization and Black Power movements in Africa and the West'.[70] In the same way that we discussed for women, this is in part a response to narrow and cultural nationalism. Huey P. Newton declared that people needed to 'deal with their insecurities' around homosexuality and that the Panthers needed to unite with gay and women's movements in a 'revolutionary fashion'. He was open about his own prejudices but made it clear that there was nothing in the Panthers' politics that was necessarily homophobic and even acknowledged that 'a homosexual could be the most revolutionary'.[71] It would be wrong to say that this demonstrates Huey's, the Panther's or Black radicalism's excellent credentials on the issue of gay liberation. While not being hostile, there has been a lack of discussion of the issue. This absence has led to calls for 'queer' Black politics.[72] Wright argues that the only way to create the concept as 'wholly inclusive and non-hierarchical is to understand Blackness as the *intersection* of constructs'.[73] In other words it can only have meaning in relation to concepts of gender, sexuality, disability and class. But the assumption that Blackness, in its radical sense, needs to be transformed is problematic.

It would be wrong to assume that because Black radicalism has not explicitly centred on LGBTQ issues it excludes those who are not heterosexual. When Africans were enslaved, or areas colonised, they didn't separate out the Black population by sexuality. People of all sexualities and gender identities were both re-created as Negroes and rose up to resist, whether in slave rebellions, anti-colonial struggles or in post-war movements. Malcolm's comments on religion could equally apply to sexual orientation: 'they don't hang you because you're a Baptist; they hang you 'cause you're Black. They don't attack me because I'm a Muslim; they attack me 'cause I'm Black. They attack all of us for the same reason'.[74] As the police killings in America demonstrate, being gay or transgender is no protection from police bullets. To underscore how the issues impact across the board, Black Lives Matter was founded by three queer women, Alicia Garza, Patrisse Khan-Cullors and Opal Tometi. Blackness cannot just exist at the intersection or it has no real meaning at all, it just becomes one of many differences. It is also true that being queer opens you to attacks that being Black and heterosexual do not, and we certainly need to understand how Blackness intersects with other oppressions; but a central feature of Black radicalism is that Blackness is *the* underlying concept that unites the Diaspora.

One of the main reasons that LGBTQ issues have not been highlighted in Black radicalism is not because of the problems themselves but because the campaigns are often based on appeals to civil rights. Seeking legislative changes on age of consent, same-sex marriage or transgender recognition may be important but these are not radical challenges to the system. The same criticisms that were levelled at civil rights campaigns for racial equality apply to efforts to make the system fairer based on sexuality. Of course there should be equality, but it is not reasonable to expect a radical politics to engage in liberal struggles with the state. Black radicalism is concerned with liberation of Black people from the West, not social equality within the system. Black radicalism also unapologetically privileges Blackness analytically. But Blackness must be a cultural and expressive blank slate upon which we can build our revolution.

There is no point in pretending that there is some Black radical blueprint for the nation after the revolution that is the model of gender and sexuality equality. But equally there is none that provides for Black straight men either. To this point Black radicalism has provided the basis and articulation for struggle but has not answered the question of what comes next. Kimberlé Crenshaw's work on intersectionality is vital in making sure we do not lose sight of the plurality of Blackness, but debating the misogyny of Black radicalism based on the past will not get us very far.[75] What Black radicalism has done is to provide the basis for liberation, with Blackness being at the centre. It is only by coming together, pushing the politics forward and articulating how the Black nation will function that we can fulfil the promise of the radical tradition. Black radicalism must be a space open to all those in the Diaspora who have felt on the outside. There can be no exclusions in what unites us in our Blackness. In terms of producing a radical culture that overcomes the centuries of Western influence, this can only be produced in the furnace of radical action. Communing together, working together and struggling together is the only way to build a society together.

In the effort to distance themselves from race and to either link, or disconnect, the various cultures of the African Diaspora, scholars have had to abandon the real world for the imagined and theoretical. Wright seriously argues that 'political traditions serve only a limited use' in understanding Blackness and privileges intellectual formations, which she locates in the literary world.[76] To effectively dismiss centuries of political resistance in order to prioritise the work of contemporary fiction writers is a dangerous indulgence in academia. Sadly, Wright is not alone in this kind of rewriting of Blackness, detaching the concept from its radical and grassroots origins. It is an ongoing 'crisis of the Negro intellectual' to be unable to articulate the radical nature of Blackness because of the limits of the White academic framework.[77] Blackness is not a theoretical, literary or abstract construct. It is a concept produced in struggle, by those facing the brutal realities of racial oppression. Perhaps it should come as no surprise that the Black intelligentsia have been unable to comprehend the basis and importance of this radical idea. I can personally testify to the assault of the Eurocentric canon and the insular nature of the academic industrial project. It is only by rooting our understandings in that knowledge produced outside of the university, in the process of struggle, that we can trace radical versions of Blackness.

The misogynistic Blackness that you have been led to believe has dominated our politics has never been at the heart of the radical project. Black political movements have been by no means perfect models of gender and sexuality equality, but Blackness provides the unifying concept that can build a truly inclusive and liberatory politics.

Chapter 6

Black Marxism

In 2012 I attended a Black History Month event in an African Caribbean community centre in Birmingham. There was nothing particularly memorable about the event itself; it was one of the many indistinguishable celebrations of Blackness that we crowd into every October in Britain. There is nothing like state funding to remind the community of their roots. This occasion stands out because a discussion arose about South African farmers who were striking over pay and conditions at the time. The strikes began organically in the Western Cape and eventually spread across the country. At the event members of the Socialist Worker's Party (SWP) were present and brought their rhetoric with them. You may well question why the SWP was at a random Black History Month workshop, but only if you have never attended a Black community event. Malcolm used to joke that the FBI always lingered at Black community meetings; in Britain it's not the feds who are ever-present, but the SWP or some other variant of the left. An undeniable part of this hyper-presence is certainly to lecture us that our problems are really about class and not race. In fact, when Critical Race Theory first emerged in Britain, every conference was attended by Mike Cole and/ or Dave Hill, Marxists sent to teach us the error of our ways.

But there is also a genuine attempt to reach out to an audience that, as we will see in this chapter, has often been overlooked or side-lined in Marxist analysis.

At this meeting the SWP was there to get support for a potential teachers' strike over pension changes. It has stuck with me because their spokesperson seriously tried to tie the fate of the South African farm workers, who were going on strike at the time, to the struggle for teacher's pensions. The argument was that these were both examples of the general oppression of the working classes. If we were supporting the South African farm workers we should also be backing the teachers. This argument demonstrates many of the problems with Marxism that we will discuss in the chapter, and as you can probably imagine did not go down very well at the event. In the simplistic calculations of groups like the SWP, we are all workers in a fight against the capitalists, and must unite to succeed. But they have neglected the privileges that those in the West receive. The case of teachers is a perfect example. The starting salary in England is over £22,000, meaning you begin your career in the top half of earners in the country. With increments and promotion you are set to end up anywhere as high as the top 5%. On the global scale that places teachers well in the upper section of earnings there is no material comparison to be made by those in a comfortable and financially sound profession fighting over their pensions, to farm workers in South Africa demanding a wage that can feed them. Worse still, teacher's salary and pension contributions come from the state and therefore tax revenue. As we have seen already, the wealth in Britain is produced by historically under-developing places like South Africa and maintaining their poverty through neo-colonial economic practices. Not only are British teachers rich in comparison to South African farmers; they have that wealth in large part *because* the farmers are poor. It is actually offensive to pretend that they are in the same struggle, and makes a complete nonsense of the idea that there is a 99% in a battle with the global elite. However, as much as the central tenet of Marxism falls apart on scrutiny, Black Marxism has historically been a dominant form of organising.

There is perhaps no more influential radical school of thought than Marxism. The *Communist Manifesto* published by Marx and Engels in 1848 is, after the Bible, the most read book in the entire world and inspired revolutions in Russia, China, Korea, Cuba and across the globe. Marx provides a searing critique of capitalism, arguing that the rich are rich because the poor are poor, and concluding that there can be no justice within its economic framework. Nothing short of a revolution can bring about a transformation of the system, and liberate the oppressed. This is a direct parallel to the Black radical position that we have discussed so far. The similarities go further when we look at the processes of historical change in Marxism.

In pursuing their exploitation of the workers, the oppressors or 'bourgeoisie' were said to be creating their own 'grave-diggers'.[1] This is often taken to mean that Marx saw the end of capitalism as inevitable, but it is actually more complicated than this. The gravediggers of capitalism for Marx were the Proletariat, but we have to distinguish this group from the working class. Marx saw the Proletariat as a 'class in itself', oppressed but also controlled by the system. In order to bring about the revolution they would need to become a 'class for themselves', and understand their place and power to form as the Proletariat. In other words, every worker is a *potential* Proletarian but they need to be educated and awakened from the delusions trained into them by the system of oppression. Brazilian educator Paolo Freire called this processes 'conscientization',[2] removing the veil of false consciousness, while Malcolm X explained the need for a programme of 'political re-education to open our people's minds to the truth'.[3]

It is not difficult to see why Marxism would be appealing to Black communities looking for liberation from oppression. In the same way as those who rebelled in Haiti took inspiration from the French Revolution, Black communities will always rally to those movements that can bring down the oppressive system. Figures like George Padmore, Paul Robeson, Angela Davis and Claudia Jones have historically been prominently involved in Marxism. The late Stuart Hall, so influential in Britain, was probably most notable for his contributions to contemporary debates in Marxism, and the Black left in this country has deep links to the tradition. That is not even to mention the Black Panther Party and revolutionary movements in colonies such as Grenada in the Caribbean,[4] or Guinea in Africa.[5] So influential was Marxism on the continent that the first president of Tanzania, Nyerere, created the concept of 'African Socialism' to apply the doctrine in the conditions outside of Europe.[6] The late Cedric Robinson's classic text *Black Marxism* captures the deep connections across history.[7] As excellent and foundational as this book is, Robinson makes the fundamental error of conflating Black Marxism with Black radicalism. Although Marxism is radical, it is not Black. There are almost as many Black activists who joined Marxist groups as who left them once they understood that the politics is undermined by how it views the questions of racism. Marxism is certainly one of the very few radical arguments, but there is a difference between Black radicalism and Black people being radical.

The Negro question

Marxism's central problem is its relegation of the question of racism. Class is the central, underlying antagonism in Marxism, which has been widely critiqued as being too simplistic.[8] It is also true that the accusation that Marx reduced everything to the economic has become an over-simplified critique that avoids engaging with Marxism's complexities. Marx died a long time ago and intellectuals such as Gramsci have done much to move away from narrow inter-pretations of his work.[9] There is some room for manoeuvre in how the question of racism is used in Marxism, and of course Black scholars have had a key influence in these discussions. We would be wrong to reject Marxism outright because it prioritises class over racism. The issue here is how and why class is given primacy and what this tells us about the limits of Marxism.

The Communist Party of the USA (CPUSA) has histor-ically been central in the discussion of race and class. As the

Western country with the largest Black population, the issue of racism in the United States was pressing. After the emancipation of enslaved Africans in America the competition between Black and White workers impacted greatly on the future formation of the nation. Dubois argued that an opportunity had been lost in the South for the workers of both colours to unite and fight the wealthy exploiters. He argued that the psychological 'wages of whiteness' had convinced the White workers to despise the formerly enslaved.[10] Resolving this conflict was seen as important because of the presence of millions of African American potential Proletarians. The CPUSA could not afford to ignore issues of race and set about discussing whether 'African Americans be considered a subject nation, an oppressed race, or simply a particularly disadvantaged section of the American working class'.[11]

The CPUSA doing the legwork on what the Communist Party as a whole called the 'Negro Question' is in itself an indictment of the party. Though Lenin had made it clear that the exploitation of the colonies was absolutely essential to the maintenance of capitalism, the Negro Question and wider issues of race were relegated to the side-lines. Communist groups in places like Britain and France were uninterested in the discussion because they had very few bodies from the colonies within their nation states. They did not have to deal with Negro workers, so they felt no urgency in addressing the issues of racism. Ironically, given that Marxism condemns the nation state, organisation of the Communist International took place firmly within the colonial national framework. Black Marxists colluded in the logic of the British and

French by seeing America as the 'headquarters and centre of political thought' for Black people.[12] The colonies were not viewed as advanced enough to be at the forefront of the revolution because the Proletariat was defined in relation to industry, which the colonies did not possess. The communist thesis on the Negro question in 1919, mostly authored by the Afro-Surinamese Otto Houiswood, acknowledged the importance of Black people worldwide but argued that their cooperation was essential to the Western 'Proletarian Revolution',[13] which would deliver the victory against capitalism. In the very formulation of the Negro question the Communist Party placed Black people on the periphery.

None of this should come as any surprise. Marx acknowledged the importance of slavery and colonialism in building the West, arguing that 'it is slavery that has given the colonies their value; it is the colonies that have created world trade, and it is world trade that is the pre-condition of large-scale industry. Thus slavery is an economic category of the greatest importance'.[14] The problem with a Marxist analysis, though, is that even though he recognised the role of slavery and colonialism, Marx saw this as 'pre-capitalist accumulation'. In the same way as you could not have capitalism without feudalism, colonialism was seen as a necessary precursor. But importantly they both lay outside of capitalism, which was seen to be more advanced and dominated by industrial relations. One of the most lasting critiques of Marx is how he downplays the role of peasants in the revolution. They are not workers in advanced economies and therefore are outside the system of capitalism. The Proletarians were meant be forged in the factories, but history has taught us it is actually that peasantry who have taken the lead. Russia, China, Grenada, Burkino Faso, Korea, Guinea, Cuba all depended on the agricultural communities. What should also stand out in this list is how little progress communism has made in the West. The biggest failing of Marx is that he 'imagined that the industrial Proletariat was the hero of capitalism and invented a history whose narrative justified this'.[15]

Far from marking a break with feudalism or colonialism, capitalism is an advanced form of the Western imperial project. It is impossible to separate what happens in the colonies from what happens in the West. While the West may have been rapidly urbanising and industrialising in Marx's time, the colonies were not. They were purposefully being underdeveloped in order to maintain control by European powers. So although the peasantry were disappearing in the West they remained a force outside of it. It is only in recent years that globally more people live in cities than rural areas. The idea that colonial rule is 'pre-capitalism' is also inadequate. It is true that capitalism was built on the wealth from slavery and colonialism, but that is just as true today as it was in the nineteenth century, in terms of the legacies of historic oppression, which can be seen in the wealth generated, and the poverty caused. Even if the end of slavery and direct rule was the end of Western exploitation, the colonies would have been put back in their development by centuries. As no reparations have been forthcoming there is clearly still a debt owed; you cannot just steal the wealth, hold on to it and then blame your victims for being poor. Actually you can, and that is the basis of the global economy, which takes it further with neo-colonial trade practices. By prioritising the experience of Europe, drawing a line between pre- and post-capitalism and pretending you can understand the economies of the West without considering their exploitation of the rest of the world, Marx was just as guilty of Eurocentrism as his more liberal contemporaries.

In fairness to Marxism, newer developments have attempted to deal with this problem. Wallerstein's World System Theory, for example, places the wealth of the West at the core in relation to the exploitation of the colonies on the periphery of global economics.[16] It is no longer controversial to argue that capitalism is a form of imperialism, rooted in the oppression of the former colonies. But it is one thing to recognise the problem of global capital and quite another to deal with the issue of racism.

It is in the mechanism for change where we can see Marxism's most fundamental error. The industrial working class has not and will never be the most exploited group in the system of imperialism, and therefore capitalism. Even though the conditions in the factories during the industrial revolution were terrible, they were a luxury compared to the enslavement of African people. Due to how dehumanising slavery was, the history has been sanitised in the collective memory. We can picture the chains, whippings and even rapes, but the scale of the torture, mutilations and genocide is mostly hidden from view. One brutal slave-owner in Jamaica, Thomas Thistlewood, as well as raping hundreds of women, invented a punishment where the enslaved 'would be beaten, and salt pickle, lime juice, and bird pepper would be rubbed into his or her open wounds. Another slave would defecate into the mouth of the miscreant, who would then be gagged for four to five hours'.[17] If we truly comprehended the horrors of slavery we would not only be saddened but sickened. We would certainly not do the history the disservice of comparing it to the labour that Europeans experienced in the workhouses. As horrible as it was, Thistlewood's Derby Dose, as he called it, was not being practised on the production line. When Europeans had exhausted the lives of the natives in the America they did not enslave poor Whites to produce their commodities. In order to extract maximum wealth they needed to create the Negro, the commodity to be bought and sold. There were some White people on the plantations and you may have come across the popular 'myth of Irish slaves'.[18] The reality is that there were some poor Europeans on the plantations who were indentured servants. They had to serve for limited periods of time, and still had human rights.[19] They were not slaves, they were not seen as beasts, or treated as subhuman. Indentured labourers were effectively serfs; by no means were they equal, and they experienced tremendous hardship, but they were not slaves. Britain did not round up its, or Ireland's, poor at the barrel of a gun and chain them into chattel slavery. Those horrors were reserved for Africans, who were used to produce the wealth that the industrial revolution developed from.

As the conditions for the working classes in the West improved, they did not do so in the colonies. In fact, the conditions in the West improved because of the continued poverty in the colonies. The wealth generated from imperialism was a key part of allowing for the abolition of child labour, the introduction of the working week and the comforts provided by the welfare state. The fear of communism after the Second World War was enough for Britain and other countries to offer social welfare, free schooling, free healthcare and to bring in more progressive taxation systems. But these benefits were not passed down to the colonies, which suffered further exploitation to secure social democracy in the West. If we take the example of Britain, at the founding of the welfare state the colonies were still controlled by the mother country and they provided the wealth and labour to make the project possible. The National Health Service was described by Labour Prime Minister Harold Wilson as 'the very temple of our social security system', providing universal, free medical care.[20] From its outset the NHS has been entirely dependent on migrant workers from the colonies and nations after independence. The only reason Black people are in the country in large numbers is because our labour was needed to build a welfare state that the colonies saw no benefit from. As is typical of the White left, they tend to celebrate these advances in progress as the result of their tireless working class campaigning. But considering the welfare state should be impossible without recognising Britain's colonial subjects. Therefore it was particularly offensive that Ken Loach's *Spirit of '45* movie, celebrating the era, was almost exclusively White.

The unfortunate truth about Marx's hero of history is that the Western working class has benefited from imperialism and forged political movements that mostly aim to distribute the wealth gained from the exploitation of darker people more equitably between Whites. Trades Unions have largely operated to 'defend the short term interests' for their members within the framework of the nation state.[21] On top of this, the unions have also been a bastion of racism and exclusion. When Caribbean and Indian workers came to Britain they found themselves subject to colour bars from both the unions and workers' organisations like social clubs.[22] Groups like the Indian Workers Association had to form because they had no representation in the mainstream unions. Even now, though we are welcome to pay our fees, I don't remember anyone ever expressing the feeling that their union was particularly supportive over issues of racism. If we are honest, the history of working class movements in the West has largely been one based on self-interest, and these interests generally do not align with the victims of imperialism. Though this has never stopped the left attempting to organise on behalf of the Black and Brown.

After the financial crisis in 2007, Western economies felt a severe impact: declines in share prices, the near collapse of Greece and banks having to be bailed out with public money. The result was the politics of austerity and a significant squeeze on public spending and resources. The credit crunch laid bare the lie of progress built on loans and the rebalancing of Western economies has been terrible for the poor. Wages have stagnated, public safety nets have been removed, houses repossessed and people are now regularly struggling to feed themselves. Unemployment in some countries has not been the problem it could have been, but underemployment is just as big an issue. Having a job that does not pay enough to live on is hardly better than not having one at all.

All of this financial chaos led to a reaction from the left and the Occupy Movement was born, rallying around the slogan 'we are the 99%'. Marxism is not in vogue at present so the movement was not keen to embrace its politics, although there is a clear influence in the idea of the elite against the rest of the world. We will not go into any depth of critique of Occupy, which has since become a distant memory, but will simply point out that all of those things that the movement were complaining about were not new to the former colonies. Poverty, food insecurity, precarious work and especially austerity have been features of the global development package for decades. It was only when these inequalities were felt in the West that people deemed it necessary to rise up. More to the point, the financial crisis did not bring anything new to Black and Brown communities in the West. Much has been made of the staggering unemployment in Southern Europe, but Black male youth unemployment has hit as high as 50% in some parts of Britain. One of the starkest figures I have seen on racial inequality recently is that, of all African Americans who have jobs in New York, half of them work in fast food outlets.[23] Austerity and the financial crisis have also hit Black communities disproportionately hard. Losing a million public sector jobs is devastating in Britain to a Black community that has relied on public sector work because of discrimination in the employment sector. To be told that we are now in a collective struggle is a bit difficult to hear when our plight has mostly fallen on deaf ears for decades.

The response to the politics of austerity has been typical of the White left through the ages: fight to get a more even distribution of the profits of imperialism, while making sure to keep the system in place. Appeals to the White working class have either been made directly on a racist, nationalist basis as we saw with Trump in America or Le Pen in France, or with calls for a return to social democracy and more equality within the nation state, as with Podemos in Spain or Corbynism in Britain. Nationalising railways and taxing the rich are good ideas but let's not pretend that they will alleviate global poverty. Britain was a social democracy when my grandmother came to Britain and faced the kind of overt racism I have only seen on screen. Gains for workers in the West have always been secured off the backs of those in the underdeveloped world. This is a necessary feature of capitalism.

A perfect example of the ignorance of racism and neo-colonialism from the left is the idea of the universal basic income (UBI). In short, the idea is to abolish welfare spending and give everyone a set income. This would mean everyone could eat, have a foothold in society and work to earn more money. It has been a part of the Green party agenda for years and the Finnish government has even run a trial. One of the justifications for UBI is that increases in robotics have eroded many of the manual jobs that were the staple of working class communities.[24] Again we see the bias towards the West because the problem in the underdeveloped world is not the loss of manual work. In fact, in many places it is the opposite, the outsourcing of manual labour to poorer countries that do not have the same working conditions and are paid far less than the Western worker. When you are paid less than a dollar a day for your ten-hour shift, robots taking your job is not your number one concern. For the African continent the problem is the complete marginalisation of the economies, where the West (and China) take the resources and do not leave enough for the native populations. The fascination with robotics is the definition of a First World problem, and UBI is the fittingly Western solution.

Even if UBI was a good idea, it would not necessarily do anything to alleviate the global issues of inequality. One of the pioneers of this idea, Guy Standing, actually researched the concept in the underdeveloped world, an ideal setting because the amount is pegged to subsistence levels.[25] In a poor country UBI is much less than in a rich one, so he did not need as much research funding for the project. Surprise, surprise, the results were positive: if you give people money their lives get a bit easier. Setting aside the ethics of giving people money in a poor country and then stopping when the research finishes, the whole notion actually reinforces global inequalities. The West gets to keep its inflated UBI, while the rest live off a much lower figure. But because no one is starving, everything is alright with the world. Worse still, the campaigns for UBI are typically at the nation state level, so there is little concern for applying the model to the globe. UBI is the perfect example of the left coming up with a solution that benefits the West and does not challenge the world system, which provides the wealth for their social safety net.

Psychosis of Whiteness

Marxism has been unable to overcome what I call the 'psychosis of Whiteness',[26] which infects Western thought.

Whiteness is actually rooted in the political economy; it is in the fabric of the institutions and social life. You cannot work the natives in the Americas to death without Whiteness. You do not enslave millions of African people and kill millions more without Whiteness. You do not steal the resources from the places of the world you have underdeveloped and then create a system of unfair trade practices without Whiteness. The modern world was shaped in the image of Whiteness. Swedish botanist Linnaeus gave the perfect illustration of the hierarchy of Whiteness in his categorisations of the species of mankind in the eighteenth century:

> Eurpaues albus: ingenious, white, sanguine, governed by law, Americus rubescus; happy with his lot, liberty loving, tanned and irascible, governed by custom, Asiatic luridus; yellow, melancholy, governed by opinion, Afer Niger; crafty, lazy, black, governed by arbitrary will of the master.[27]

Europeans perceived themselves as superior and built a world in the image of this belief. It is telling that the hierarchy outlined by Linnaeus is a very good approximation of global poverty. The wealth in the West is built and maintained off this embrace of Whiteness. The West never needs to account for its multiple sins because the poverty in the developing world is attributed to the inadequacies of the Black and Brown victims of the system. Western governments can brush off any claims for reparations for transatlantic slavery because it all happened so long ago that we should have pulled ourselves together by now. The ideology of Whiteness, the irrational set of ideas that distances White people from blame for the ills of the world, are absolutely essential to maintaining the system of imperialism. If White people were to acknowledge their role in the world, the blood and destruction upon which their liberty is built, then the whole system would come tumbling down. So Whiteness becomes ingrained in not only the political economy but also the intellectual ideas. The Enlightenment provides the knowledge necessary for science and progress in Europe, while at the same time cementing the hierarchy of Whiteness into how we understand the world. The idea of Europe being the centre of knowledge, which shines its light out onto the darker, savage parts of the world, is absolutely central to both the Enlightenment as a project and the West in general. It was no contradiction for John Locke to believe in freedom for all, but make money from the slave trade and be opposed to rights for Native Americans.[28] He did not view the savage as worthy of the same liberty as Whites. Kant's much praised writings on pure reason are of course in no way in conflict with his numerous clearly racist writings on the human family. Whiteness is not a reasonable frame, and once you exalt Europeans to a different level of existence you understand that liberty and freedom have never been meant for us. These are not just ideas; Whiteness is in the DNA of the social system. Therefore overcoming Whiteness is impossible because it is a product of the structural condition, a psychosis caused to ensure that the system remains intact.

There is no reasoning with a psychosis, just as there is no point in engaging in a rational debate with Whiteness. So embedded within the fabric of society is the psychosis that it even frames the critical Whiteness Studies literature. Much has been written on critical Whiteness Studies in the last few decades, identifying Whiteness that privileges White skin.[29] When Whiteness is produced, it becomes normalised and invisible to the White population.[30] The concept is not static, it shifts in time and space, in terms of who is and who is not included in the exclusive club.[31] Whiteness has also been acknowledged as a key to a global system of oppression by the West over the 'rest', being used to mobilise the 'civilised' over the 'uncivilised' world.[32] However, the wealth of writing on the subject has remained too optimistic on the issues of Whiteness.

In identifying Whiteness as an issue, the solution has often been to engage in critical pedagogy, to make people realise their Whiteness so that they can remedy it.[33] If only Whiteness could be taught out of White people then they could play an important part in the 'liberation of people of colour around the globe'.[34] To see Whiteness as something that can be trained out of the poor souls infected by it is to locate the source of the problem in the wrong place. Unfortunately, this is a dominant theme in the literature, most perfectly represented by the so-called 'new abolitionists'.

Whiteness is something that can be abolished according to scholars such as Ignatiev, who argued that 'so-called whites must cease to exist as whites in order to realize themselves as something else … White people must commit suicide as whites in order to come alive as workers … fully developed human subjects'.[35] This is the classic Marxist appraisal of the problem of Whiteness, which is betrayed later in the talk by his assertion that by committing 'race treason' and defying 'White rules', poor White people would realise 'their real condition of life'. In other words, Whiteness is nothing more than the false consciousness of working class Whites, who have been tricked into being racist by their capitalist oppressors. This theme is recurrent in the work of Ignatiev, who is famous for his *How the Irish Became White*,[36] where he argues that the immigrants from Europe to America were not always accepted as White, but became so by embracing racism and defining themselves in opposition to African Americans. If Whiteness can be learned, then presumably it can be undone, if people are treasonous to their supposed race.

Like all Marxist arguments in regard to racism, it misses the point and importance of the concept. The Irish did not become White in America, they arrived as White and were eventually accepted into the national framework. It is vitally important that we distinguish analytically between racism and xenophobia in this discussion. The Irish have undoubtedly historically experienced xenophobia in America and Britain. As foreigners they have been derided, scorned and faced discrimination. In competing for resources with those already inside the nation state they have faced marginalisation and had to overcome this to become part of the respective societies. This is a process that any migrant community has to go through and is distinct from racism, which works on a different set of metrics. Those groups that are not White will face the xenophobia of being a foreigner, but racism is more elemental than this. It is tied to and written on the body, it is rejection for having difference rooted in biology. Racism cannot be overcome through integration into the social system. While the Irish assimilated into America and Britain, Black people in both countries have largely remained marginalised. Even though I was born in Britain, and I am relatively successful, my children are still Black British, and will never fully be granted equality in the national picture. Structurally, the Irish are now indistinguishable from White people in general, while Black people remain subject to severe disadvantage. The idea that the Irish were not White before they arrived in America is also typically ahistorical. There is a reason that Irish people migrated voluntary to America on boats, while Africans were stolen and taken there in chains.

The very notion that it is possible to abolish Whiteness speaks to how little weight is truly given to both the concept, and issues of racism in general. Abolition ties into the myth that anything other than one form of racial oppression was ended with the so-called emancipation of enslaved Africans. Rather than being the solution to the problem of racism, abolition just heralded the dawn of new ways to oppress Black people. But it is also the perfect metaphor for the new abolitionists, the illusion of progress while ignoring the structural issues of racism. Even better, abolition is the definition of the White saviour discourse, celebrating the White heroes who abolished the evil system of slavery. Central to the psychosis of Whiteness is that White people are the key agents of history, the ones who decide the future of the world, for all of us.

Importantly, the psychosis of Whiteness is not limited to those whose skin is white. Whiteness is rooted in the political economy of the West and not only White people benefit from this. From the very outset of the imperial social order there were those who were bought off by Western interests, or elevated into positions of authority in order to manage the imperial system for the West. The former colonial elite very much exists today, allowing the West to leech off the homelands for a small share of the spoils. Those of us who reside in the West must also accept our collusion in the global system of oppression. While racial oppression is endemic for Black people in the West, we are mostly spared the harshest forms of brutality. Many of us have integrated to the point where we comfortably benefit from the fruits of imperialism. So we are also not immune to the psychosis of Whiteness. There are many Black members of the Conservative party; Black entertainers get rich living up to racial stereotypes; and everyone apparently lost their minds thinking that Barack Obama was going to end racism. Black Marxists have also fallen into the trap of the psychosis.

In the 1920s African American scholar Abram Harris accused those who embraced race consciousness as being in the grip of 'colour psychosis' and needing to gain an 'aware-ness of working-class-consciousness' in order to join the real struggle.[37] For Marxism, class always trumps race, and the history of Black Marxists lecturing those who cannot accept that equation is well worn. Garvey's principle of 'race first' was the subject of scorn by Marxists, including the African Blood Brother (ABB). However, both the ABB and the CPUSA attempted to infiltrate the UNIA and convert the members to communism.[38] Garveyism attracted the Black masses because it resonated with the situation they found themselves in.

Instead of engaging with why this was, the Marxists sought to play the role of the revolutionary vanguard and lead the people to where they thought they needed to be, in desperation to provide the theoretical basis for solidarity with the White workers. Harris also wrote that 'the negro was not enslaved because of his complexion'.[39] It is here we see the fundamental fallacy at the heart of the Marxist discussion of race.

In Eric Williams' Black Marxist classic *Capitalism and Slavery* he repeats this idea when he argues that 'slavery was born not of racism; rather racism was the consequence of slavery'.[40] In this logic racism was justified after the decision was made to enslave countless African people. As we have noted earlier, this logic cannot be defended. The brutality of slavery was only an inevitable feature of capitalism because Whiteness was already driving the process of imperialism. In fact, racism actually pre-dates class in a Marxist sense, shaping the development of the system that will eventually lead to the Proletarian revolution.

Williams goes into a lot of detail explaining how White indentured servants were not treated in the same way as enslaved Africans, and were even a 'democratic force in society'.[41] However, the main thrust of his argument is that the enslavement of Africans 'seen in its historical perspective, forms a part of the general picture of the harsh treatment of the underprivileged classes'.[42] Denying the particular experience of enslavement to Black populations is a particularly insidious form of the psychosis of Whiteness. Even more harmful in terms of activism is the reduction of Blackness to a product of class.

By arguing that racism is produced by capitalism, race consciousness becomes problematic. Steeped in the psychosis of Whiteness, Marxists can only see the production of race through European eyes. The Negro is a product of racism, produced in the image of Whiteness. In that sense we are racialised through the eyes, oppression and institutions of Western society. Indeed, racialisation has become a central way in which academia understands the issue of race.[43] The fundamental logic of Marxism is therefore to abolish Blackness and join the ranks of the oppressed workers. But, as we explored in the last chapter, Blackness was never created by Whiteness; it is a rejection of it. I am not racialised into Blackness; I am Black. My Blackness is a declaration of self and resistance, not a position of victimhood and oppression. The same cannot be said for the White working class who from the outset have been racialised into Whiteness. Far from breaking down this racialisation Marxism tends to feed it, transforming the White workers from collaborators in the system of oppression into the vital hero of the story. The White working class is part of the problem of imperialism; it does us no favours to pretend they will be the solution. But Black Marxists have been unable to break free of the illusion that the White working classes are a 'sleeping beauty' of allyship. It's time to realise they have no intention of waking up.[44]

African socialism

As well as embracing Marxism in the West, Black activists in the colonies have attempted to apply the theory to their conditions. Walter Rodney's *How Europe Underdeveloped Africa* was an essential text in applying a material analysis to the problems in the colonies. The idea of analysing the situations in the colonies through the lens of Marxism was a powerful one. The Communist bloc presented an alternative to Western imperialism and the Soviets, Chinese and Cubans also provided key support to African and Caribbean revolutionary struggles. For instance, before the hero of the Cuban revolution Che Guevara was assassinated in Bolivia, he spent part of 1965 in Congo trying to support the revolutionary movement.[45] The failure of this mission could stand as a metaphor for communism in Africa, but there was a time when the struggle between capitalism and communism was uncertain. Africa was a central battlefield given the continent's wealth of material resources, so Marxist revolutions in places like Angola, Guinea and Mozambique were a clear threat to Western dominance.

In adopting Marxism, efforts were made to adapt its core principles. Africa was not in an industrial stage of development and had vastly different social and cultural norms to Europe. Amilcar Cabral, who led the revolutionary struggle in Guinea and Cape Verde, also developed a significant analysis of Marxism on the African continent. Rather than dismiss colonialism as a prior force to capitalism he explained that 'what commands history in colonial conditions is not the class struggle ... it is the colonial state'.[46] Colonialism is at the heart, not the periphery of the analysis and is the foundation of the class system. He explored the elevation of some tribal leaders into a managerial class overseeing Portuguese rule and the creation of a city-dwelling class to serve the Portuguese residents. The marginalisation of the rural peasants was total and they were locked away from any social advancement, even literacy. In presenting these class distinctions Cabral importantly does not conclude that the African petty bourgeoisie, who collude with the Portuguese, are a counterrevolutionary class. In fact, he argues that it is this class that is absolutely essential for the revolutionary struggle, because although they based the 'whole armed liberation struggle on the peasantry', the leadership was drawn from the petty bourgeoisie.[47] National liberation became the primary objective in the colonial struggle and in order for this to occur all the classes of Black people in Guinea had to unite. The picture Cabral draws is very similar to the unity of the enslaved, Mulattoes and free Blacks that we examined in the Haitian revolution. However, this struggle for national liberation was not in itself Marxist, because to hope that the petty bourgeoisie 'will just carry out a revolution when it comes to power in an undeveloped country is to hope for a miracle'.[48] Classical colonialism stifled the petty bourgeoisie in African countries, but they could be bought off by the colonial powers offering them a place in the global elite with trappings of state power. Guarding against neo-colonialism, therefore, became key in the revolutionary struggle.

In reinterpreting Marxism through the colonial relationship, Cabral based the revolutionary struggle on the immediate evil facing the African continent. In the 1980s, in Burkino Faso, Thomas Sankara would blend Marxism in a similar manner, in order to 'eliminate imperialist domination and exploitation; and to purge the countryside of all social, economic, and cultural obstacles that keep it in a backward state'.[49] Not only should this be a reminder that the material relations in the colonies are vastly different to those in the West, but it raises questions about whether Marxism in the African context is even the same concept.

Cabral attempts to link the struggle in Africa to the West, arguing that 'neo-colonialism is more of a defeat for the international working class than for the colonised people'.[50] If the welfare state was founded off the back of Empire in the 1950s, it should come as no surprise that social democracy starts to fall apart after independence movements in the colonies. Neo-colonialism marks a shift to the dominance of the economic over the political in the West as well as the colonies: corporations, globalisation of trade and the ability to move production to poorer countries. All of these undermine the post-war settlement that kept the natives in the industrialised West happy. We are still seeing Western governments try to come to terms with this new reality of a smaller state, less unskilled work and a rampant and unpretending class of profiteering, tax-dodging elites. So we could be seeing the convergence of the interests of White workers in the West with the oppressed in the global South. However, this view would be ahistorical and overly optimistic.

Levels of inequality within the West have risen to their highest since the 1920s. A detached elite rubbing the faces of the poor in the dirt is not a production of neo-colonialism. The welfare state was founded off the back of the colonies, but not because of classic colonialism. It was the fear of the spread of communism that led to the gains after the Second World War. The collapse of the global revolution and the Soviet Union is the reason that the elite gorged themselves on the proceeds of inequality. Once there is an organised push-back the elite will make some concessions, which will no doubt placate the working classes in the West. There is no evidence, either historical or current, that the Western working class is throwing its lot in with the Black and Brown wretched of the earth.

Cabral effectively spells out a vision that allows for African agency in the liberation struggle and also to remain non-aligned from the Soviet Union. This is very different to how Marxism was often applied in Africa. Socialism became a foundation of the left in the Pan-African movement. Nkrumah died in Bucharest after his exile from Ghana and even DuBois turned to China and Marxism in the end. Just as we explored in Chapter 2, Pan-Africanism was ultimately an imperial project, and even its embrace of socialism took this form. Dubois' vision of socialism involved leaning on both West and East to provide the necessary support for Africa. In climbing into bed with China many African countries have now found themselves on the receiving end of imperialism under a different guise.[51] Truly revolutionary projects like Cabral's were not allowed to continue and the socialism that was largely embraced in Africa actually hindered any radical progress.

Similar to how calls for Pan-Africanism became empty rhetoric, so did the call for socialism. It allowed leaders to sound progressive, without actually committing to socialist principles. Twenty years after independence 'none of the states implemented policies which would qualify as effectively fighting for socialism'.[52] The extent of socialism for many countries was to allow China to interfere in their economic affairs. Whether by accident or design, when socialism was applied in the African context it largely became devoid of its revolutionary politics. Nyerere's African socialism is an example of these limitations, being rooted in connecting communism to the communalism of traditional African society. In the village everyone's fate was tied together. If the crop failed, the chief and the servant both suffered due to the nature of communal living. But the differences between communism and communalism are stark and undermine the radical nature of Marxism.

In a society based on the communal production and distribution of food, where housing and clothing can be built within the family unit, communalism can thrive. Crops failing will be devastating to everyone, so it makes sense to pool resources. But there is no comparison of this situation to that of industrialised, mass production with wealth that far outstrips subsistence levels. Providing the basic material of life is no longer done on the village scale. Think of the complex system that gets milk to someone in the city. You need the farmer, farm machinery, the market, infrastructure, mechanics, vehicles, and the list goes on. There is not one aspect that everyone contributes to, which everyone relies on for the system to work. If one farmer has trouble and goes out of business, there is another one to take their place. Rich and poor are perfectly possible. The very individual idea of profit that underlines the system runs contrary to communalism.

Once you base a system on the idea of individual wealth you structure inequality into social life. To argue that there is something innately African about sharing this wealth is to grossly oversimplify the situation.

The limits of Nyerere's concept of African socialism can be seen in his discussion of the role of individuals in socialism:

> In the individual, as in the society, it is an attitude of mind which distinguishes the socialist from the non-socialist. It has nothing to do with the possession or non-possession of wealth. Destitute people can be potential capitalist exploiters of their fellow human beings. A millionaire can equally well be socialist; he may value his wealth only because it can be used in the service of his fellow men.[53]

Socialism is reduced to a mere state of mind, detached from all economic analysis. To argue that someone who is destitute is equally capable of being a capitalist exploiter as someone who is wealthy is to remove any Marxist analysis from socialism. It is this thinking that makes the bourgeoisie comfortable in their oppression, because if they do not hold capitalist attitudes then they can feel on the right side of history. By invoking platitudes about traditional African life and removing any material analysis, African socialism becomes a tool for maintaining the economic status quo of the imperial social order.

Marxism on the African continent becomes so transformed that it is not recognisable to the Eurocentric doctrine. In the revolutionary case like Cabral the theory has to be changed, almost beyond recognition, or we are left with meaningless platitudes like Nyerere's African socialism. Marx never had a monopoly on the concept of universalised resources, so it is best to abandon the label in order to build an alternative and Black radical economic analysis.

Black Panther Party for Self-Defense

Untangling Marxism from Black radicalism is difficult because of the crossover and linkages, as the Cabral discussion demonstrates. The Black Panther Party for Self-Defense is perhaps the best example of the complexities here. The Panthers were an openly Marxist-Leninist organisation that saw itself as part of the vanguard of the global revolution. The party first raised funds by selling copies of Chairman Mao's *Little Red Book* to college kids.[54] Fred Hampton, a leader in Chicago who was famously murdered by the police while he slept,[55] declared 'I am a revolutionary … I am the proletariat, I am the people'. He even predicted that he would 'die a revolutionary in the international revolutionary proletarian struggle'.[56] The influence of their contemporary neo-Marxists on the Panthers was also keenly felt. Suspicions about Eldridge Cleaver aside, he penned a piece 'On Lumpen Ideology', where he argued that the pampered working classes in the West would not lead the revolution.[57] Instead, it would be the lumpen proletariat, those Marx called the 'the dangerous class, the social scum, that passively rotting mass' at the bottom of the society.[58] The Panthers believed they could reform the dealers, robbers, murderers, pimps and put them in service of the revolution. Huey P. Newton was famous for long and theoretical speeches about Marxism, and he eventually completed a PhD on the Panthers with neo-Marxist Erik Olin Wright.[59] There is absolutely no doubt that the Panthers were an avidly Marxist organisation, in theory at least. But we need to separate the practice of the Panthers to understand why they lie firmly within the Black radicalism.

Organisationally it is important that the Panthers were not part of any overarching communist body. While they preached the international struggle and made links with communist groups, they were never part of, or led by them. In contrast, the African Blood Brotherhood was founded in 1919 but folded into the CPUSA by 1924. The independence of the Panthers is important because they maintained Black leadership and therefore went beyond the limitations of seeing Black people as a 'class fraction' of the wider struggle.[60] Unlike the framing of the 'Negro question', the Panthers always prioritised the issues of racism. In fact none of the key activities of the Panthers were Marxist in orientation.

In the last chapter we debunked the masculine history of the Panthers, drawing attention to the newspaper, the free breakfast programmes, the liberation schools and free health clinics. The paper and the school could fit into Marxism with their political re-education to fight against the ideological tyranny of the elites. But providing free breakfast and medical care is not a classically revolutionary act (though we will pick up this discussion in Chapter 8). The Panthers also used violence for self-defence and spent most of the time organising programmes for survival; tactics which are not, in isolation, those of the Marxist-Leninist revolutionary vanguard.

None of this should come as a surprise because the Panthers were the self-proclaimed 'children of Malcolm',[61] and Malcolm's fundamental influence was Garveyism. Ignore the Marxist rhetoric and you see the tools of Garveyism at work, the newspaper and the programmes that were aiming to make the Black community self-sufficient and able to survive America. Bobby Seale running for mayor and Elaine Brown for city council in 1972 fit perfectly into this Garveyite scheme, pulling the levers in order to generate power for the Black nation.

The Panthers also inspired movements outside of America. In Britain, the Black Panther Party was founded in 1968 by a group including Althea Jones-LeCointe, Eddie Chambers and Darcus Howe. It is telling of their legacy that the Marxist rhetoric was even less present. The group set about campaigning on issues of policing, housing and immigration, following the lead of being rooted in the concerns of Black communities.

Marxism is appealing because it offers a searing analysis of the problem of exploitation, tied directly into the material conditions people face. Black people are all too well aware of how inequality is woven into the fabric of society and therefore the need for a revolution. Black Marxism may well be an avenue to revolutionary overthrow and I have avoided getting into a discussion of the merits and logic of Marxist analysis. The aim of the chapter is to demonstrate that despite all of its appeal, Marxism remains a fundamentally Eurocentric paradigm. Robinson's *Black Marxism* attempts to deal with the Eurocentric bias of Marxism by centring on Black activists rather than the European working class.[62] But to do so changes the nature of Marxism to the point that it becomes a different political ideology. This is why we have seen Black activists often break away from Marxism or stretch it beyond its meaning; perhaps maintaining the rhetoric, but in reality engaging in other forms of engagement. Whether or not Marxism can produce revolution, it is a different project to Black radicalism.

The categorical difference to Marxism is that Black radicalism does not rely on White agency. If the White working classes surprise the world and join the fight against imperialism then of course that would be welcome. But Black radicalism is based on seeing the fundamental contradiction in society as that of racism, Whiteness, hierarchy. The Black revolution will destroy this foundation and alter the lives of the working classes in the West, but it is just as likely (if not more so) that they will be a central component of the reactionary response. Increasingly this is also the case with workers in China, India and the rest of 'dark mankind'. Black Marxists may have far more faith in the workers of the world, which is commendable, but the politics of Black radicalism has no room for this optimism.

Chapter 7

Liberal Radicalism

Since being placed on the FBI's most wanted list in August 1970, Angela Davis has been an iconic figure in radical circles. Davis was on the run because she had bought the gun that seventeen-year-old Jonathan Jackson had used to take a judge, prosecutor and three jurors hostage. Jackson was hoping to use the hostages to bargain for the release of his brother George and fellow 'Soledad Brothers' who were facing charges of murder for the death of a guard at Soledad Prison, in California.[1] The situation did not end well; after a shootout with police as they were trying to escape, the judge and the three Black Panthers were dead.

Davis had developed a relationship with George while he was in prison, and Jonathan served as her bodyguard. By 1970 Davis was heavily involved with the Communist Party and had been fired from her role as assistant professor at UCLA because of her politics. When she was caught, President Nixon celebrated the 'capture of the dangerous terrorist' and a mass campaign to free Angela spread across America and the world.[2] One of the iconic images from the Black Power era is of Angela Davis, with her immaculate Afro, confronting the system of racism. Following her acquittal on all charges Davis resumed an academic career, writing on feminism, liberation and becoming one of the strongest critics of the 'prison industry complex', arguing that prisons should be abolished.[3] Her work and activism make her one of the most sought-after speakers today and an inspiration to countless generations.

For all these reasons I was extremely excited to get the chance to hear Davis speak at the Black Matters conference at the University of Texas in 2016. It will become apparent in this chapter, if it has not already, that my biggest struggle is reconciling my role as an academic with the radical politics that I believe in. Universities are a central part of the system that oppresses Black communities. The very idea of race, the hierarchy of White supremacy, was produced and maintained by universities. Universities have continued to produce the knowledge that supports ideas of White supremacy, and are the peak of a school system that is the enemy of Black progress on a global level. Universities are as institutionally racist as the police force, so in the same way that a Black cop is always problematic, so too is a Black academic. I was fortunate enough to get to ask a question so I used the opportunity to ask Angela Davis how she had maintained being a radical, while being an academic. In my experience these two are entirely contradictory and it is a constant struggle to negotiate the academic industrial complex and maintain radical commitments. Much to my surprise her response was to explain that she 'did not see the contradiction', and that maintaining links outside of the university was the solution.

Davis also raised the fact that as an academic she had been attacked by politicians and fired for her radical political beliefs. But it is precisely here that we can see the contradiction of the academic. When Davis was an active member of the Communist Party and providing the weapons for attempts to break Black Panthers out of prison, she was hunted down and arrested, and of course not permitted into the hallowed halls of the academy. When she shifted to writing, speaking and theorising revolution from the comfort of the university Professor Davis was no longer hounded by the state. In fact, she is one of the most celebrated academics in America. To be unable to see this contradiction demonstrates the level to which we can easily fall into the trap of liberal radicalism; to embrace radical theory, but ignore radical solutions because we benefit from the liberal system.

Symptom-free racism

One of the statements that Davis made in 2015, while in Berlin, is a good starting point in this discussion. After speaking to refugee activists and being taken to see one of the housing facilities, Davis remarked that 'the refugee movement is *the* movement of the 21st century. It's the movement that is challenging the effects of global capitalism, it's the movement that is calling for civil rights for all human beings'.[4] Due to the sheer numbers of people fleeing their homelands in search of refuge, immigration has become a priority issue across the globe. Not only in terms of refugees, who are in fear for their safety, but millions of people are seeking economic stability and escaping the biting poverty that exists where they were born. Despite the media panic, the majority of displaced people reside in countries in the global South. Turkey, Pakistan, Lebanon, Iran, Uganda and Ethiopia are the nations that house the most displaced people.[5] The refugees and economic migrants who do make it to the West face hostility and a range of different laws aimed to keep them out.

In Berlin, Davis was greeted with stories of discrimination and saw the squalid living conditions that migrants faced in the city. This should come as no surprise given the anti-migrant feeling that has become a mainstay of political discourse in the West. The European Union reducing support for search and rescue in the Mediterranean is indicative of the callous approach to migrant life of Western governments. So keen are they to keep people out, they use floating bodies as a deterrent to migration. Britain has a particularly inhumane system for those who wish to claim asylum. People are prevented from working and forced to live on an income far below the poverty level while their cases can take years. During this time they are incredibly insecure and in danger of being apprehended at a moment's notice if their case fails. Detention centres are used to house families and unaccompanied minors, and deporta-tions are carried out by private security firms. Put this together with a hostile media and suspicious public and life for migrants in Britain should bring shame to us all. Davis is right when she compares the refugee movement to those campaigns for civil rights. The quest is for decency and dignity to be applied to all. But if this is *the* movement of the twenty-first century then we have given up on radical change.

The plight of refugees is not *the* problem, it is a symptom of the wider structural issues. Rather than trying to simply deal with how migrants are treated in the West, we must be trying to prevent their arrival in the first place. In truth, there is too much migration, which is caused by the imbalances of global inequality. This is a resources issue, though it is not that migrants are stealing from the West, but the exact opposite. Due to the continued imperial global order the West enriches itself from the poverty and instability that is driving millions to flee their homes. We should be trying to stop there being any need to flee in the first place, not just trying to make the process of moving easier. Radical arguments seek to cure society, not just alleviate the suffering.

Unfortunately, the desire for *symptom-free racism* is strong and at the core of much of our politics, activism and theory. We focus on surviving by treating the symptoms rather than the disease. Police brutality, educational inequalities, unemployment, migrant rights, and the list goes on. By engaging our energies in the symptoms we can convince ourselves that we are healing, without having to address the fundamental concern. We build a politics that helps us live with the disease of racism, rather than overcome it. This is the liberal individual approach to tackling racism. Our aim is to make the effects of racism as little seen in our lives as possible, to push it to the side-lines. We know we will not avoid the symptoms forever, but as long as they only act up every so often we can deal with it.

The quest for symptom-free racism is most keenly felt in the Black bourgeoisie, those who have managed to alleviate some of their condition. Unsurprisingly, then, symptom-free contagion is rampant in Black academia. The best example of this would be the theorisation and focus on 'micro-aggressions',[6] which are the slights of everyday racism; the subtle papercuts that as they accumulate do enormous damage to the psyche. Any Black person in a professional job will testify to the pain caused by micro-aggressions. People are often surprised when I explain I have a 'uniform' for work. I always go to the office in smart trousers and shoes because I have been scarred by being treated as a student by both the security and my colleagues. Any Black male academic will have a story of being harassed while carrying out their job because they simply did not fit the expected profile of an esteemed academic. For the first year as an academic I made sure to wear my staff card around my neck, because the treatment was so noticeably different when I did not. Having to adjust to the constant slights in the corridor, in meetings and in general takes its toll. But as my mother said when I tried to explain micro-aggressions to her, 'that's just what being Black is'. The micro-aggressions are a symptom of racism, and unless we thought the disease had gone away there is no reason we should expect not to suffer from its effects.

As symptoms go, micro-aggressions are incredibly mild ones. I have to deal with slights and stresses at work, but I do not get harassed by the police; I am in one of the best paid professions in the world and reap the societal benefits that such an income provides. If the only symptoms of racism that we experience are micro-aggressions then we should be thankful, because we are extraordinarily privileged. In a world where a child dies every ten seconds because they cannot eat we should be grateful for the papercuts of racism. Instead, and I won't name names here because the individuals are not important, many of us dedicate our privileged academic lives to researching and writing about micro-aggressions. Papers, books, inaugural lectures on how bad we have it because of the everyday slights and the pressure it puts us under.

It is impossible to eradicate micro-aggressions and making them the focus of our work is the worst and most insular way we could approach the issue. Micro-aggressions are a reminder that we are Black, that no matter how far we have come we cannot cure racism within this system. We should use this reminder as our way of connecting to struggles off-campus, not indulge ourselves in trying to treat our minor symptoms. I can already hear the howls of disapproval from colleagues affected by micro-aggressions and fighting to stay sane in the halls of privilege. But the radical analysis has always been based on the liberation of the masses. You cannot build a revolution by trying to make it more comfortable for the lucky few to endure the master's house.

Symptom-free racism is by no means confined to Black academia. Much of the criticism that applied to cultural nationalism in Chapter 3 would apply here as well. The idea that we are a broken people who first need to be fixed is the perfect example of putting the symptoms before the disease. Cultural nationalists focus on those aspects they deem problematic like absentee fathers, substance abuse, violence and even dietary choices. To the extent that these are problems within Black communities, they are the symptoms of racism. For instance, Amos Wilson insightfully explored how the disproportionate numbers of Black people killing each other (a phenomenon we see across the globe) are caused by the destruction of Black selfhood in this system of oppression.[7] Cultural nationalism can never be radical because it presents treating the symptoms as *the* solution to racism. In reality, embracing a new world view may make you feel better individually but it does nothing to end the problem of racism. We may well be a broken people but we cannot be fixed within a system of oppression.

Treating the symptoms of racism necessarily locates the issues at the individual level. Even when we attempt to apply the treatment on a mass scale it often results in trying to inoculate individuals. We work with young people to help them navigate the school system, or avoid getting caught up in gangs. We mentor, coach and inspire people to survive and resist. There is nothing wrong with any of this work; it is vital given the conditions that find ourselves in. But we have to acknowledge that we are treating the symptoms and never the disease. The whole voluntary and not-for-profit sector is set up to be this way. The state, businesses, philanthropists and communities put resources into dealing with the results of racism but never the oppression itself.

Medical metaphors are fitting here because there has been a push for 'self-care' in activist circles,[8] ensuring that we have the resources and time to recharge our batteries. Before we can love the people, we first need to love and look after ourselves. Again, there is nothing wrong with this in principle; running yourself into the ground is not a great strategy for social change. Though it may be a good idea, it is certainly not a radical one, and the self-care paradigm can easily cross over into the indulgent politics of self. No one individual is so vital to the revolution that they need to be pampered and cherished. Radical engagement must be built on collective agency. Also, the idea of sacrifice has always been at the basis of radical politics. When Assata Shakur threw off her slave name, she purposefully picked the name meaning 'she who struggles' in order to connect to the politics of the movement.[9] We call it the struggle for a reason. It is uncomfortable, unforgiving and exposes you to all kinds of danger. Newton talked about the need to commit 'revolutionary suicide', to give your life to the people.[10] We used to be prepared to die for the people, now we are not even committed enough to be stressed and overworked. It speaks to what we have on the line, the comforts of the West that we are so keen to cling on to.

Self-care is also problematic because it again treats the symptoms, not the disease. There is no sanctuary within this imperial system; there is no respite, no safe space. We can only ever partially heal when we are constantly living under oppression. Our spaces of healing may enrich us individually, but they are a mirage and in the long term no more useful than the distant dream of paradise on the horizon. Rather than trying to escape from feelings of despair, anger, anxiety and depression, we should lean into them. Given the state of the world these are all appropriate responses. I keep coming back to dead children because the image is so stark. In the time it will take you to read this book the number of children who have been killed by this political and economic system would be overwhelming. If you do not despair at the brutal reality of the system then you either do not appreciate the depths of it, or are somewhere on the psychopathy scale. We should use our discomfort to challenge us, to propel us, to keep us on edge. We should be 'angry', we should be 'hot' and we must be 'uncompromising'.[11] At its worst, self-care can act as a pain-killer against the racial oppression that we face. Malcolm used the metaphor of the dentist applying novocaine to your gums to stop you fighting them pulling out your teeth. He warned that the worst we could do as a community was to take the novocaine and 'don't stop suffering – just suffer peacefully'.[12] Embracing our suffering is key to our resisting it. We should not wallow in our pain, or be consumed by it. We must use it as the driving force to push us into building a radical alternative. Once we get too comfortable, we stop struggling, but struggle is the only route to freedom.

Flight is not freedom

In his book *Freedom as Marronage*, Neil Roberts made the argument that 'freedom is not a place, it is a state of being'.[13] The book offers a fascinating account of maroon experiences, with a particular focus on Haiti. Maroon refers to communities of the formerly enslaved who liberated themselves from slavery and set up villages, towns and settlements out of the reaches of the slaving powers. Wherever there was slavery there were maroons. We have talked already about Queen Nanny Jamaica. The Quilombo settlements in Brazil were home to thousands of escaped Africans, with the largest, Palmares, operating as a republic that was hundreds of miles long and home to 30,000 people, from 1600 to 1694.[14] In America, Harriet Tubman is the most notable maroon, who freed hundreds of the enslaved using the Underground Railroad. Roberts argues that refusing to be enslaved and reclaiming their bodies gave the maroons a measure of freedom. But flight is not the same as freedom, and Roberts recognises this when he distinguishes different forms of marronage. Petit-marronage was temporary flight, where the enslaved would leave the plantation from a few hours to a week, but return. Grand marronage was the quilombos and maroon communities who never returned to the plantations. But his highest form is sociogenic marronage that he models after the Haitian revolution, which by 'abolishing slavery outright' marked 'a radical move'.[15] That is precisely because fleeing the plantation did not bring freedom. The plantation continued to shape social life for the maroons. It defined where and how they could live and they had to constantly be vigilant for fear of raids and capture. The lack of freedom meant that many maroon communities signed treaties with the colonial powers in order to protect themselves. Under these treaties the maroons would have to agree not only to stop attempting to free the enslaved but also to return any runaways to the plantations. Collusion between some maroons and the imperialists ran so deep that it continued even after the end of slavery. Paul Bogle, who started the Morant Bay Rebellion in Jamaica in 1865, was captured for the British by maroons.

Flight may be a rational response, but it is not a radical one. By leaving the system of slavery intact the maroons could never be free from it. This is an extension to the problem of narrow nationalism that we discussed in Chapter 1. Separation can never solve the problems, it just relocates them. This was even true for Haiti because the republic could never succeed, surrounded as it was by the imperial might of the

West. Freedom can only be won by overturning the system that oppresses you. Flight, as part of a process of liberation, should never be confused with the condition of freedom. Roberts ends the book by connecting Rastafari into the history of marronage, and it works as the perfect case for its limits.

In rejecting the language, culture and mind-set of the West, or the Babylon system, Rastafari represents cultural flight. At the birth of the movement Rastas also lived apart from the crazy baldheads in the city and survived off the land. In Chapter 3 we covered how the increasing cultural nationalism of the movement took it away from the Black radical tradition. But even in its most political sense Rastafari is based on fleeing Babylon rather than conquering it. The notion of 'chanting down Babylon' plays a key part in Rasta practice,[16] using culture to transform the Black population and eventually to destroy the wicked system. But Rastafari offers a primarily 'ideological assault' and alternative cultural and value system as the solution.[17] No matter how free Rastafari may make you feel, it cannot provide liberation.

Attitudes to Rastafari by the mainstream have also dramatically changed. At one point the Jamaican government was in open warfare with Rastas and in Britain dreadlocks were synonymous with crime and drugs.[18] In Britain, Rastafari became closely associated with the uprisings against police racism that shook Britain in the 1980s. Rasta's overt connection to radical liberation struggles marked it out as something to be opposed. But as the movement took on more cultural nationalist overtones, the mainstream embraced Rasta, or at least the symbols of it. In Britain, dreadlocks, dub and parts of the Reggae scene have become gentrified. They are now markers of the White, middle class youth who are bravely reclaiming inner city spaces. Rastafari has become firmly a part of brand Jamaica, with the global success of Reggae being seen as a boost to the tourism industry. Undoubtedly, the diluted version of the culture being taken on in the mainstream bears no resemblance to the roots of Rastafari, but the fact that the movement is no longer seen as dangerous tells us its radical limits.

Rastafari should remind us that there is no way to check out of the system. It is almost impossible not to engage in Babylon. I have seen all sorts of strategies for avoiding the system, including destroying your birth certificate and refusing to register your car, or even your child. None of these take you out, or put you beyond the reach of, the system. It may feel liberating to reject the formalities but you are still just as much a part of system as anyone else.

Assata Shakur is probably the best example of a modern-day maroon.[19] Assata was part of the Black Liberation Army, active in the 1960s and 1970s in America. Along with her comrades Sundiata Acoli and Zayd Shakur, Assata was involved in a shootout on the New Jersey Turnpike with State Trooper Werner Foerster in 1973. Both Zayd and the officer were killed and Assata was badly injured, arrested and eventually convicted of murder. But in 1979 she was broken out of prison and escaped to Cuba, where she still lives with political asylum.

Technically, Assata is free, out of prison and away from the clutches of the American state. But her entire existence remains framed by America. There is currently a $2 million bounty on her head and she is on the FBI's Most Wanted Terrorist List. Therefore she has to remain in hiding in Cuba and have limited contact with family and the outside world. She cannot leave the island or lead anything remotely like a normal life. Cuba is effectively a prison for Assata, so it should be no surprise that when asked what freedom meant to her, she responded 'you asking me about freedom? I know a whole lot more about what freedom isn't than about what it is'.[20] Flight can never bring about freedom, because the act of running ensures that the system of oppression remains. Freedom is not a process, it is not the struggle. Freedom is the dream that we struggle for.

Misuse of 'revolution'

Radical dreams of freedom are uncompromising, totalising and demand the complete transformation of the social, political and economic order. For radicals the only solution is revolution, in order to 'overturn' and 'destroy' the existing system.[21] But Malcolm warned that 'many of our people are using this word "revolution" loosely',[22] lightly embracing radical rhetoric without truly taking on board revolutionary practice. This critique definitely applies to Black politics and theory, where to be radical or revolutionary appears to mean adopting a position that differs somewhat from the norm. Part of the misuse of the term revolution is closely tied to the idea that change must come from within before it can lead to social transformation. For cultural nationalists that is the spiritual and cultural transformation; in academia we focus on the ideas, the knowledge to produce change.

While acknowledging that Cesaire's negritude movement was 'never intended to be a road map or a blueprint for revolution', Kelley contends that his classic work *Discourse on Colonialism* was 'poetry and therefore revolt'. He goes further to argue that the book was an 'act of insurrection … a hand grenade thrown with deadly accuracy, clearing the field so that we might write a new history with what's left standing'.[23] Cesaire is the perfect figure to explain the limits of intellectual radicalism. As we explored in Chapter 3, his work was hugely influential, with Fanon crediting him for transforming how Black subjects of colonialism saw themselves. But we also discussed how Cesaire was a French republican to the core, who did not see liberation from France as being desirable. Negritude was about claiming Black personhood in order to integrate more equally into the Western ideal. There is nothing radical or revolutionary about the project. Just because it went against the prevailing ideas of the time (that Black people were inferior) that does not make it radical. To judge the radical nature of an argument we have to engage in the 'new history' that it writes, not just its condemnation of the old one.

To be revolutionary also means going beyond deconstructing the present and offering abstract visions of a different future. This clearly applies to a range of post-structural theoretical reminiscences on society that even if they were written intelligibly would make little sense. In terms of Black radicalism the more common misuse of revolutionary relates to giving too much power to music and popular culture. Moten argues that 'Black radicalism is (like) music. The broken circle demands a new analytic (way of listening to the music)'.[24] He spends a lot of time making the argument that Black music with its different arrangements, soulful cries and boundary-breaking forms of expression represent the 'aesthetics' of Black radicalism. Kelley speaks of the 'revolutionary nature of the blues',[25] and the power of the surreal in transforming our vision for reality. A lot of emphasis is placed on this work in the idea of desire, fantasy and soul being alternative concepts to build our understanding on rather than European ideas of rationality. To be a blues people is to embody a different form of being, and can perhaps lead to a revolutionary transformation of society based on 'love and creativity'.[26]

There's certainly something romantic about the idea of the artists, writers, poets and musicians being the revolutionary vanguard, painting a new vision for the future and calling us to its tune. However, in reality this is just an intellectual version of cultural nationalism. We know society is corrupt but instead of trying to overthrow it we seek solace in the beauty that has been created in the hideous. We can affirm ourselves by getting lost in the sorrow songs, fiction and poetry or watching the achingly beautiful choreography of the Alvin Ailey Dance Theatre. But none of this culture, no matter how beautiful or genre defying, is revolutionary. It does not pave the way for revolution, or even in itself open up possibilities. Culture is always a product of the political moment. Slavery and marronage make the blues; the New Negro movement shapes the Harlem Renaissance; Pan-Africanism calls into existence Afro-beat; Rastafari and Garveyism produce Reggae; and Black Power creates the

Black Arts movement. Even the lack of cohesive Black political movements can be traced to the commercialisation and gangsta-isation of Hip Hop. In a memorable quote from the James Baldwin documentary *I am Not Your Negro*, he explains that he was a 'witness' to the political events that shaped his work. The film is based on a book he was writing about Malcolm X, Martin Luther King and Medgar Evers. Unlike those three he was not a leader in any organisation, and he did not pay with his life for his commitment. Baldwin was on the side-lines, linked in but not fully part of the movements. This is not to belittle or downplay Baldwin's role, but to recognise it. Artists document the political moment, they do not create it. It is a vital role, but not a revolutionary one.

Perhaps the loosest use of the term revolution I have come across is in Shayne Lee's *Erotic Revolutionaries*. Lee argues that 'erotic revolutionaries ... effectively wage war against the politics of respectability and challenge traditional scripts offering women a greater space to indulge in a fuller range of sexual expressiveness'.[27] His revolutionary vanguard includes singers, video vixens and models who blaze their transformative trail against sexual conformity. It is almost too obvious that this version of revolutionary is not radical, and is probably not meant to be. I doubt even Lee believes that doing video blogs giving tips on how to improve your sex life is a revolutionary act on a par with trying to bring down a political and economic system that kills children. But the redefinition of revolutionary is important to discuss because it has implications for Black political movements, particularly in the West where revolutionary overthrow is not an option.

One of the most fundamental problems with Lee's argument is his obsession with the politics of respectability and therefore the need to move beyond it. Respectability politics refers to the notion that Black people must represent ourselves as upright and decent citizens to counter the negative stereotypes of the lazy and deviant Black person. There is long history of respectability in Black politics, with Booker T. Washington and the 'pull yourself up by your bootstraps';[28] and Dubois' notion of the 'Best of the Race'. For radical figures such as Garvey and even Malcolm, the idea of being clean-cut and upright was seen as paramount in how we portrayed ourselves. For more conservative versions of Black politics, it is not just a question of appearance but the idea that acting, dressing and talking 'right' is the key ingredient to success in society.

One of the best examples of this poisonous logic was when Bill Cosby used his speech at the fiftieth anniversary of the desegregation of schooling to attack the 'people with their hat on backwards, pants down around the crack'. He launched a tirade against women with their 'dresses all the way up to the crack' and 'five or six different children' with 'eight or ten different' fathers. He even goes as far as to blame victims of police killings for their deaths, using the hypothetical example of people getting upset over the police shooting someone who was stealing pound cake. The problem is not the police but that they 'were holding the pound cake' in the first place.[29] Respectability politics is a problem with vastly negative consequences for Black politics and also has particular implications for gender.

Rosa Parks was not the first Black woman in Montgomery, Alabama to refuse to give up her seat to a White passenger. Nine months previously Claudette Colvin had been carried off a bus in handcuffs after she asserted her constitutional right to a seat. She sought the support of the civil rights apparatus but they did not want to use her as a test case. Claudette was fifteen and pregnant, the opposite of the steadfast Black working woman they would later use as the symbol of the campaign.[30] Rosa Parks is the embodiment of what Lisa Thompson calls the 'Black lady' archetype, a representation that 'relies heavily on the aggressive shielding of the body concealing sexuality; and foregrounding morality, civility and intelligence'.[31] Claudette was too much the stereotype, not respectable enough as the face of the campaign. In order to have the necessary esteem in the eyes of the public and the state they needed to call in the Black lady.

Lee rails against how the Black lady has dominated not just Black political representation but also Black feminist scholarly work. Seminal scholars such as Patricia Hill Collins have forensically analysed how mainstream culture provides limited 'controlling images' of Black women. From the sexless, nurturing 'mammy' figure to the deviant, oversexed 'jezebel',[32] the Black female body has been policed in popular culture. Lee is critical of how scholarship has overdetermined the role that sexualisation of Black females has played and therefore limited the space for Black female sexuality to be appreciated on its own terms. There is some truth to this; the Black lady in particular is an over-correction to the negative representations of mainstream culture. But we have to view it as a response and a resistance to this cultural oppression.

Sexual abuse of Black female bodies has historically been so central to racial oppression that it is difficult to overstate. Rape was part of the fabric of plantation life. The gruesome world tour that Saartije Baartman was subjected to, paraded naked in a cage to show off her big breasts and large backside, is testament to the powerful image of Black female sexuality underlying mainstream discourse. The controlling image of deviant Black people is not just used to make White people feel superior, but also to justify oppressive treatment. If Black women are sexual vixens then they cannot be raped. Embracing the image of the Black lady was a political manoeuvre in part enacted to protect Black women, to desexualise and make them less of a target of unwanted desire. Of course, this is a limited kind of defence and you could even argue it perpetuates rape myths about people bringing on their own assaults. But the reality is that the Black lady, and the politics of respectability in general, however misguided, are a defence mechanism. It is a symptom and not the disease. Therefore rejecting it is not a revolutionary act of liberation, just a correction of a problem-atic political position that arose in the struggle.

It is also completely incorrect to paint the Black lady as the dominant form of Black female representation. Perhaps in the Black church, or even within some Black community circles this may be the case, but most certainly not in mainstream culture. Scholars object to seeing Black women's bodies being displayed with same contempt for Black female sexu-ality as Saartije Baartman experienced, as they rightly should. Black female sexuality has been given space to be explored in popular culture, through the lens of White oppression. There is absolutely nothing new or transformative about the presentation of Nicki Minaj, or the plethora of video vixens. The only difference is that now they are paraded on screen, rather than in a cage.

Liberation is not rebelling against Black political formation. Of course we need to refocus our lenses, learn from mistakes of the past and reject conservative ideas. But the trend that views Black politics as *the* problem is disturbing. If we strip back much of Lee's argument we see an embrace of the individual, with Black women being restricted in their sexuality by the moralising Black feminists who take a more collective position on representation. There is an urge to free Black women to fulfil their desires and sexual fulfilment. Similar to cultural nationalism or finding solace in the break of the beat, this is an illusion of freedom. Revolutionising your sex life is not a radical act.

More problematic from a Black radical perspective is how this is yet another example of forgoing the collective for the individual revolution. Broader critiques about the industry and the way that the Black female body is used are not about policing representation. You can believe that Nicki Minaj's representation is problematic, while defending her right to pursue her career in whatever way she sees fit. But her individual career choices are not so sacred that they are above criticism and when they reproduce harmful controlling images we should have the right to critique those decisions. More importantly, to reassert Black radicalism we have to push back against the corrosive idea that there can ever be an individual revolution, whether centred on culture or the body.

Part of the desire to shift the terrain to newer sites of resistance is because of the perceived gender dichotomy between the public, private and even personal spheres. This follows on from the discussion in Chapter 5 about the critique of the masculine history of Black political movements. Opening new terrain for radical politics can be seen to break the gendered binary that placed men on the front lines and women on the domestic front. Recasting domestic labour as a site of resistance is an important project.[33] If the kitchen is a radical space then the labour within it can be revolutionary. As we will discuss in the next chapter, redefining what we mean by revolutionary labour is vital to understanding Black radicalism. The Panthers' survival programmes, which fed children and provided medical care, were just as revolutionary as their armed patrols of the police. But that does not mean that all domestic labour is revolutionary. The women who were cooking and cleaning for the men in Karenga's US Organisation were not revolutionaries because they were contributing to a cultural nationalist and regressive project. Worse still, they were reproducing the gendered politics that have held back Black political progress. To embrace the domestic sphere as a potentially revolutionary site does not mean necessarily to cast it as one. Doing so runs the risk of further gendering the political movements. A radical role for women is carved out but *only* in the home, doing so-called women's work. There is no real difference to the idea that the woman's place in the struggle is to support her man, and to raise the family. The same danger is present in the idea of an erotic revolution.

If the body can be a terrain for liberation, then embracing different forms of expression can be seen as a radical act. Egalitarian sexual relations and overcoming the misogyny that has been present in Black political movements are certainly necessary for revolutionary practice. Our visions of freedom must liberate all Black people, not just recreate patriarchal hierarchies. But this does not mean that every embrace of sexual freedom is revolutionary. Reproducing racialised gender norms would clearly be counterrevolutionary, as would embracing the individualism of desire at the expense of collective engagement. More importantly, radicalism means those politics that aim to overturn the existing system. If one of the goals of Black radicalism is to fundamentally transform patriarchy then no amount of individualised expression of desire and sexual liberation will achieve this. The same structure that produces the celebrity of video vixens, modern-day Saartije Baartmans and places celebrities as spokespeople is the very one that needs to be overturned. Revolutions in Black sexual expression will never happen in mainstream media, in the same way that 'a chicken will never lay a duck egg'.[34]

Maintaining this gendered binary also misses how supposedly feminine notions have been debated within Black politics. Love, for instance, has been frequently used in Black politics, with the difference being in how it is mobilised to distinguish radical from liberal movements. Martin Luther King believed in 'love power', in a soul force that could transform society by reaching the hearts of the oppressor. He argued that 'we will meet the forces of hate with the power of love ... we must say to our white brothers all over the South, we will match your capacity to inflict suffering with our capacity to endure suffering ... Bomb our homes and we will still love you'.[35] King's conception of unconditional love for the oppressor was a central concept underlying the political nature of the civil rights movement. In its focus on being a part of society, civil rights had to appeal to White people to let us in. Unconditional love was not just a moral issue of non-violence and Christian ethics, it was the only way that the movement could make sense. Forgive them father for they know not what they do, and if we just keep loving them eventually they will come to their senses. Unsurprisingly, Black radicalism takes a different approach to love.

In complete opposition to King's approach, Malcolm declared 'you don't have a revolution in which you love your enemy'.[36] In complete contrast to King's politics, Malcolm was clear that 'you don't have a revolution in which you are begging the system of exploitation to integrate you into it'.[37] King's unconditional love was that of the supplicant House Negro who 'loved their master more than they loved themselves'; who was desperate to remain on the plantation. For Black radicalism, embracing the oppressor is the antithesis of revolutionary love. Instead it is essential to ground the politics on an 'undying love for the people'.[38] The radical commitment is to the grassroots, the masses, to build the unity that is necessary to create the world anew. There is no space to love the oppressor. We cannot indulge in love for ourselves. It is love for the people, for the Black nation, that is absolute essential to bring about the Black revolution.

Limits of Critical Race Theory

Looking for revolution in aesthetics and desire expresses the cultural turn that we have seen in both academic and some activist circles. The result is to switch the terrain of revolution by removing the gaze from the structural concerns of Black radicalism. The most frustrating bodies of thought are those that embrace the radical analysis of Black radicalism but do not engage in the revolutionary solutions. There is a tendency for this kind of liberal radicalism to be present in Critical Race Theory (CRT), which has become a well-used paradigm for understanding racism in America and Europe.

Critical Race Theory represents some of the best scholarship on the foundational role that racism plays in society. The movement emerged out of critical legal studies in America and the dissatisfaction once scholars realised that the momentous civil rights legislation many had devoted their lives to had failed to improve the conditions for most African Americans.[39] Derek Bell, the late founder of CRT, argued that Black people will 'never gain fully equality' in America because racism is a permanent feature of society.[40] It is not so much that civil rights legislation failed, but that it was never meant to make society more equal. For Bell, even the most progressive legislation is meant only to further White interests. He explains that the motivation behind the 14th Amendment, which guaranteed citizenship to the formerly enslaved, was not equality but for the Northern states to prevent the South from exploiting the labour of African Americans by paying them inhuman wages. But the implications are far worse than simply empty legislation; the law is used to provide the illusion of equality and therefore discrimination becomes more effective because it is covert, and harder to prove. In a quote that I always use in talks, Bell explains how this basic framework means that 'what we designate as "racial progress" is not a solution to that problem. It is a regeneration of the problem in a particularly perverse form'.[41]

One of the reasons I appreciate CRT so much is that it is an academic articulation of many of the key Black radical ideas. These concepts were not alien to me when I came across them, but felt familiar. In fact, Malcolm's condemnation of the civil rights movement pre-dates Bell by almost thirty years. We have already discussed Malcolm's dismissal of the March on Washington as farce, in Chapter 3. Without the benefit of hindsight he saw that the best Black people could hope for was second class citizenship in America. The problem with CRT is that though it eventually embraces the analysis it does not adopt the revolutionary solution.

Education has been a key site of CRT research in Britain. The longstanding racial inequalities in terms of both Black attainment and higher exclusion rates have persisted, despite funding and attention from policy makers. All that the money has done is 'altered *the processes and experiences* of minority young people' but 'done little to alter the *outcomes* recorded for them'.[42] CRT is useful because it removes the need for evil intent to reproduce racism; as Gillborn argues, the situation is 'worse than that'.[43] Britain is no different from any other nation in regard to schooling inequalities facing Black students. Even with good intent from teachers and policy makers, racism is reproduced because it is a necessary feature of the system. Once we have established the permanence of racism in schooling then surely we need to radically rethink how we educate our children.

A mainstay of the educational response to the challenge of CRT has been to develop strategies of critical pedagogy. Often this entails using the school system to transform the understandings of White students by getting them to think critically about their own experiences and privileges of Whiteness.[44] Also, by presenting counter-narratives and alternative understandings from marginalised communities critical pedagogy aims to be 'productive of empathy' and promote 'awareness of racism in society'.[45] The only problem is that the theory of CRT tells us that awareness of racism could not possibly solve the problem because even with positive intent racism is reproduced. In a study of teachers' racial attitudes this is exactly what was found:

> awareness did not lead to empathy amongst teachers, but resulted in a reinvention of meaning that reified existing, culturally constructed, racist frameworks … racism adapts to any new ideology introduced, accommodating the discourse within a framework of continued racial supremacy.[46]

The problem has not been that people are unaware, but that they are fully aware and yet continue to reproduce a racist society even with the best intentions. As we discussed in Chapter 6, Whiteness is a psychosis; it is entirely irrational and immune to logical thought or persuasion. By presenting itself as some kind of solution to an issue it can never solve, critical pedagogy is in fact a 'regeneration' of the problem that is 'particularly perverse' because of its good intent while actually contradicting the core theoretical foundations of CRT.

Further contradictions in the theory and practice of CRT emerge when it comes to the idea of social justice. The term is littered through the writings of CRT and much progressive research. Milner sees the role of CRT as being to 'assist social-justice-oriented individuals in organising to actively do something, to change racist systems, policies and practices'.[47] What is meant by social justice is unclear, and also what it means to 'do something'. Civil rights activists were no doubt 'social justice oriented' and certainly did 'something' to change racist systems; however, CRT is founded on the basis of critiquing these actions. In order to overcome the permanence of racism in society it must therefore be far more complex than supporting those with good intentions. Milner acknowledges 'interests and their ideological convergence that are most profound for movements to be successful',[48] but this then precludes embracing the social justice mantra. CRT cannot at once be in support of ideologically committed and interest driven groups, while simultaneously agitating for vague coalitions of the well intentioned. But this is precisely what CRT often becomes, a method for diagnosing systemic inequality and championing solutions that contradict its own theory.

Bell somehow argues that 'we *de*legitimate it [racism] if we can pinpoint it', and appears to present CRT as a claim of truth to power where stating the reality of oppression loudly and firmly is advanced as noble action. Bell's paradox is most clearly demonstrated in his embrace of both the permanence of racism and the constant struggle against it. He bleakly contends that we must come to '*both* the recognition of the futility of action … *and* the unalterable conviction that something must be done, that action must be taken'.[49] Cheerfully singing into the abyss is not the foundation of a radical politics and here is where we find the fundamental limit of CRT. A body of thought produced in the university is liberal by its very nature. So while CRT can appreciate radical rhetoric it can never make the next logical step to revolutionary practice. To do so would undermine the very foundation upon which the idea was produced in the first place.

Universities are built on the basis of separating thought from action, of the intellectual from the communities they serve. The role of the academic is not to bring about social change but to reproduce the status quo, 'the social relations of oppression and exploitation'.[50] By becoming part of the academic furniture it is debateable to what extent we have changed our traditional oppressive function. By remaining largely detached from the movements for social change we cannot produce the knowledge of liberation. This is what separates Malcolm from CRT and why he was able to foresee the limits of the civil rights movement. He was with the grassroots, trying to enact change so understood how the system would react. Rather than producing knowledge that is engaged in social change, academics often prefer to take the traditional role of the intellectual. Gloria Ladson-Billings does not even see the academic's role as necessarily creating the limited critical pedagogy. Instead, she argues that 'CRT's project is to uncover the way pedagogy is racialised and selectively offered to students according to the setting';[51] in other words, we just provide the analysis not the solution. Trapped in the academic industrial complex, our internal bubble where we write, speak and engage with the same audience, Bell's theoretical cul-de-sac is transformed from a paradox into business as usual. We were never meant to actually solve the problem, so we can be content diagnosing the need to act, and the futility in doing so.

Racism is a permanent feature of Western society, but we only become resigned to it if we cease to imagine the alternative. We make a fatal error to conflate this society with the only possible one. Taking on board the radical analysis and refusing to consider its solution means that we become trapped in a black hole, unable to see any real hope. Academic versions of radicalism therefore become hallmarked by either a misplaced optimism or an inherent pessimism.

Orlando Patterson argued that slavery was a state of 'social death', being reduced to the subhuman, with no rights or full claims to humanity.[52] The notion that this social death is the basis of Black life in the Western world is the foundation upon which Afro-pessimism is based. As Sexton argues, 'black life is not social, or rather that black life is lived in social death' because society is built on, and therefore permeated by, anti-Blackness.[53] Afro-pessimism has been critiqued because it associates with the negative connotations of Blackness and appears to offer no hope of redemption.[54] In keeping with a radical analysis, Afro-pessimism refuses to ignore the brutal reality of racism. One of the most enduring strengths of Blackness is its ability to endure and to create beauty in spite of oppression. But the fact we have survived while suffering such abuse does not negate the realities of that torment. As we discussed in Chapter 6, the Negro was a creation of the West with real consequences, and social death still exists today. Afro-pessimism is an 'affirmation of pathological being' in order that we comprehend the total incompatibility of Black life with Western society. As Sexton argues, 'Blackness is not the pathogen in afro-pessimism, the world is', it is an indictment of the society that creates Blackness as social death. But Afro-pessimism suffers from the same fundamental flaw as many analyses of racism emerging from the academy, in that it gives too much emphasis to how White society has conceived of Blackness.

Negro-ness is a state of social death, the construction of non-humanness by the West. Blackness is rejection of the Negro and therefore the cure to the disease of racism. Blackness is the opposite of social death; it is the rejection of the condition imposed by the West. Not in the sense of being proud, or finding moments in cultural resistance, but in proclaiming an uncompromising commitment to the Black revolution. Ruminating on how social death still frames Black life is not the Black radical project. Calling into being the methodologies, strategies and politics for overturning the political system and building the Black nation is the work that needs to be done.

Black radicalism is one of the most optimistic politics that exists. While recognising the totality of oppression that Black people face, it refuses to lose faith that the problem of racism can be solved. Given the nature of our oppression, and how far the condition has spread, this might seem unlikely. In fact, this is one of the main reasons that we have generally stopped fighting for a cure and tried to make ourselves as comfortable as possible. But we are not resigned to treating the symptoms or relieving our pain with cultural palliative care. As Malcolm put it, 'we don't want to hear nothing about the odds are against us'.[55] Black radicalism is built on a revolutionary vision that provides the antidote to racial oppression.

Chapter 8

Black Survival

When Malcolm X died in 1965 the world was at a tipping point. Revolutions raged across Africa and the West was terrified that much of the continent would turn to communism and add to the powerful Eastern bloc. America was still entangled in the bloody conflict in Vietnam and European empires were losing control of their colonies. The Bay of Pigs fiasco in Cuba in 1961 showed just how close the world was to nuclear war. Capitalism was in crisis and overturning Western imperialism was a tangible possibility. The Black revolution was not some far-off fantasy, but a political reality. Malcolm's optimism in the Organisation of African Unity and the United Nations must be seen in this context. With the right politics and strategy, the West could have been taken down. A unified Africa could have provided a new model for society, free from the domination of the West.

Malcolm also died before the realisation of most civil rights legislation. There was little pretence of equality in the West; until 1965 it was legal to discriminate on grounds of race in Britain. It was only in the 1960s that many colonies achieved their so-called independence and before this it was obvious that they were exploited by colonialism. Black people were not accepted into the system in any meaningful way and therefore the idea of revolt was attractive. One of the reasons that the Garvey movement managed to build a membership of five million people before the internet was that it did not need to convince Black people that they had no place in the West. It was blindingly obvious due to the conditions of racial oppression.

In the ensuing fifty years both the probability of revolution and the conditions that would lead those in the West to embrace regime change have steeply declined. Revolutionary movements were violently put down across the African Diaspora and the globe. The Western political consensus dominates to the point that the 'end of history' has been declared due to the lack of viable alternatives.[1] Communism is now symbolic, after the collapse of the Soviet Union and China's integration into the capitalist system. In the current context, the Black revolution can seem like a distant, utopian dream to those of us suffering the brunt of institutional racism. The realities of racism mean that there are any number of struggles on a daily basis that need to be resisted that do not necessarily aim to overturn the system. I was in fact once accused by a high-profile professor of 'abandoning my sons to racism' at home by focusing on the fantasy of revolution.

Black radicalism also seems distant because for all of the racism we suffer, we have also become a part of the system. Alongside destroying revolutionary movements, the powers that be also offered just enough of a glimmer of access to provide the illusion of hope. Civil rights, race relations and so-called independence have blinded us to the totality of our oppression. As we discussed in the last chapter we are seeking to relieve the symptoms and not treat the disease of racism. We are trapped in a paradox, where we see no prospect for liberation and so cling to an illusion of false hope offered by our improved access to the system, and those who have benefited from it. In this limiting framework we are left with recognising the 'historical limitation of the "new" black petite bourgeoisie' but arguing that they 'play a crucial role' in the Black struggle. According to none other than Cornel West, the 'Black middle class – preachers, teachers, lawyers, doctor, politicians – possesses the requisite skills and legitimacy' that are essential for Black progress.[2] In reality the Black middle class possesses the skills necessary to succeed within Western imperialism, a system opposed to Black freedom. We are deluding ourselves if we are looking for the House Negro to solve the problems of the plantation.

Now all this may appear contradictory coming from a card-carrying member of the Black middle class. I have a level of income and privilege which would make it absurd for me to claim any other location than that firmly entrenched in the master's house. It is a contradiction that none of us unfortu- nate enough to suffer the symptoms of racism in the West can escape from: from activists celebrating the smartphone, which is built off Black suffering, to the academic getting paid through the taxes from a system that kills Black children. The Black revolution is based on the idea of creating a world entirely independent of the oppression of the West, making it difficult to chart a radical politics by those who live off the teat of imperialism. In this chapter we will discuss how to navigate that contradiction and build a Black revolutionary politics that can deal with local symptoms and the global disease of racism.

Separateness is not a problem

Black separatism has been a central feature of Black Nationalism, as we discussed in Chapter 1. But we must distinguish these calls from the independence that lies at the heart of Black radicalism. Before we do so, it is necessary to offer a defence of the idea of separation, while recognising its limitations. Separatism has been used as an example to point to the obvious extremism of those who want to live apart. We reduce the debate to civil rights, love thy neighbour, integrationists vs. Black Power, hate Whitey, separatists. Separation is seen as problematic because it must prevent our progress in society. But the discussion on separateness is based on ideology, not evidence. Ironically, many of the arguments against separatism are actually harmful to Black progress even within the system.

In Britain, the idea of communities living separate or 'parallel' lives is seen as not only problematic for integration but also as an essential element in the breeding of terrorists.[3] Separate and isolated communities will obviously not be able to integrate and of course develop a mistrust of mainstream society. In the 1960s when Britain was first having to deal with large numbers of Black and Brown children, it was a left-wing government which issued an edict that schools could have no more than a third of students from a migrant background.[4] In the cases where the numbers exceeded this limit, minority children were bussed to other schools. It was inconceivable that these migrant children could learn the culture and the language to fully assimilate into a British identity if there were too many of them in the schools. Britain has a limited history of bussing,[5] but there is a much stronger legacy of the practice in America.[6] In desegregating schooling and trying to create a racial mix, bussing was the perfectly liberal response to the problem of racial inequality. The aim was to give Black children access to the cultural resources of Whiteness so that all the good cultural capital could rub off onto the kids, who could then better integrate into mainstream society.

Underlying the concept of bussing, and fear of separateness, is the wrongheaded idea that racism is located at the level of the individual and mostly caused by ignorance. Seeking increased contact between people from different backgrounds is meant to educate racism out of people as well as integrate minorities. Up until riots in the north of England in 2001 that pitted largely British Pakistani and Bangladeshi youth against White racists, Britain pursued a race relations policy of multiculturalism. In this doctrine the local and national state supported the development of Britain into a 'community of communities' where support was offered for different ethnic groups.[7] But after the riots, the 'death of multiculturalism' was proclaimed because it was seen as culpable in the unrest.[8] Under the so-called community cohesion agenda the state is unlikely to provide funding to specific minority groups in order to prevent segregation. In the new paradigm cross-cultural initiatives with White and Muslim young people became a fixture of state-funded programmes.[9] Such cross-cultural initiatives typically occur within cities between deprived communities, focusing on educating the White formerly working class who often display the most open and aggressive forms of racism. This is patronising and wrongheaded for a number of reasons.

White working class racism is certainly problematic, vocal and distressing. In Britain, marches for far right groups such as Britain First and the English Defence League are filled with White people who feel dispossessed. This group also has real political clout, fuelling the success of the UK Independence Party, the vote for Brexit and the shift to the right on immigration for all the major parties. The same is true in America, with the Rust Belt providing Trump with his surprise presidential victory and his calls to Make America Great [White] Again. A section of poor Whites have always played this role in maintaining racist societies, but poor Whites embracing the wages of Whiteness is a symptom of racism. As we explored in the last chapter, we love nothing better than ignoring the disease and treating the symptoms. Whenever there is a fascist demonstration, there is an anti-racist response to let the 'scum' know that they are not welcome in our cities. These confrontations have become a staple of anti-racist movements. But they are more to salve the conscience of the protesters rather than to make meaningful change. The skinheads are not going to change their minds or stop acting out. We just give them attention so that we feel as though we are doing something active in the struggle. People count their anti-fascist demos like tours of duty in an actual conflict. The problem is that the White people in the streets are not the real enemy; they have little power and embrace their bigotry mostly out of frustration. I am writing this in the days after the Charlottesville White supremacist march in 2017, and the counter anti-racist mobilisation. My twitter feed has been full for days with people dumping on Trump for not explicitly condemning the far right. The problem with this approach is that people are looking at Trump as though he is somehow distinguishable from the violent racism of White supremacy; that as odious as he is, he is somehow above the hideousness of the Klan. Not only did Trump court the very constituency he eventually came out to condemn, he actually represents the disease of racism far more than they do. Racism is systemic, not symbolic, vocal or overt, and Trump has been implicated in perpetuating the system of racism, first as a business guru and now as president. If Trump can gain some sort of credibility by disavowing White nationalist protests it tells us just how distorted our view of racism is. He is the embodiment of White nationalism, not the White masses on the street who have no other voice but to hold a rally and cause trouble. The real problem with racism lies with the privileged and it is here we can see the anti-separateness logic fall to pieces.

The people who choose to have the least contact with ethnic minorities are typically not the White formerly working class. Due to residential segregation there are certainly areas that are predominantly White and deprived. But particularly in the major cities in countries like Britain, minorities have historically moved into areas that are occupied by those Whites with less resources. Contact in this context is competition, and highly unlikely to produce friendly relations. A major cause of the tensions has been based around the idea of migrants taking the jobs and resources from the supposedly native White folk. Even for those who have very little contact with minorities, they have been told they are in conflict with the hordes of undeserving migrants who are stealing their resources. As nonsensical as these notions are, they did not just emerge through the ignorance of the poor. Politicians have learnt to play the politics of like a drum creating the fear of the dark invaders in order to boost their electoral prospects. Thatcher talked about Britain being 'swamped', and Trump was elected on a solidly White nationalist platform. For all the middle class handwringing about separate lives and the need for contact between different communities, the most self-segregating group is always, without question, the White middle class and elite.

Inner city areas in Britain are not dominated by minorities by accident. This was the housing that was available to us when we migrated and there was a strict colour bar as to where we could live. For example, when Birmingham City Council wanted to put a boarding house for Caribbean men in the then affluent Northfield, the residents protested and the residence ended up in the inner city area of Handsworth.[10] Around 80% of inner city Birmingham is now ethnic minority (an ironic term given the numbers), not from our choice but because as we moved in the White people who could afford it moved out. White flight is the only way to explain how areas that were once entirely populated by White people have been almost completely emptied of the so-called native population. The most segregated areas in Britain are not those spaces inhabited by minorities but the almost exclusively White middle class enclaves that are self-selecting. In Birmingham the only area where over 90% of the population is one ethnicity is Sutton Coldfield, the Whitest part of town. Even in affluent neighbourhoods, there was a slight increase in the Indian population because some managed to afford to move in and the area has ceased to be the chosen destination for the White middle class. Now it is the villages in the commuter belt that are the dream, away from the hustle, bustle and darkness of the city. They don't call the hit TV show, where people try out expensive homes in rural areas, *Escape to the Country* for nothing. White people with money get as far away from minorities as they can. In America this trend is even more pronounced, as the White middle class has effectively abandoned the city limits entirely in major cities and resides exclusively in the commuter belt, with the good (White) public schools and picture book homes. Residential segregation is so acute in America that the public schools are now more segregated than they were before the supposedly momentous decision of *Brown vs Board of Education* in 1954.[11]

If separateness really were seen as a problem in itself then the focus of the concern would be entirely with the middle class and their parallel lives. Instead, in Britain there is constant handwringing about self-segregating minority communities that are failing to integrate properly. The 2016 government review into integration led by Dame Casey opined that there were seventeen out 9456 local electoral wards where the non-White British population was over 90%. The report neglected to count the number where the inverse of this is true, but given that half of all minorities live in three cities,[12] we can assume that there are thousands of electoral wards where more than 90% of the population is White. While the big inner cities might have very few White people in them, they are incredibly diverse. Migrants and their descendants from hundreds of different countries live side by side and manage to get on just fine. But the rhetoric from the government and the press is how multiculturalism has damaged the fabric of the great nation. This fear of separateness is really about ideology.

The inclusion logic is not about separation itself but about *who* is living apart. There is no problem with White people, particularly those with money, living separately because they obviously have the correct values and identity in the first place. There is no need for them to mix with minorities to learn about tolerance, compromise and how to live with diversity because these can be taught in exclusively White neighbourhoods, schools and universities. They are the solution to the problem, not the cause of it. The anti-separateness agenda is fundamentally based on the politics of assimilation, trying to ensure that minorities can become sufficiently like White people to be a part of society.

Railing against separateness is also problematic because it ignores all the available evidence as to how minorities succeed in a society, even when integration is your goal. The discrimination that new migrants feel in any country is acute and debilitating. Therefore a sensible and common practice is for communities to form, to support and protect each other. This process is no different for White migrants than it is for those of colour, as we discussed in Chapter 1. The idea of a Black, residentially segregated community coming together to support each other is not a radical but rather a rational response to the situation that any minority group finds itself in. Part of the problem with Black communities is that we have been so busy trying not to be separate, we forgot to focus on uniting to change the conditions we find ourselves in.[13] Integration can also have negative effects. A much ignored impact of the infamous *Brown vs the Board of Education* decision was the closure of the Black schools that children were segregated into. These were deemed inferior and Black students were integrated into the supposedly better White institutions. In the aftermath of the decision, thousands of Black teachers lost their jobs in the South, and African Americans remain significantly underrepresented in the profession.[14] In chasing the dream of integration African Americans undermined the systems of support they had built up within the Black community.

Separation to independence

As much as we must defend the notion of separation, we must also acknowledge its limitations. Separation is similar to flight in that you may feel liberated because you are out of the direct clutches of the oppressor, but it does not provide freedom. As long as the system that oppresses you remains in place you cannot be free from it, no matter how separate you feel. For Black people in the West, separation is a misguided goal. We are in the belly of the beast and cannot separate from it. We should certainly use the resources that we have better, and unite to improve our conditions, but we should never confuse relieving the symptoms with curing the disease.

After leaving the Nation of Islam, Malcolm understood that separateness was not enough. He argued that 'this word separation has been misused … a better word than separation is independence'.[15] Black independence is the basis of the politics of Black radicalism: aiming not just at being apart from the West, but being immune to its poisonous influence by being completely independent from it. As explored in Chapter 3, this is why Africa is so important for the Black revolution. Not only is independence possible, but it would cripple the Western empire, which is so dependent on the exploitation of the resources of the African continent.

Black independence in the West is impossible, and the biggest paradox for Black radicalism is that we are part of the system (and therefore the problem), so how can we be engaged in bringing it to an end. Everything we do to improve our conditions here further embeds us into the system that we are aiming to fight against. Black businesses, Black schools, Black political parties, and every other attempt to be outside of the mainstream, ultimately can never be independent. We need to expand Malcolm's metaphor of the House and Field Negro. On the plantation the divide was very clear and remained so after emancipation. Those who were locked out of the system were in the Field and those who managed to find some foothold in professional or political classes were in the House. But the situation has now changed with civil rights legislation that has opened up the doors to the House to many more than before. Make no mistake, there are plenty in the

Field, poverty and mass incarceration ensure that. However, the distinction between House and Field now mostly needs to be made on the global level. The conditions facing Black people outside the West are not comparable, and explain why millions risk life and limb trying to escape the global South. Our relative prosperity in the West is based on the exploitation of Black people outside of our national and experiential borders. Worse still, we can unconsciously create a politics that is dependent on the exploitation at the heart of the West.

Black Lives Matter has re-energised Black political movements by reshaping how we experience racial state violence. No longer do we hear about atrocities committed by the police through the news, or by word of mouth. We witnessed live on Facebook Philando Castile bleeding out after being shot by police. The ability to broadcast video and images across the globe instantly without a mainstream press filter has made state violence accessible. None of what people are protesting against is new, we just live in an age where it is impossible to hide the violence, and the exposure has reignited protests.

Due to social media, the ability to mobilise and organise has also been key. Black Lives Matter emerged from a tweet by Patricia Cullors who used the phrase in a poem after the killing of Trayvon Martin. The hashtag was added to the phrase by a friend and the tagline grew into a movement. Social media allowed for Black Lives Matter to spread across the globe, connecting an array of local and national movements. We are also able to follow the protests from the perspectives of the activists and avoid the mainstream media's lazy demonisation of peaceful protesters as rioters.

Black Lives Matter is in many ways the product of social media, which has led to criticism of the substance of the movement and the limits of 'clicktivism', where people will commit only in the digital realm where there is little real at stake.[16] This kind of criticism is unfair when levelled at Black Lives Matter given the record of street protests and the platform 'Movement for Black Lives', which outlines a clear agenda for the movement. The success of Black Lives Matter has been to transform what began as a hashtag into a meaningful network of local movements, bringing publicity and funding to the cause. From a radical perspective the issue is not with the digital beginnings of the movement but the contradictions of that digital platform.

The smartphone is the key piece of technology that has facilitated the move, allowing instant access to video and content, streaming police brutality live wherever you are. Reverend Gregory Drumwright, who organised a protest in Washington, noted that the device meant 'society has a body camera' and Erica England, one of the protesters, explained that 'it's important to have a smartphone … It can mean life or death'.[17] But the smartphone is also one of the most direct symbols of African oppression. The technology is only possible and so widely available because the raw materials necessary are stolen from the African continent in the neo-colonial economic arrangement. Worse still, many of the key minerals are mined by young children who are not only exploited by the companies but risk death in their labour.[18] The smartphone is the definition of what Audre Lorde called the master's tools and Black Lives Matter cannot be for all

Black lives if it relies on technology that oppresses African children. This does not of course mean that the movement cannot deal with this contradiction. We must struggle where we are and with the resources we have at our disposal. But it should be a reminder of Lorde's warning that the 'master's tools will never dismantle the master's house'.[19]

The challenge for Black Lives Matter, or any movement that was born in the West, is to build meaningful connections to the African Diaspora. This does not mean abandoning oppressive instruments like the smartphone, but building a political connection that can transcend their limitations. As we have seen so far, it is easy to fall into narrow nationalist movements that only try to overcome problems for Black people within nation state boundaries. Black radicalism offers a blueprint for overcoming this contradiction.

In the constitution of the Organization of Afro-American Unity (OAAU), Malcolm concretely tied Black progress in the West to that on the African continent. In the first article, 'Establishment', the importance of this connection was embedded in the organisation:

> Anyone of African descent, with African blood, can become a member of the Organization of Afro American Unity, and also any one of our brothers and sisters from the African continent. We must unite together in order to go forward together. Africa will not go forward any faster than we will and we will not go forward any faster than Africa will.[20]

Importantly, this is not just a rhetorical connection to Africa but an organisational one. Not only was Malcolm encouraging African brothers and sisters to join, he also spent months of his last year on earth travelling and making connections with African leaders and freedom fighters. A key component of Black independence in the West is to be independent of the colonial nation state narrative that limits our politics. We must go beyond the idea of political alliances with the Diaspora and build a complete political movement. Only then can we overcome the contradiction of our successes being built on the Black people who live in poverty in the global South.

As discussed in Chapter 3, the OAAU aimed to be the global organisation that could transcend the nation state. But its appeal and programme was hyper-local as well as attending to the global Black nation. Malcolm explained that 'we start in Harlem with the intention of spreading throughout the state, and from the state throughout the country, and from the country throughout the Western Hemisphere'.[21] Building the organisation from the grassroots outwards was absolutely essential to creating a strong foundation.

There were four areas that the OAAU staked its ground on. The first was on the issues of self-defence, given the brutality that Black people were facing from racist mobs, during protests and from the police. The infamous battle between violence and non-violence had to play out at the organisational level. For Malcolm, not to defend yourself and your community was cowardly and criminal. A solid commitment to self-defence is very clearly stated early on in the charter for the OAAU. As we will see later in the chapter this was picked up by the Panthers after Malcolm was assassinated. But in spite of the prominence that self-defence has in much of Malcolm's rhetoric and in the founding of the OAAU, it is not fundamental to the programme of the organisation. The idea was for the OAAU to create departments that would organise in the key areas of struggle; there was no self-defence department and concrete proposals are conspicuous by their absence. Self-defence appears more as a philosophy, a mindset, rather than a practical reality. To understand this we must look at the context in the West. We are a minority in the most violent system that has ever existed on the planet. Engaging the state in violence is always going to be a losing battle. The downfall of the Panthers is a testament to this; many of them were murdered by the state. Malcolm talks about self-defence in the context of protecting protestors in the South against White racists, and not taking on the state. When it comes to state violence this forms part of the political programme, exerting pressure over officials and politicians. Even the notion of self-defence is a particular form of violence reserved for the West. The goal is for protection, reacting to the violence from others. This is not the revolutionary violence that Malcolm endorses on the African continent where overthrowing the state is possible. For the other key objectives of the OAAU there is a more fully formed programme of action.

Education was a prominent feature of the organisation because of the substandard schooling that Black people have historically received. One of the aims of the OAAU was to gain representation on school boards and take over 10% of the schools in New York, with the idea being to provide a platform for Black education. A department of education was seen as essential in terms of taking over Black schooling but also in providing a 'political re-education' for the community as a whole. A Black education, independent of the mainstream, was vital to connect the community to a political programme for revolutionary change, rather than just for Black people to succeed in America. So we must distinguish the call of the OAAU from the more liberal and even conservative ideas of Black education that seek to fix perceived deficits in the Black children, rather than the system.

My first book, *Resisting Racism*, studied the Black supplementary school movement in Britain, which began in the 1960s to counter the racism of the mainstream schools.[22] Supplementary schools are the definition of a grassroots movement, with projects springing up in people's houses, community centres, churches and school buildings as the community sought to respond to the crisis of racism in the school system. In the archives I came across teachings on Malcolm, Garvey, the Panthers and Caribbean and African histories. There were exercises where the students did reading comprehension with excerpts from George Jackson's *Soledad Brother*. At one of the oldest supplementary schools, the Sankofa Sesh, run by the African Caribbean Self Help Organisation (ACSHO) in Birmingham since 1967, they talked about the battles they had with the local education authorities and the police in setting up the school. Their curriculum included not only Black radical thinkers but also lessons on Marxism-Leninism and revolutionary theory. ACHSO was also connected to the Pan-African Congress Movement in Britain, and was a hub for Black radical organising in the city and country. The building that housed the school was the same venue where figures from the Black liberation movement worldwide would come and give talks. For example, Herman Chitepo, who was a key figure in the Zimbabwean freedom struggle, visited ACSHO weeks before he was assassinated in Zambia in 1975. ACSHO has organised the Africa Liberation Day celebrations in Birmingham since 1977, annually bringing figures from the Black world into the city. Such a political organisation running a supplementary school for Black children was seen as dangerous by the state, which in the words of Bini Brown, one of the founders of the organisation, tried to 'smash' Sankofa Sesh. Given this history I was expecting to find in the movement a location for contemporary politics of Black radicalism. Instead, I found the opposite.

Alongside the radical histories there was always a more conservative trend, a split between the 'official' and 'self-help' projects.[23] Sankofa Sesh represents the self-help group of schools, independent from the state and its politics, while the official projects are those that take funding from the state and are often run by Black schoolteachers. These official projects may or may not have Black Studies curricula and are very much focused on mainstream subjects and success. The purpose of these schools is to boost the grades and performance in mainstream schools, not to provide Black education. Over the years the official sector has come to dominate the movement and radical education has almost disappeared. In its place is often a focus on culture, but lacking any concrete commitment to politics. Black Studies becomes about teaching Black children to know themselves and their history so that they will have the confidence and self-esteem to achieve mainstream success. Where once there was a movement indicting the mainstream school system, the focus now has moved to critiquing the community and the investment by parents in their children's schooling. Black supplementary schooling is a perfect example of how the state funds and then accommodates a grassroots movement into the system. The Black independent education that the OAAU called for sought to reject this process by remaining financially, as well as politically, independent.

Culture played an important part in the OAAU, with its own dedicated department. Malcolm envisioned a 'cultural revolution to unbrainwash an entire people' and start the 'journey to our rediscovery of ourselves'.[24] Opening a cultural centre in Harlem was seen as a key step in this cultural revolution, and towards regaining the power to shape Black representation. Importantly, culture was not seen as a solution in itself, as in cultural nationalism. The role of culture was to educate people regarding their history and selves so that they would commit to 'action'. Embracing Black culture was also central in building the connection back to Africa, not only historically but for constructing the global Black nation politically. Culture is crucial to any revolutionary politics, and Black radicalism is no different.

A department for political action was also seen as essential to develop the OAAU. Just as with the rest of the organisation, the aim here was to build political independence within the Black community. Stressing local concerns, the goal was to 'organize the Afro American community block by block' and to form independent Black political clubs.[25] Assessing the situation in New York in particular and America in general, the OAAU sought to capitalise on the possibility of building electoral power through the ballot box. Residential segregation provided possibilities for electoral gains at every level of local, state and national government. These opportunities have been seized upon, with a raft of Black elected officials, but the OAAU was against signing up to the politics of either Democrats or Republicans. The aim was to support Black politicians independent of the main parties, with the logical conclusion being an OAAU party. It may seem liberal and contradictory to the radical philosophy behind the OAAU to engage in the corrupt electoral system, with voter registration drives and running candidates. But again, we have to respond to the conditions that face us. While we are in the West a key lever of power is electoral, and therefore to create as independent a Black political front as possible is essential. But mainstream political representation was not seen as a solution to any of the problems facing Black people. I met Gus Newport, who was formerly mayor of Berkeley and knew Malcolm. He explained that people were trying to convince Malcolm to run for Adam Clayton Powell's seat in Congress. Powell represented Harlem in the House of Representatives and if there was any seat that Malcolm could win, it would be the place he had become a legend. Newport was convinced that Malcolm was seriously considering the prospect and may well have run had he not been assassinated. As much as the move may have been tempting and would have provided some financing and a national platform, I just cannot see how it would fit into Malcolm's politics. Wielding a limited influence in Congress and having to submit to the confines of a role so deeply imbedded in the political system runs contrary to the ethos of the OAAU. Malcolm could not have maintained the radical nature of the OAAU while representing Harlem in Congress. It is entirely possible that Malcolm would have run for Congress but, make no mistake, to do so would have been a betrayal of the Black radical politics he so well defined. Unfortunately, history is littered with examples of people who blazed radical trails and ended up dissolving into the very systems that they were trying to overturn. Given the ground-work laid in the OAAU I have faith that Malcolm would have stayed true to his Black radicalism and used the engagement in mainstream politics as a tool to further the liberation of Black people worldwide.

Another area where the OAAU firmly staked a claim was in economics and as we saw in Chapter 1 this is also an issue where radical sentiment can bleed into liberal action. The desire to create Black businesses can often descend into Black capitalism, changing the colour of the skin of the people who are exploiting the community. There are plenty of Black millionaires, but if they refuse to support Black people then they are no better than anyone else who profits from the community. In the economic programme for the OAAU, building Black business and cooperatives certainly comes up as a focus, but does not have the prominence that may have been expected. Particularly while in the Nation of Islam, Malcolm professed the need for Black businesses and

continued to do so once he left.[26] Key to economic empowerment is being able to provide jobs for Black people when
others will not. Economic independence is utterly reliant on
building a base of Black businesses that support the community. But the focus on the launch of the OAAU was far more on
stopping economic exploitation in housing, and the proposal
to coordinate a Harlem-wide rent strike to respond to the
economic injustice of high prices for substandard living. We
can see that the economic programme was integrally tied to
political action, moving beyond just empowerment to a political agenda.

Perhaps the most important aspect of the OAAU was the
funding model for the organisation. Malcolm was critical of
the National Association for the Advancement of Colored
People (NAACP). He criticised the $2.50 annual membership
and explained that it was this figure which meant that they had
to always go begging to White liberals for support. Malcolm
knew that whoever funded the organisation would own and
control its message. Instead of charging a small fee and having
to find funding from elsewhere to survive, Malcolm insisted
that the Black community must fund the OAAU. Membership
was set at $2.50 *a week* to ensure that the organisation was
self-sufficient. This funding model is absolutely essential to
making the politics of the OAAU different from other organisations. You could challenge the radical credentials of an
organisation that does voting drives, plays electoral politics,
organises rent strikes and supports Black business. As I have
been at pains to explain throughout this book, none of these
activities are radical as they involve engaging with, rather than

overturning, the system. In fact, a number of organisations that I have been highly critical of in this book are engaged in similar activities. But being independently sourced from the grassroots changes the complexion of all these activities. Combined with the radical and Diasporic politics professed in the organisation, the independent funding means that these measures can be seen as tools to progress Black liberation, the sum being far greater than the parts. Remember that the New York chapter of the OAAU was only ever meant to be one of many dotted across the African Diaspora, all of which were dealing with local concerns but connected into a global movement for Black liberation. The aim was to build a power base within New York and spread the model out to other locations. Only from that position of power could the necessary revolutionary work take place. In the West, independence means taking as much control over our political and economic destinies as possible but always putting this in service to the wider global Black nation.

Survival

Strategies for Black independence in the West contain a fundamental contradiction in terms of their radical nature. Uniting and mobilising the community to gain political and economic power will undoubtedly improve the conditions facing Black communities. History suggests that once people are doing better they are less likely to revolt against a system they are making gains in. The biggest recruiter for Black politics has always been racism, and if the symptoms are lessened we are more likely to want to keep reaping the benefits of the master's house. We should not delude ourselves into thinking that Black prosperity in the West is any more righteous than when White people enjoy the spoils of racial capitalism. The most likely outcome of a successful OAAU-type organisation is that it better integrates us into the system of oppression, creating more opportunities for symptom-free racism. That is why the political education and organic links to the global Black nation are so vital. But we also need to amend the equation away from independence, because self-sufficiency is impossible and the rhetoric allows us to believe we can be free within the belly of the beast. Once we accept that we are simply trying to survive, rather than thrive, we have an avenue to frame supporting Black communities in the West, while recognising that we must always internationalise the struggle.

Survival itself is a testament to the endurance that has kept the spirit of resistance alive in Blackness. After centuries of unimaginable oppression we are still standing and have never just accepted our treatment. But survival is not enough and certainly does not on its own represent a radical political stance. It may sound contradictory to all the rhetoric put forward so far, but Black radicalism necessitates creating structures in the West to help us survive the system, allowing those of us located here to play our part in the global revolutionary struggle. The debate about the revolutionary nature of survival played out most publicly in the Black Panther Party.

Huey P. Newton strongly advocated for the Panther survival programmes, which included providing free breakfasts for children, free medical care and liberation schools. He equated the programmes to a life raft for the struggling Black community and argued that they were part of a revolutionary process, 'a means of bringing the people closer to the transformation of society'. But this point was not accepted by all members of the Panthers. Eldridge Cleaver's mentality was that you 'either pick up the gun or remain a snivelling coward' and that the survival programmes were a distraction from the revolutionary work of the party.[27] During his exile in Algeria he very publicly split with the party over this issue of revolutionary tactics, and took the New York chapter with him.

Tensions had been brewing between Newton and Cleaver over the issue of tactics. Cleaver argued it was necessary to create a guerrilla army and wage direct war against the American government. Geronimo Pratt was expelled from the party by Newton for trying to raise an army of the vanguard. Further divisions were caused when Newton expelled the New York-based Panther 21, which included Tupac's mother, Afeni Shakur. The Panther 21 were on trial for allegedly planning to target and kill police officers. Much of the discord in the party was stoked by the FBI and its counterintelligence programme (COINTELPRO), which fed misinformation and lies throughout the party. The FBI sent false letters between Panthers and started rumours that the Newton and Cleaver factions were planning to kill each other.[28] As I made clear in Chapter 6, I am sceptical about Eldridge's motives in relation to the party and firmly believe that his role in splitting the Panthers was no coincidence. The authorities took an ideological rift and helped create a chasm. In 1971 Newton hoped to heal the problems with Eldridge and arranged a phone call mediated by a San Francisco television presenter, live on air, between the two of them. The scene descended into farce, with Eldridge insisting that the Panther 21 be reinstated and calling for the resignation of the central committee of the party, which he deemed inadequate. The end result was Newton expelling Eldridge from the party, and Eldridge declaring that Newton was no longer fit to lead and doing likewise. The resultant chaos severely damaged the party and, combined with the continued assault from the state, it never fully recovered.

We should not be surprised that the FBI used this ideological split over tactics to divide the party. Guerrilla warfare with the American state apparatus is clearly a cul-de-sac, a blind alley with no possible exit. Not only is toppling the state in that manner impossible, but efforts to do so also provided the FBI and police with the perfect cover to destroy the Panthers. Picking up the gun in that way makes you an easy target for police repression, and COINTELPRO made sure that these aspects of the Panthers were always at the forefront of the public consciousness. J. Edgar Hoover, head of the FBI, called the Panthers 'the greatest threat to the internal security of the country'.[29] But America did not fear the Panthers because of the threat of some fantastical violent overthrow of the state.

Hoover highlighted the free breakfast programme as particularly problematic because it gave the Panthers too much good publicity and built close connections to Black communities.[30] The authorities were terrified a Black organisation that could rally the masses would emerge and present a serious threat to the status quo. The Panthers knew that dealing with the day-to-day concerns of the people was absolutely essential to build any meaningful political programme. After the split of the guerrilla-obsessed Panthers the party launched the slogan 'survival pending revolution',[31] which perfectly captures Black radical efforts in the West.

Every political movement has to embed itself in the community it serves. To have 'love for the people' means that you have to address the very real and present suffering. Black radicalism cannot just operate on a theoretical or impractical level. Revolution is essential but there are stages that we need to take to get there. One of those stages is to organise Black people in every street, neighbourhood, city and nation where we reside. The only way to do this is to meet people where they are, to address the issues that impact on people's lives. The Panthers increased popular support because they knew that there can be no revolution without survival as popular support is necessary in order to overthrow the system.

So the day-to-day, the small acts and confronting racism where we find it, play an essential role in Black radical politics; but again we have to be aware of our privileges here. The Panthers sought to provide the fundamentals of food, education and healthcare to the Black poor. Survival programmes aimed at that purpose, to support those people who were being failed on a basic level by the state. Free legal advice and patrols of the police also served to help people survive the system. There is a stark difference to these programmes and efforts to integrate Black people into the mainstream through mentoring programmes or support to get youngsters into elite universities. We must also draw a strong distinction between the focus on micro-aggressions, the middle class problems of the aspiring Black bourgeoisie. Survival has to be aimed at those who are struggling to make ends meet, not those with the means suffering through the process of meeting them. Black politics must always root its authenticity in serving the least of those in our communities. Survival should also force us to take a global perspective on Black politics. Racism has a life or death impact on Black people, with children dying by the second due to entirely preventable causes on the African continent. Once we commit to the politics of survival we have to internationalise the struggle and make solving the problems of the whole Black nation our concern.

Taking a global rather than a national view of revolution means understanding that the Black revolution will take place on the African continent. This is the only means of securing Black freedom and building an independent political and economic system. But that does not mean that we have no role to play if we reside outside of Africa. Those in the Diaspora have the responsibility to build up the resources and organisations to support the eventual revolution on the continent. It also does not mean that our struggles in the West are not relevant. We must build a movement that connects the grassroots struggles across the global Black nation to a cohesive politics of revolutionary resistance. None of this is new; we just need to go back to the politics of Blackness, which connected the Black nation into the same struggle for freedom. The OAAU is the perfect vehicle for the Black radical politics that we need, combining local concerns with a global politics of revolution. The blueprint is there and has been for the last fifty years. There is a reason that the organisation has been wiped from the collective memory of Malcolm X.

Considering Malcolm was working on building the OAAU at the time he was being interviewed by Alex Haley for the autobiography, it is astounding that it receives scant attention in the book. Given the history of infiltration and subversion by the authorities into the workings of Black organisations and their leaders, we would be foolish to view this glaring omission as a coincidence. We also know that there are missing chapters and notes in the book on the OAAU that were never written up.[32] The OAAU, with Malcolm's links across the Diaspora, represented the organisation that could have built the global Black nation into a truly revolutionary force that threatened the West. Simply assassinating the character of Malcolm, controlling how he is remembered, and removing his radical programme of action from that memory is the perfect way to dismantle his political agenda.

We have been taught to misunderstand and fear the politics of Black radicalism. We have been told that the ideas are unworkable and dangerous; that the leaders were irresponsible, misogynistic and violent. Black radical movements were attacked through spies and propaganda as well as with oppression and murder. We have been sold a distorted legacy, while being promised a slightly bigger slice of the diseased pie of capitalism. We need to reject the illusion of equality and the idea that Black radicalism has had its day. We must re-engage with the politics that so terrified those responsible for maintaining the status quo. We must organise for 'survival pending revolution' and pick up the baton from those who have gone before. We need to go back to Black.

Epilogue

It's Already Too Late

Black radicalism is an unapologetic politics that leaves little room for either practical or theoretical compromise. I have tried to match that approach in this book, clearly distinguishing radical politics from those that may clothe themselves in revolutionary rhetoric, but in reality offer nothing but maintaining the status quo. Critiquing movements like narrow Black Nationalism, cultural nationalism and even Pan-Africanism will likely bring howls of disapproval from the conscious community. Undermining the liberal radicalism of Black academia and challenging intellectual movements I have contributed to is also unlikely to be well received by my academic peers. But that is precisely the point of the politics of Black radicalism: to trouble and disturb, to shake us out of our complacency, especially that induced when we presume we are 'awake'. The undeniable truth is that we are not on the right track. Whatever we are currently doing is not enough and is taking us no closer to the liberation of Black people worldwide. We need to rethink, reset and regather ourselves and our movements by facing the radical critique. This is not something that can ever be done comfortably. If you read a book on radicalism and it did not make you uneasy and cause you to question your basic assumptions then it could only be masquerading as revolutionary. There are very few radical politics for a reason: because revolution overturns everything we have come to accept. It is a lot to expect people to risk however little (or much) we have managed to claim to mobilise for a world that offers no promises, only the dream of liberation. It's far more rational to try to improve what we have, to convince ourselves that this system that so reviles us can be redeemed. But we have to understand that there is no prospect of racism being eradicated from capitalism. One cannot exist without the other; racism *is* the system. Malcolm argued that we needed an 'it's already too late philosophy' in order to push us towards the Black revolution,[1] and accept nothing less than complete and total liberation.

Liberty or death

We opened the book with a discussion of nationalism and the need to break beyond the limits of the colonial national state. If you were just to focus your attention on Black people in Britain, Europe or the West you might see enough glimmers of progress to maintain the delusion that freedom is possible: the emergent Black middle class, Black millionaires and even a Black president. In Britain in particular, we make up only 3% of the population; even if we will never have full equality the harsher edges of oppression could be softened. But we do not need to look far to see futility of this logic. For the vast majority of us in Britain our roots lie in the Caribbean or Africa. As I have explained in detail throughout the book, the conditions facing our relatives there make the racism we experience here look like a privilege.

Epilogue

In Chapter 1, we explored the bleak future prospects for places like Jamaica, and in Chapter 3 how neo-colonial trade policies keep most Africans in the grip of poverty. We have to build a politics that recognises the nature of the plight we are in and can deliver liberation for Black people across the globe. The West was built by reducing us to the Negro, the Nigger, devaluing our lives to the point where we could be treated as less than human. Nothing has changed in this regard, and we see the deadly results. We can mobilise against micro-aggressions in middle class jobs all we want, but it is already too late for the millions of children who die on the African continent because of the wealth exploited by the West. In the time it has taken you to read this book the number of Black children who have died because of our relative prosperity would form a pile so large that the thought of it should sicken you.

It is already too late for the hundreds of thousands who have died by violence in South Africa since apartheid ended due to the utter failure to provide a state that can work for all. Make no mistake, it is life and death for many of those in the West. It is already too late for the thousands that die by the gun not only in the developing world but also for African Americans who have been killed at unimaginable rates. It is already too late for those who have died at the hands of, and in the custody of, police. It is already too late for those bodies left floating in the Mediterranean after trying to cross the sea to find some sanctuary in Europe. These are the stakes; it is liberty or death, not as a battle cry but the simple description of the state of the Black nation. Without liberation we will continue to die in the millions due to racial oppression.

When we comprehend the struggle in terms of life and death it becomes easy to see the limits of most of our approaches to racial justice. Black capitalism actually makes the conditions outside of the West worse, feeding the system of economic exploitation. Subscribing to cultural nationalism, by dressing, talking and praying 'African', helps only to heal your psyche and does nothing to reduce the pile of dead children, which is added to by the second. Seeking liberation in our individual joy or experience offers nothing to those who do not have the luxury of existence, let alone desire. Trying to make ourselves safe in bourgeois institutions, or being represented in the mainstream of social and political life, is a lucrative cul-de-sac. We might be able to get some of the benefits of the system but it will always be oppressive to us and deadly to those who look like us but are not as fortunate. It's already too late to try to reform a system built on our oppression. Freedom can only be found in overturning the Western imperial status quo. To do so means adopting an uncompromising politics, the radical politics of Blackness.

Blackness is essential as a concept because it can be nothing other than political. To truly claim Blackness is to recognise our situation and ultimately commit to a revolutionary politics. Black is not negative. It is not taking on the words of the oppressor. It is not to be racialised. If you believe we need to go beyond Blackness then you simply do not understand the politics of the word. Faced with White oppression and the disregard for our African-ness there were many possible avenues for resistance. We could have tried to maintain ties to tribe, or region. We could have sought refuge in our individuality and tried to elevate our position within the system. We could have given in to desperation and ended it all. We could have focused on surviving, making sure that we prevailed. All of these were and still are tactics used to navigate racism. Embracing Blackness means uniting around not only our oppression but also our connection via Africa. It means taking on the responsibility for all those in the global Black nation. Blackness is a choice, a commitment to the 'dead and unborn' to engage in a politics of true liberation.[2] Black is crucially different to African in this regard. Black is a politics, Africa is place. It is only a political statement to say you are African if you were born in the Diaspora. On the continent it is a description, and as we saw in Chapter 2, one of the main limitations of Pan-Africanism is the lack of any ideology. It is not an achievement to be African and there are many versions of African-ness that are just as bad for Black people as Whiteness. The radical politics of Blackness is just as necessary on the African continent as it is in the Diaspora. As Malcolm made clear, 'if you're Black, you should be thinking Black, and if you're not thinking Black at this late stage I'm sorry for you'.[3]

Thinking Black at the intersection

To be clear, 'thinking Black' is not about how you dress, talk, walk or who you choose to sleep with. Thinking Black is solely about politics and not culture. It is about uniting around our Blackness to organise and mobilise. That Blackness must be open to diverse cultural and representational forms. We explored, in Chapter 5, how patriarchy and homophobia has infected Black political movements, something that cannot be accepted. Freedom for all of us must mean liberation for everyone. We need to recognise that our Blackness connects us across location, age, gender, sexuality, disability and the rest of our differences. That does not mean that those differences are not important, just a recognition that our Blackness is a connection that goes beyond them. Audre Lorde offered a warning that 'there is no such thing as a single-issue struggle because we do not live single-issue lives'; the key is to stop thinking of Blackness as a single issue.[4]

Hopefully, the systemic analysis that Black radicalism insists on has been apparent in the book. White supremacy is an essential part of the political economy and therefore our Blackness cannot be reduced to the cultural or representative. Our position within the system is as essential to its maintenance as the location of the heart in the body. There is no way to understand how class, gender, sexuality or disability impacts on a person without considering how this intersects with Blackness. You do not escape the oppression that comes from being Black because you are a woman or queer. For instance, no matter your gender identity you are more likely to be killed by the police. Being a man does not guarantee me typically male benefits; for example, Black men in Britain are less likely to be employed than women. As Malcolm put it, 'we are all in the same boat and we're all going to catch the same hell'.[5]

Being Black obviously does not prevent us from experiencing the oppression that goes with being a woman or not

being heterosexual, but it is the same society that discrimi-
nates on the grounds of gender and sexuality. You could argue
then that we need allies across different struggles and communities to support the Black struggle. But anti-discrimination
movements are not immune from Whiteness. Feminism has
been accused of maintaining Whiteness from ignoring the
pleas from activists like Ida B. Wells over lynching,[6] to taking
the same stance today on mass incarceration. Gender, sexuality and disability equality can be achieved for some without
solving any of the issues facing the Black segments of these
communities. In the same way that you are always a Black +
nationality, you are always Black + discrimination. Coalitions
can be important strategically but we must always remember
that there can be no liberation within this political and
economic system for Black people. Therefore we must always
be agitating for revolution and building an alternative that can
bring us freedom. It is vital that in building the alternative, it
is one rooted in a Black politics open to all its various mani-
festations. But losing sight of our Blackness risks the global
solidarity necessary for the revolution.

Of course it is not just Black people who suffer horrif-
ically at the hands of the West. The children that die every
six seconds for lack of access to food are spread across the
global South. In resisting Whiteness we could re-engage
with calls for Third World solidarity and the global majority
of people of colour. But there is little more harmful we can
do than base our political identity solely in relation to Whiteness. Blackness is of course relational, in the sense that if
we were all the same colour it would not be a concept, but

it is not just relational to Whiteness. To claim Blackness as the link to Africa is to tie ourselves into a shared heritage, the 'unbreakable umbilical cord' across the Diaspora.[7] It also distinguishes us from other groups that have sought to exploit the continent, like the Arab invaders into North Africa who instituted their own slave trade.[8] As much as the hierarchy of White supremacy ultimately oppresses all those who are not White, that does not mean it cannot be amended to give additional benefits to some over others. The reason that China was not wholly supportive of the anti-apartheid movement was because it was busy integrating itself into the economy of the West. It is true that the majority of Chinese are viciously oppressed both by their government and global system of capitalism that relies on their poverty wage labour. But given China's exploitation of Africa's resources it is also not hard to imagine the nation lifting its people out of poverty off the back of the continent. Capitalism has always required an army of destitute labourers and most of the world's population growth will be in Africa over the next fifty years. If Africans are again to be the source of labour for capitalism, the whip may not be yielded by White hands.

All of this is a speculative but necessary reminder that it is a delusion to think that people will not exploit us just because they are also not White. That is why independence is so important to the politics of Black radicalism. We of course have solidarity with oppressed people across the globe and the Black revolution will end the system that exploits them. But the only way to ensure Black liberation is to build the Black nation into one that can stand on its own two feet.

Drawing these sharp lines around Blackness can lead to accusations of separatism and divisiveness that typically we can brush away. But this does pose a serious question. I have been asked a lot about where people of mixed heritage fit into the equation. Most often this is put to me as a question of choosing sides, as if embracing Blackness goes against White or other heritages that a person may possess. The choosing side's metaphor demonstrates the way that rather than challenging the binary view of race, much of the rhetoric of mixedness reinforces it. At times it seems as though we are talking of a combining of oil and water, substances that can never truly mix but remain separate from one another in the same body. The reality is that the vast majority of those descended from enslaved Africans are mixed to some extent, so the idea that when you are half and half you are in a new category of 'mixed' is highly problematic. The uncomfortable truth is that our conceptions of mixedness are directly linked to racial categorisations from slavery. On British plantations the racial categories that deemed those with one White and one Black parent a Mulatto through successive generations could produce offspring who came closer to Whiteness. Having a Mulatto and 'Negro' parent, though, meant you were a 'Sambo', remaining firmly on the Black side of the dividing line.[9] No different than today, on the plantation a White grandparent meant you were Black, but a White parent represented being mixed. Part of the embrace of a mixed identity is to resist the legacy of the 'one drop rule', which in America both during slavery and segregation meant that any African heritage marked you as a Negro and restricted your legal status. Even on British plantations, though being mixed afforded advantages, to be in one of the many categories was still to be different and oppressed. The way to overcome the racist categorisation is to abandon the logic, not embrace it.

Blackness is a rejection of race and so makes no claims to unity based on biological purity. You are no more or less likely to think Black based on your complexion. Blackness is rooted on our connection to the Diaspora and so the 'one drop' is the link to the Black nation. But this does not determine your biological or cultural destiny. Blackness is a choice, embracing the importance of that link as the basis for political mobilisation. You could argue that it may be more difficult with people of mixed heritage to embrace that connection, but some of the darkest skinned people on the African continent are less Black (politically) than some of the lightest people of mixed heritage. Make no mistake, Black radicalism does mean choosing sides: either maintaining faith in a system based on White supremacy or embracing your African descent to unite and struggle against that racist system. It really is that simple and is a choice that will not depend on how mixed you are, or are not. There may once have been a time where the system could have developed along a different path, and a melting pot society where these distinctions did not matter could exist. But it is already too late be deluded by that fantasy.

Beyond repair

We find ourselves at a turning point. In the 1960s we were poised for a revolution that could have toppled the West.

But state violence, race relations legislations and so-called independence of the colonies offered a glimmer of hope that the system could be redeemed. Fifty years later it must be blatantly obvious that the promise was a mirage, a delusion to keep us surviving but still suffering. However, leaving the door ajar has given some of us access to resources and even some levers of power. Let's not pretend that we are not still under surveillance and that the state will not use violent means to suppress any real opposition. But we are afforded platforms and technologies for building unity that we never had before. Yet so complete is the domination of our politics, economics and even intellectual life that we ourselves have stopped agitating for revolution, keeping faith in some faint hope in transforming the system from within.

We are currently in the United Nations Decade for People of African Descent (2015–2024). It is mostly symbolic, with no funding provided and only a suggestion given to the nation state governments that they should provide resources. UN Resolution 69/16 of the General Assembly, which outlines the programme for the decade is strongly worded and advises member states to consider affirmative action, and for those states that have not have not yet 'expressed remorse or presented apologies' or paid reparations for slavery 'to find some way to contribute to the restoration of the dignity of victims'.[10] This focus on reparations has been pushed by grassroots activists to the point where Caribbean nations are pressing Europe for compensation for centuries of enslavement. The Movement for Black Lives in America and the Pan-Afrikan Reparations Coalition in Europe (PARCOE) also demand reparatory justice. In Britain there is an annual march and many organisations, including Rastas, ensuring reparations are on the agenda.

The case for reparations is indisputable. In reality there is no credible argument that reparations are not due. Current wealth in the West is built off riches deriving from the enslavement of African people. Port cities like Bristol and Liverpool in Britain simply would not exist without the wealth from the triangular trade, and my hometown of Birmingham has its roots in the guns and shackles needed to subdue the enslaved.[11] The industrial revolution was fuelled by the proceeds and also products of enslavement, with the steam engine processing cotton from the Americas. Finance capitalism engorged itself on the trade, with Britain's biggest corporation, Lloyds of London, founded on insuring the merchant (slave) trade. The banking sector has so many links to slavery that it may as well sign all the companies over to the global Black nation. The church, the political class, the elites all owe their wealth in large part to the enslavement of African people. When slavery was abolished it was so lucrative that the British government paid the equivalent of £2 billion in compensation to the slave owners for their losses. Researchers at University College London have tracked where that money went and it demonstrates just how deeply implicated in slavery was a whole swathe of British society. Every other slave-trading nation will have similar stories, and even those that were not directly part of the trade benefited directly and indirectly from it. Swedish companies, in that social democratic beacon of justice, made a fortune selling iron ore to Britain for the manufacture of guns and chains. In return for building the West our ances-tors received nothing. The bill for unpaid labour for centuries of work runs into the countless trillions. In America alone it is estimated that Black people are owed anywhere between $5.9 and $14.2 trillion in back pay,[12] not including damages for murder, rape and torture. A staggering figure, but more so when you consider that less than 20% of enslaved Africans ended up in America, not counting the millions who perished during the middle passage or fighting to remain free in Africa.

A debt is clearly owed, and nothing short of full payment could even come close to repairing the damage that has been done. But rather than pushing for payment in full the repa-rations debate has now changed to being no longer 'all about money'. The demands of the Caribbean Community and Common Market (Caricom) include a call for the end of debt repayments, an apology and a literacy programme. The Movement for Black Lives asks for free college tuition. In Britain we also hear appeals for educational and even psycho-logical repair. What all these demands have in common is that they seek to reform the system. They retain hope that our relationship to the West can be healed. But the paradox of the reparations debate should tell us that this kind of repair can never happen.

Reparations are long overdue and also impossible. Forget the logistics of where the money would go, the massive transfer of wealth necessary for reparatory justice would cripple the Western economy. Exploiting African flesh is one of the key foundation stones of the political economy, and to have to account for it would inevitably bring the house of cards tumbling down. Even if we could imagine that it was possible to transfer the wealth, we have to acknowledge that slavery was just a mechanism of our oppression, not the basis of it. The reality is that our lives are worth less and can therefore be exploited and discarded. After slavery the mechanism for this became direct colonial rule. As we discussed in Chapter 2, once the façade of so-called independence was granted, neo-colonial economic rule became the method. So the wealth that would be transferred would be based on a system that still oppresses us on the same basis for which reparations would be paid. If we used the wealth correctly we would eradicate the problems that inflict us, making it impossible for the West to continue to exploit us. Capitalism that had to pay fair price for the resources of Africa is not a feasible economic project. The West is not going to destroy itself paying off the debt, and even if it did the complete collapse of the economy would make the wealth meaningless. Once we understand that the entire political and economic system is based on our oppression then we should come to the realisation that it is already too late to be asking for reparations.

The danger in the mobilisations for reparations are that the West complies with the demands but in a way that does not solve any of the problems. It may offer an apology, cut some debt and provide some (mostly privately funded) aid initiatives for the Caribbean. Given the trickery of Western states this is the most likely outcome of the campaigns. A big ceremony and display will be made about how the West is atoning for its original sin and making peace with Black communities and nations. Nothing substantive will be passed over, no repair will be made but we will have been lulled into thinking that we have made progress. The best possible outcome of the campaign for reparations is 'not a solution … but a regeneration of the problem in a particularly perverse form'.[13] I do not mean to argue that there is no value in the reparations movement. There has been excellent and tireless activism around this issue for decades that should never be downplayed. Reparations are the perfect tool for the political education necessary to explain the depth of our plight to Black communities. When used as a tool to mobilise Black people into radical action then reparations is an incredibly powerful campaign. But campaigns for reparations that expect to achieve repair from the West are the definition of liberal radicalism.

Blueprint for Black radicalism

Black radicalism is its own ideology and way of understanding the world. We must separate it out from more reactionary and liberal forms of Black politics. Throughout this book I have tried to be as precise, and unsentimental, as possible in distinguishing Black radicalism as its own ideology. My aim was to provide a blueprint that we can use to move forward, which deals with the critiques I have heard over the years. Many of those critiques were in fact of other politics I have never identified with, but others' criticisms have shaped how I have come to understand the need for and process of the Black revolution. For me it has been at times an uncomfortable journey, having to unlearn and challenge my own position.

The chapter on Pan-Africanism was probably the hardest because I had always been invested in Pan-Africanism as the solution to the Black struggle. That the opposite was true was a difficult, but necessary, realisation. The more I have written and talked about Black radicalism the more I have also become discomforted by my position. As an academic I am the model of the liberal radical I so criticised in Chapter 7. A semi-elite that makes a good living off talking about revolution, while reaping the benefits of racial oppression. My hands are just as soaked as anyone else's in the blood of those who die by the second because of the relative wealth I enjoy. That realisation creates a jarring jolt of guilt, anguish and pain. I fully understand why people seek refuge in culture or religion, or convince themselves that we can be part of the system and part of the solution. I can see why people go off the grid and try to escape Babylon by rejecting it. But deep down all of those responses are to make us feel better because we do not believe that the system can change. We have learnt helplessness and either seek to escape or conclude that doing something, no matter if it makes little or no difference, is better than doing nothing. Instead of ignoring or debating our complicity, we need to embrace it. It is the feelings of anguish that will never let us be comfortable in this wicked system. We can turn the pain into anger, to fuel our constant movement towards liberation. More than anything, we must use the priv-ileges we do have to build the politics of Black radicalism. We cannot change the system from within, but we can leverage the resources we have access to in support of mobilisations on the outside.

What we can never do is lose hope that revolutionary change is possible. Fifty years is a long time. In the 1960s we were on the cusp of the Black revolution and we are now further away than we have ever been. In the next fifty years the world can be a completely different place if we choose to build it. The West was built on our backs because they have been able, through various means, to control us. But we have always had the power to bring the system crashing down, which is why they invested so much effort in shackling us. I do not pretend to present any new ideas in this book because that it is not what we need. Black radical politics has always been there; we have just not looked hard enough. What I have tried to do is to dust off, re-package and re-articulate the radical basis for the Black revolution. We need to go back to this politics, retrace our steps to the last turning point in the 1960s where we headed down the cul-de-sac of integrating into the system of racial oppression. The blueprint exists to build a grassroots organisation based on uniting the global Black nation; one which embraces a vision of Blackness that includes all of our cultural, social and representational forms and is rooted in providing for those suffering the worst oppression. There can be no shortcut to our liberation, no freedom without sacrifice. We cannot theorise or perform our way to revolution. When Kwame Ture visited Birmingham in 1983 his message was simple: 'if you're not part of an organisation then you are against your people'.[14] The only vehicle to liberation is building an organisation that can empower the global Black nation. No excuses about how organisations have failed in the past, or how we have tried this before, will do. It's already too late to be standing on the side-lines waiting to see whether you should commit.

It is only by rejecting the system of Western imperialism that we can ever be free. But as we leave the house we must bring it crashing down in order to truly liberate not only the Black nation, but all oppressed peoples.

Notes

Prologue

1   Andrews, K. (2016) Black is a country: Building solidarity across borders. *World Policy Journal* 33(1): 15–19.

2   Taylor, K. (2016) *From #BlackLivesMatter to Black Liberation*. Chicago: Haymarket Books.

3   Malcolm X (1963) Message to the grassroots. Speech at the Negro Grass Roots Leadership Conference, Michigan, 10 November.

4   Malcolm X (1963) Excerpt from interview with Louis Lomax. Greenwood, IN: Educational Video Group.

5   CNN Politics (2009) Most blacks say MLK's vision fulfilled, poll finds, 19 January.

6   Malcolm X (1963) The Black revolution. Speech, Abyssinia Baptist Church, New York, 23 January.

7   KRS-ONE (1993) Black cop. *Return of the Boom Bap*. CD Album, Jive Records.

8   Griffin, C.L. (1996) Angela Y. Davis. In Leeman, R.W. (ed.) *Afro-American Orators: A Bio-Critical Sourcebook*. Westport, CT: Greenwood Press.

9   Beckford, R. (2007) *The Great African Scandal*. Directed by Kirby, K. Channel 4.

10 Nkrumah, K. (1998). *Africa Must Unite*. London: Panaf Books, 27.

11 Malcolm X (1964) The ballot or the bullet. Speech at Cory Methodist Church in Cleveland, Ohio, 3 April.

12   Carmichael, S. (1971) *Stokely Speaks: From Black Power to Pan Africanism*. New York: Vintage Books, 206.

13   Malcolm X, Message to the grassroots.

14   DeCaro, L.A. (1996) *On the Side of My People: A Religious Life of Malcolm X.* London: New York University Press, 253.

15   Boyd, H. (2004) *We Shall Overcome*. Naperville, IL: Sourcebooks, 192.

16   Malcolm X (1964) Speech at the Militant Labor Forum. New York, 29 May.

17   Shelby, T. (2005) *We Who are Dark: The Philosophical Foundations of Black Solidarity*. Cambridge, MA: Belknap Press, 6.

Chapter 1

1   Hopkins, S. (2016) Veteran British racism campaigner has message to Black Lives Matter ahead of London riots anniversary. *Huffington Post*, 30 July.

2   Kraszewski, J. (2002) Reconceptualizing the historical receptions of Blaxploitation: articulations of class, Black nationalism and anxiety in the genre's advertisements. *The Velvet Light Trap* 50: 48–61, 57.

3   Shelby, *We Who are Dark*, 6.

4   Joseph, P.E. (2010) *Dark Days, Bright Nights: From Black Power to Barack Obama*. New York: Basic Books, 4.

5   Malcolm X, Ballot or the bullet.

6   Hill Collins, P (2006) *From Black Power to Hip Hop: Racism, Nationalism, and Feminism*. Philadelphia: Temple University Press, 96.

7   Tushnet, M. (2004) Clarence Thomas's Black Nationalism. *Howard Law Journal* 47(323), 2.

8   Rossiter, B. (2012) 'They Don't Care About Us': Michael Jackson's Black Nationalism. *Popular Music and Society* 35(2): 203–222.

9   Shelby, T. (2003) Two conceptions of Black Nationalism: Martin Delaney on the meaning of Black political solidarity. *Political Theory* 31(5): 664–692, 667.

10   Brown, R.A and Shaw, T.C. (2002) Two attitudinal dimensions of Black Nationalism. *The Journal of Politics* 64(1): 22–44, 27.

11 Shelby, Two conceptions.

12 Brown and Shaw, Two attitudinal dimensions.

13 Du Bois, W.E.B. (1935) A Negro nation within the nation. *Current History* 42(3): 265–270, 267; emphasis added.

14 Carmichael, S. and Hamilton, C. (1968) *Black Power: The Politics of Liberation in America.* Harmondsworth: Penguin, 60–65.

15 Malcolm X, Ballot or the bullet.

16 Malcolm X (1964) Speech at the Audobon. New York, 20 December.

17 Malcolm X, Ballot or the bullet.

18 Kunjufu, J. (1991) *Black Economics: Solutions for Economic and Community Empowerment.* Chicago: African American Images, 161.

19 Ibid., 160.

20 Valls, A. (2010) A liberal defense of Black Nationalism. *American Political Science Review* 104(3): 467–481.

21 Glaude, E. (2002) *Is it Nation Time? Contemporary Essays on Black Power and Black Nationalism.* Chicago: University of Chicago Press.

22 Joseph, *Dark Days, Bright Nights.*

23 Taylor, *From #Blacklivesmatter*, 140.

24 Ibid.

25 Ibid., 103.

26 Ibid., 83.

27 Mulloy, D. (2010) New Panthers, old Panthers and the politics of Black Nationalism in the United States. *Patterns of Prejudice* 44(3): 217–238, 237.

28 Van Kessel, I. and Oomen, B. (1997) 'One chief, one vote': The revival of traditional authorities in post-apartheid South Africa. *African Affairs* 96 (385): 561–585.

29 Plaatje, S. (2007) *Native Life in South Africa.* London: Echo Books.

30 Lipton, M. (1972) The South African census and the Bantustan policy. *The World Today* 28(6): 257–271.

31 Piper, l. (2002) Nationalism without a nation: The rise and fall of Zulu nationalism in South Africa's transition to democracy, 1975–99. *Nations and Nationalism* 8(1): 73–94.

32 Mzala (1998) *Gatsha Buthelezi: A Chief with a Double Agenda.* London: Zed Books, 231.

33 Piper, Nationalism, 79; original emphasis.

34 Mzala, *Gastha Buthelezi.*

35 Jeffery, A. (1997) *The Natal Story: Sixteen Years of Conflict.* Johannesburg: South African Institute of Race Relations.

36 Mandela, N.R. (1996) *Long Walk to Freedom.* London: Abacus Books.

37 Muhammad, E. (1997) *Message to the Blackman in America.* Maryland Heights, MO: Secretarius MEMPS Publications, 222.

38 Stuckey, S. (ed.) (1972) *The Ideological Origins of Black Nationalism.* Boston: Beacon Press, 6.

39 Shelby, Two conceptions.

40 Ibid.

41 Shelby, *We Who are Dark*, 42.

42 Guyatt, N. (2016) *Bind Us Apart: How Enlightened Americans Invented Racial Segregation.* Oxford: Oxford University Press, 4.

43 Essien-Udom, E.U. (1970) *Black Nationalism: A Search for Identity in America.* New York: Dell Publishing.

44 Powell, E. (1968) Rivers of Blood. Speech to Conservative Association, Birmingham, 20 April.

45 Horne, G. (1994) *Black Liberation/Red Scare: Ben Davis and the Communist Party.* London: Associated University Presses, 68.

46 Guyatt, *Bind Us Apart.*

47 Malcolm X, Black revolution.

48 Malcolm X (1963) Speech at UC Berkeley, 11 October.

49 Marable, M. (1998) Black fundamentalism: Farrakhan and conservative Black Nationalism. *Race and Class* 39(4): 1–22, 5.

50 Ibid., 16.

51 Berger, D. (2009) 'The Malcolm X doctrine': The Republic of New Afrika and national liberation on U.S. soil. In Dubinsky, K. Krull, C., Lord, S., Mills, S. and Rutherford, S. (eds) *New World Coming: The Sixties and the Shaping of Global Consciousness*, 46–55. Toronto: Between the Lines.

52 Malcolm X, Ballot or the bullet.

53 Anderson, C. (2003) *Eyes off the Prize: The United Nations and the African American Struggle for Human Rights, 1944–1955.* Cambridge: Cambridge University Press.

54 James, C.L.R. (1938) *The Black Jacobins.* London: Penguin.

55 Roberts, N. (2015) *Freedom as Marronage*. Chicago: University of Chicago Press.

56 Levi, D. (1992) Fragmented nationalism: Jamaica since 1938. *History of European Ideas* 15(1–3): 413–417.

57 Editorial (2015) Out of many, one people: Motto or myth? *Jamaican Observer*, 2 August.

58 Walker, C. (1999) When is a nation? *Ethnic and Racial Studies* 13(1): 92–103.

59 Thornton, R. (1987) *American Indian Holocaust and Survival: A Population History Since 1492*. Norman: University of Oklahoma Press.

60 Williams, *Capitalism and Slavery*.

61 Malcolm X, Ballot or the bullet.

62 Robinson, J.W. (1994) Lessons from the structural adjustment process in Jamaica. *Social and Economic Studies* 43(4): 87–113.

63 Index Mundi (2016) Jamaica economy profile 2016. Available at http://www.indexmundi.com/jamaica/economy_profile.html

64 Dearden, N. (2013) Jamaica's decades of debt are damaging its future. *Guardian*, 16 April.

65 World Travel and Tourism Council (2015) *Benchmark Report – Jamaica May 2015*. London: WTTC.

66 Jessop, D. (2012) Tourism's downside: Lack of hard data. *Jamaica Gleaner*, 15 April.

67 Index Mundi, Jamaica.

68 Haughton, D. (2012) Here's why things are so bad in Jamaica today. *The Gleaner*, 12 December.

69 Shridath Ramphal Centre (2010) *Caribbean Fishing Industry: A Brief Overview*. Cave Hill: University of the West Indies.

70 Ministry of Foreign Affairs and Foreign Trade (2015) *National Diaspora Policy*. Kingston: Ministry of Foreign Affairs and Foreign Trade, 4.

71 Ibid., 25.

72 Ibid., 25.

73 Ibid., 1.

74 Ibid., 14.

75 Ibid., 20.

Chapter 2

1   Carmichael, *Stokely Speaks*, 206.

2   Andrews, K. (2015) We need to revive the revolutionary spirit of the Pan-African congress. *The Guardian*, 15 October.

3   DuBois, S.G. (1971) The liberation of Africa: Power, peace and justice. *The Black Scholar* 2(6): 32–37, 33.

4   Malcolm X (1964) 2nd Founding Rally of Organisation of Afro-American Unity. Speech, New York, 28 June.

5   Garvey, M. (1967) *The Philosophy and Opinions of Marcus Garvey: Or Africa for the Africans*. London: Routledge, 1.

6   Part of this argument is also developed in Andrews, K. (2017) Beyond Pan-Africanism: Garveyism, Malcolm X and the end of the colonial nation state. *Third World Quarterly*, 38(11): 2501-2516

7   Ackah, W. (1999) *Pan-Africanism: Exploring the Contradictions: Politics, Identity and Development in Africa and the African Diaspora*. London: Routledge, 12.

8   Enaharo, A. (1962) Comments. In American Society of African Culture (ed.) *Pan-Africanism Reconsidered*, 69–73. Berkeley: University of California Press, 69.

9   Fanon, F. (1967) *Towards the African Revolution*. New York: Grove Press.

10 Shepperson, G. (1962) Pan-Africanism and 'Pan-Africanism': Some historical notes. *Phylon* 23(4): 346–358.

11 M'Buyinga, E. (1982) *Pan Africanism or Neo-Colonialism? The Bankruptcy of the OAU*. London: Zed.

12 Kinyatta, M. (1973) Dialectical reality of the African revolution. *The Black Scholar* 4(10): 20–23, 21.

13 Adi, H. and Sherwood, M. (1995) *The 1945 Manchester Pan-African Congress Revisited*. London: New Beacon Books.

14 Sherwood, M. (2011) *Origins of Pan-Africanism: Henry Sylvester Williams, Africa and the African Diaspora*. London: Routledge.

15 Logan, R.W. (1962) The historical aspects of Pan-Africanism, 1900–1945. In American Society of African Culture (ed.) *Pan-*

Africanism Reconsidered, 29–52. Berkeley: University of California Press, 38; emphasis added.

16 Garvey, *Philosophy and Opinions*, 138.

17 Martin, T. (1976) *Race First: The Ideological and Organisational Struggles of Marcus Garvey and the Universal Negro Improvement Association*. Dover, MA: The Majority Press.

18 Shilliam, R. (2006) What about Marcus Garvey? Race and the transformation of sovereignty debate. *Review of International Studies* 32(3): 379–400.

19 Garvey, A.J. (2014) *Garvey and Garveyism*. Baltimore: Black Classic Press.

20 Shepperson, Pan-Africanism.

21 Garvey, *Philosophy and Opinions*.

22 Makalani, M. (2011) *In the Cause of Freedom: Radical Black Internationalism from Harlem to London, 1917–1939*. Chapel Hill: University of North Carolina Press.

23 DuBois, W.E.B. (1903) The talented tenth. http://teachingamericanhistory.org/library/document/the-talented-tenth/

24 Hunter, M. (2007) The persistent problem of colorism: Skin tone, status, and inequality. *Sociology Compass* 1(1): 237–254.

25 Sherwood, *Orgins of Pan-Africanism*.

26 Geiss, I. (1969) Pan-Africanism. *Journal of Contemporary History* 4(1): 187–200.

27 Nyerere, J.K. (1974) Speech to the congress. *The Black Scholar* 5(10): 16–22.

28 Kendhammer, B. (2007) DuBois the Pan-Africanist and the development of African nationalism. *Ethnic and Racial Studies* 30(1): 51–70, 61.

29 M'Buyinga, *Pan-Africanism*, 160.

30 Nyerere, Speech to the congress, 16.

31 Dubois, W.E.B. (2007) *The World and Africa*. Oxford: Oxford University Press, 188.

32 Ibid., 197.

33 Kendhammer, Dubois, 59.

34 Adi and Sherwood, *The 1945 Manchester*.

35 Emerson, R. (1962) Pan-Africanism. *International Organization* 16(2): 275–290, 276.

36 Apter, D. and Coleman, J. (1962) Pan-Africanism or nationalism in Africa. In American Society of African Culture (ed.) *Pan-Africanism Reconsidered*, 81–115. Berkeley: University of California Press.

37 Emerson, Pan-Africansism, 290.

38 Diop, C.A (1987) *Black Africa: The Economic and Cultural Basis for a Federated State*. Chicago: Lawrence Hill Books.

39 Adogamhe, P. (2008) Pan-Africanism revisited: Vision and reality of African unity and development. *African Review of Integration* 2(2): 1–34.

40 Malcolm X, 2nd Founding Rally.

41 Anderson, *Eyes off the Prize*.

42 Malcolm X, Black Revolution.

43 Apter and Coleman, Pan-Africanism.

44 M'Buyinga, *Pan-Africanism*, 176.

45 Adogamhe, Pan-Africanism, 27.

46 Malcolm X, 2nd Founding Rally.

47 M'Buyinga, *Pan-Africanism*.

48 Malcolm X, Message to the grassroots.

49 Horne, D.L. (1974) The Pan-African Congress: A positive assessment. *The Black Scholar* 5(10): 2–11.

50 Ofari, E. (1974) A critical review of the Pan-African Congress. *The Black Scholar* 5(10): 12–15.

51 Shepperson, Pan-Africanism, 348.

52 Garvey, *Philosophy and Opinions*.

53 Martin, *Race First*.

54 Shepperson, Pan-Africanism.

55 Nyerere, Speech, 17.

56 Toure, S. (1974) Speech to the Congress. *The Black Scholar* 5(10): 23–29, 28.

57 Ofari, A critical review.

58 Prashard, V. (2007) *The Darker Nations: A People's History of the Third World*. New York: The New Press.

59 Wright, R. (1954) *Black Power*. New York: Harper Perennial.

60 Garvey, *Philosophy and Opinions*, 6.

61 Editorial (2001) Africa's plan to save itself. *Economist*, 5July.

62 Adoghame, Pan-Africanism, 16.

63 Rostow, W. W. (1990) *The Stages of Economic Growth*. Cambridge: Cambridge University Press.

64 Thornton, R. (1987). *American Indian Holocaust and Survival: A Population History since 1492*. Norman: University of Oklahoma Press.

65 Williams, *Capitalism and Slavery*.

66 Rodney, W. (1972) *How Europe Underdeveloped Africa*. London: Bogle-L'Overture Publications.

67 Ismi, A. (2004) *Impoverishing a Continent: The World Bank and the IMF in Africa*. Halifax, Canada: Halifax Initiative Coalition.

68 Rostow, W.W (1962) Some lessons of history for Africa. In American Society of African Culture (ed.) *Pan-Africanism Reconsidered*, 155–168. Berkeley: University of California Press.

69 United Nations, Funding for NEPAD — Africa still waiting for genuine 'partnership'. http://www.un.org/en/africarenewal/sgreport/repdfs/partners.pdf

70 Ibid., 2.

71 Loxley, J. (2003) Imperialism and economic reform in Africa: What's new about the New Partnership for Africa's Development (NEPAD)? *Review of African Political Economy* 30(95): 119–128.

Chapter 3

1 Smith, A. (1995) *Nations and Nationalism in a Global Era*. Cambridge, MA: Polity Press, 86.

2 Part of this argument is also developed in Andrews, K. (2016) Black is a country: Black people in the West as a colonised minority. In Andrews, K. and Palmer, L. (eds.) *Blackness in Britain*, 50–63. London: Routledge.

3 Shilliam, What about Marcus Garvey?

4 Cameron, D. (2014) Scottish independence. Speech at Better Together Campaign, Aberdeen, 15 September.

5 Beck, U. (2007). The cosmopolitan condition: Why methodological nationalism fails. *Theory, Culture and Society* 24: 286–290, 286.

6   Ting, H. (2008) Social construction of nation: A theoretical explo-
     ration. *Nationalism and Ethnic Politics* 14(3): 453–482, 453.

7   Walby, S. (2003). The myth of the nation-state: Theorizing society
     and polities in a global era. *Sociology* 37(3): 529–546.

8   James, *Black Jacobins*.

9   Allen, R.L (2001) The globalization of white supremacy: Toward
     a critical discourse on the racialization of the world. *Educational
     Theory* 51(4): 467–485, 470.

10   Bauman, Z. (1989) *Modernity and the Holocaust.* London: Polity Press.

11   Andrews, K. (2016) The psychosis of whiteness: The celluloid
     hallucinations of Amazing Grace and Belle. *Journal of Black Studies*
     47(5): 435–453.

12   Pinderhughes, C. (2011) Toward a new theory of internal coloni-
     alism. *Socialism and Democracy* 25(1): 235–236.

13   Carmichael and Hamilton, *Black Power*.

14   Ibid., 26.

15   Ibid., 26.

16   See Blauner, R. (1969) Internal colonialism and ghetto revolt.
     Social Problems 16(4): 393–408; Tabb, W.K. (1971) Race relations
     models of social change. *Social Problems* 18(4): 431–444.

17   Allen, R.L. (1990) *Black Awakening in Capitalist America.* Trenton:
     Africa World Press.

18   Malcolm X, Message to the grassroots.

19   Blauner, Internal colonialism and ghetto revolt.

20   Burawoy, M. (1974) Race, class and colonialism. *Social and
     Economic Studies* 23(4): 521–550, 521.

21   Bailey, R. (1973) Economic aspects of the Black internal colony.
     Review of Black Political Economy 3(4): 43–72.

22   Tabb, Race relations, 435.

23   Phillips, D. (2007) Ethnic and racial segregation: A critical perspec-
     tive. *Geography Compass* 1(5): 1138–59.

24   Tabb, Race relations.

25   John, G. (2005) This conflict has been 20 years in the making. *The
     Guardian*, 26 October.

26   See Dove, N.E. (1993) The emergence of Black supplementary
     schools: Resistance to racism in the UK. *Urban Education* 27(4):

430–447; Graham, M. and Robinson, G. (2004) The silent catastrophe: Institutional racism in the British educational system and the underachievement of Black boys. *Journal of Black Studies* 34(5): 653–671.

27 Maylor, U. (2009) What is the meaning of 'black'? Researching 'black' respondents. *Ethnic and Racial Studies* 32(2): 369–387, 373.

28 Martinez, G.A. (1998) African-Americans, Latinos, and the construction of race: Toward an epistemic coalition. *Chicano-Latino Law Review* 19: 213–222, 222.

29 Lopez, I.H. (2003) White Latinos. *Harvard Latino Review* 6: 1–7.

30 Deliovsky, K. and Kitossa, T. (2013) Beyond Black and White: When going beyond may take us out of bounds. *Journal of Black Studies* 44: 158–181.

31 Waterson, A. (2006) Are Latinos becoming 'white' folk? And what that still says about race in America. *Transforming Anthropology* 14(2): 133–150, 144.

32 Joseph, P.E. (2008) *Waiting 'til the Midnight Hour: A Narrative History of the Black Power in America.* New York: Henry Holt and Company.

33 McManus, E. (1966) *A History of Negro Slavery in New York.* Syracuse, NY: Syracuse University Press.

34 Andrews, Psychosis of whiteness.

35 For the US see Carter, P. (2003) Black cultural capital, status positioning and schooling conflicts for low income African American youth. *Social Problems* 50(1): 136–155. For the UK see Carby, H. (1983) Schooling in Babylon. In Centre for Contemporary Cultural Studies (ed.) *The Empire Strikes Back*, 212–235. London: Hutchinson; and Figueroa, P. (1991) *Education and the Social Construction of Race.* London: Routledge.

36 Nkrumah, *Africa Must Unite.*

37 Singh, N.P (2005) *Black is a Country: Race and the Unfinished Struggle for Democracy.* Cambridge, MA: Harvard University Press, 197.

38 Attributed to Kenyatta.

39 Campbell, H. (1997) *Rasta and Resistance from Marcus Garvey to Walter Rodney.* St John's, Antigua: Hansib Caribbean.

40 See Murrell, N.S., Spencer, W.D. and McFarlane, A.A. (eds) (1998) *Chanting Down Babylon: The Rastafari Reader.* Philadelphia: Temple University Press.

41 Seife, H. (2010) A new generation of Ethiopianists: The Universal Ethiopian Students Association and *The African: Journal of African Affairs*, 1937–1948. *African and Black Diaspora* 3(2): 197–209.

42 Garvey, *Garvey and Garveyism*.

43 Andrews, Black is a country.

44 Garvery, *Garvey and Garveyism*, 23.

45 Washington, B. (1901) *Up From Slavery.* New York: Doubleday.

46 Martin, *Race First*.

47 Campbell, *Rasta and Resistance*.

48 Saidi Masawanya of the Tanganyika National Union (1962) Comment. In American Society of African Culture (ed.) *Pan-Africanism Reconsidered*, 132–134. Berkeley: University of California Press, 134.

49 Malcolm X, Ballot or the bullet.

50 Marable, M. (2011) *Malcolm X: A Life of Reinvention.* London: Allen Lane.

51 Malcolm X (1965) Not just an American problem, but a world problem. Speech, Corn Hill Methodist Church, Rochester, New York, 16 February.

52 Carmichael, *Stokely Speaks*, 198.

53 Essien-Udom, *Black Nationalism*.

54 Malcolm X (1965) After the Bombing. Speech at the Ford Auditorium, Detroit, 14 February.

55 Malcolm X, Militant Labor Forum.

56 Malcolm X, Ballot or the bullet.

57 Malcolm X, Message to the grassroots.

58 Ibid.

59 Younge, G. (2013) *The Speech: The Story behind Martin Luther King's Dream.* London: Guardian Books.

60 Malcolm X. (1964) *The Autobiography of Malcolm X.* New York: Ballantine Books, 281.

61 Makalani, *In the Cause of Freedom*.

62 Malcolm X, 2nd Founding Rally.

Chapter 4

1   Woodard, K. (1999) *A Nation Within a Nation: Amiri Baraka (LerRoi Jones) and Black Power.* Chapel Hill: University of North Carolina Press.

2   Seale, B. (1970) *Seize the Time: The Story of the Black Panther Party,* New York: Random House, 18.

3   Ogbar, J. (2004) *Black Power: Radical Politics and African American Identity.* Baltimore: Johns Hopkins University Press.

4   Woodard, *A Nation.*

5   Newton, H.P (1968) To the Black Movement. Speech, 15 May.

6   Robinson, C.J (1983) *Black Marxism: The Making of the Black Radical Tradition.* London: Zed Books, 83.

7   Strausbaugh, J. (2007) *Black Like You: Blackface, Whiteface, Insult and Imitation in American Culture.* London: Penguin.

8   Clark, K.B. and Clark, M.P. (1940) Skin colour as a factor in racial identification and preferences in Negro children. *Journal of Experimental Education* 8: 161–163, was the original experiment, which has been repeated at various times since.

9   Hilliard, A. (1998). *SBA: The Reawakening of the African Mind.* Gainesville: Makare Publishing, 15.

10   DeGruy, J. (2005) *Post Traumatic Slave Syndrome: America's Legacy of Enduring Injury and Healing.* Portland: Joy Degruy Publishing.

11   Carmichael and Hamilton, *Black Power,* 69.

12   Asante, M. (2003) *Afrocentricity: The Theory of Social Change.* Chicago: African American Images, 1.

13   Bekerie, A. (1994) The four corners of a circle: Afrocentricity as a model of synthesis. *Journal of Black Studies* 25(2): 131–149, 140.

14   Boyd, A. and Lenix-Hooker, C.J. (1992) Afrocentrism: Hype or history? *Library Journal,* 177(18): 46–49.

15   Karenga, M. (2016) Kwanzaa, the Nguzo Saba and our constant striving: Repairing, renewing and remaking the world. *Los Angeles Sentinel,* 22 December.

16   Malcolm X, 2nd Founding Rally.

17   Grant, C. (2010) *Negro with a Hat: The Rise and Fall of Marcus Garvey.* London: Vintage Books, 139.

18   Fanon, *Towards the African Revolution*, 22.

19   Ibid., 26.

20   Asante, *Afrocentricity*, 27.

21   Mazrui, A. (2005) Pan-Africanism and the intellectuals: Rise, decline and revival. In Mkandawire, T. (ed.) *African Intellectuals: Rethinking Politics, Language, Gender and Development*, 56–77. London: Zed Books, 57.

22   Mwaubani, E. (2001) *The United States and Decolonization in West Africa, 1950–1960*. Rochester: University of Rochester Press, 21.

23   Kinyatta, M. (1973) Dialectical reality of the African revolution. *The Black Scholar* 4(10): 20–23, 21.

24   Hill Collins, *From Black Power*, 82.

25   Makonnen, R. (1973) *Pan Africanism from Within*. Oxford: Oxford University Press.

26   Karenga, Kwanzaa.

27   Asante, *Afrocentricity*, 136.

28   Mazama, A. (2002) Afrocenticity and African spirituality. *Journal of Black Studies* 33(2): 218–234, 232.

29   Asante, *Afrocentricity*, 131.

30   Ibid., 113.

31   Marley, B. (1973) Get Up, Stand Up. *Burnin'*. Tuff Gong.

32   Malcolm X, Ballot or the bullet.

33   Malcolm X (1971) *The End of White World Supremacy: Four Speeches*. New York: Merlin House, 51.

34   Muhammad, *Message to the Blackman*.

35   Malcolm X, *End of White World*, 64.

36   Hutton, C. and Murrel, N.S. (1998) Rastas' psychology of Blackness, resistance, and somebodiness. In Murrell, N.S., Spencer, W.D. and McFarlane, A.A. (eds) *Chanting Down Babylon: The Rastafari Reader*, 36–54. Philadelphia: Temple University Press.

37   Campbell, *Rasta and Resistance*.

38   Nettleford, R.M. (1998) *Mirror, Mirror: Identity, Race and Protest in Jamaica*. Kingston, Jamaica: LMH Publishing; Owens, J. (1976) *Dread: The Rastafarians of Jamaica*. Kingston, Jamaica: Sangster's Book Stores.

39   Campbell, *Rasta and Resistance*.

40 Warren, N. (1990) Pan-African cultural movements: From Baraka to Karenga. *The Journal of Negro History* 75(1/2): 16–28, 26.

41 Brown, S. (2005) *Fighting for US: Maulana Karenga, the US organisation and Black Cultural Nationalism.* New York: New York University Press, 21.

42 Ibid., 39.

43 Ibid., 46.

44 Ibid., 66.

45 Woodard, *A Nation.*

46 Warren, Pan-African, 21.

47 Woodard, *A Nation*, 132.

48 Malcolm X, After the bombing.

49 Alexander-Floyd, N.G. (2003) We shall have our manhood: Black macho, Black Nationalism, and the Million Man March. *Meridians* 3(2): 171–203, 185.

50 Farrakhan in 2016 interview with Jamilah Lemieux for *Ebony* magazine.   http://www.huffingtonpost.com/ebonycom/farrakhan-remembers-the-d_b_8258032.html

51 Marable, Black fundamentalism, 4.

52 Alexander-Floyd, We shall have our manhood, 188.

53 Marable, Black fundamentalism, 5.

54 Woodard, *A Nation*, 189.

55 The Gary Conference Report: National Black Political Agenda (1972) *Black World* 11(12): 27–31, 29.

56 Woodard, *A Nation*, 227.

57 Ibid., 246.

58 Asante, *Afrocentricity*, 126.

59 Ibid., 130.

60 In Flores-Pena, Y. and Evanchuk, R. (1997) Kwanzaa: The emergence of an African-American holiday. *Western Folklore* 56(3/4): 281–294, 282.

61 Joseph, *Waiting 'Til*

62 Brown, E. (1994) *A Taste of Power: A Black Woman's Story.* New York: Anchor Books

63 Washington Post (1997) Interview: Farrakhan plans to wed 20,000 on mall in 2000, 16 October.

64 Reynolds, T. (2005) *Caribbean Mothering: Identity and Childrearing in the UK*. London: Tufnell Press.

65 Brown, *A Taste of Power*, 56.

66 Ibid., 56.

67 Asante, *Afrocentricity*, 73.

68 Ibid., 74.

69 Baruti, K. (2003) *Homosexuality and the Effeminization of Afrikan Males*. Np: Akob en House.

70 Nkrumah, *Africa Must Unite*.

71 Tsri, K. (2016) Africans are not black: Why the use of the term 'black' for Africans should be abandoned. *African Identities* 14(2): 147–160, 147.

72 Shakur, T. (1993) Speech at Indiana Black Expo, http://www.youtube.com/watch?v=Z7zmKOGEPaE

Chapter 5

1 Moore, S. (2016) Black pride at the Super Bowl? Beyoncé embodies a new political moment. *The Guardian*, 8 February.

2 Kornhaber, S. (2016) Beyoncé's radical halftime statement. *The Atlantic*, 8 February.

3 CBS News (2016) Beyonce's Super Bowl show brings praise and criticism, 9 February.

4 Andrews, K. (2016) Beyonce's 'bootylicious' sexualisation of black women isn't inspiring. *Independent*, 11 February.

5 hooks, b. (2016) Moving beyond pain. bell hooks Institute. http://www.bellhooksinstitute.com/blog/2016/5/9/moving-beyond-pain

6 Wallace, M. (1979) *Black Macho and the Myth of the Superwoman*. New York: The Dial Press, 13.

7 Ibid., 35.

8 Ibid., 36.

9 Wright, M. (2015) *Physics of Blackness: Beyond the Middle Passage Epistemology*. Minneapolis: University of Minnesota Press, 13.

10 Carby, H. (1998) *Race Men*. Cambridge, MA: Harvard University Press.

11 Cleaver, K. and Herve, J. (1971) Black Scholar interviews: Kathleen Cleaver. *The Black Scholar* 3(4): 54–59, 59.

12 Cleaver, E. (1970) *Soul On Ice.* London: Jonathan Cape.

13 Seale, *Seize the Time*, 18.

14 Spencer, R. (2016) *The Revolution has Come: Black Power, Gender and the Black Panther Party in Oakland.* Chapel Hill, NC: Duke University Press.

15 Cleaver and Herve, Black Scholar interviews, 55.

16 Brown, *Taste of Power*.

17 Matthews, M. (1979) 'Our women and what they think': Amy Jacques Garvey and 'The Negro World'. *The Black Scholar* 10(8/9): 2–13, 6.

18 Ibid., 4.

19 Carby, *Race Men*.

20 Malcolm X, Message to the grassroots.

21 Thomas, D. (2017) Cedric Robinson's meditation on Malcolm X's Black internationalism and the future of Black radicalism. In Johnson, G.T. and Lubin, A. (eds.) *Futures of Black Radicalism.* London: Verso [Kindle], Loc 3148.

22 Walker, R. (2005) *When We Ruled: The Ancient and Mediaeval History of Black Civilisations.* London: Every Generation Media.

23 Hart, M. (2014) *Gold: The Race for the World's Most Seductive Metal.* London: Simon and Schuster, 195.

24 Wright, *Physics*, 5.

25 Malcolm X. (1971) *The End of White World Supremacy: Four Speeches.* New York: Merlin House, 91.

26 Roberts, *Freedom as Marronage*.

27 James, *The Black Jacobins*.

28 Malcolm X, Message to the grassroots.

29 Fanon, F. (2004) *The Wretched of the Earth.* New York: Grove Press.

30 Malcom X, Ballot or the bullet.

31 Wright, *Black Power*.

32 Andrews, K. (2016) The problem of political blackness: Lessons from the Black Supplementary School Movement. *Ethnic and Racial Studies* 39(11): 1–19.

33 Wright, *Physics*, 4.

34 Gilroy, P (2002) *The Black Atlantic: Modernity and Double Consciousness.* London: Verso, 34.

35 Shelby, Two conceptions, 683.

36 Martin, *Race First.*

37 Marable, Black fundamentalism.

38 Toure, Speech to the congress, 27.

39 Malcolm X, *End of White World*, 51.

40 Malcolm X, *Autobiography*, 170.

41 Cross, W.E. (1971) The Negro to Black conversion experiences. *Black World* 20: 13–27.

42 Cross, W.E. (1991) *Shades of Black: Diversity in African American Identity.* Philadelphia: Temple University Press.

43 Appiah, K. (1992) *In My Father's House: Africa in the Philosophy of Culture.* Oxford: Oxford University Press, 39.

44 Ibid., 40.

45 Wright, *Physics.*

46 Mutwa, V.C. (1998) *Indaba My Children: African Tribal History.* Edinburgh: Payback Press.

47 Mbaye, B. (2006) The economic, political, and social impact of the Atlantic Slave Trade on Africa. *The European Legacy: Toward New Paradigms* 11(6): 607–662.

48 Mandela, *Long Walk to Freedom*, 698.

49 Appiah, *In My Father's House*, 42.

50 The title of a poem by that venerated British hero Rudyard Kipling.

51 Hochschild, A. (1999) *King Leopold's Ghost: A Story of Greed, Terror and Heroism in Colonial Africa.* New York: Mariner Press

52 Fanon, F. (1984) *Black Skin, White Masks.* London: Pluto Press, 84.

53 Hall, S (1991) Old and new identities, old and new ethnicities. In King, A.D. (ed.) *Culture, Globalization and the World-System: Contemporary Conditions for the Representation of Identity*, 41–68. Binghamton: NY Press, 53.

54 Fanon, *Towards the African Revolution*, 26.

55 Wright, *Physics*, 18.

56 Glaude, *Is it Nation Time?*, 2.

57 Shelby, Two conceptions, 665.

58 Reed, A. (2002) Black particularity revisited. In Glaude, E. (ed.)

Is it Nation Time? Contemporary Essays on Black Power and Black Nationalism, 39–66. Chicago: University of Chicago Press, 55.

59 Robinson, D. (2001) *Black Nationalism in American Political Thought.* Cambridge: Cambridge University Press, 2.

60 Anderson, E. (2011) *The Cosmopolitan Canopy: Race and Civility in Everyday Life.* New York: W.W. Norton Company, 249.

61 Hall, S. (1992) New ethnicities. In Donald, J. and Rattansi, A. (eds) *'Race', Culture and Difference,* 126–148. London: Sage Publications.

62 hooks, b. (1990) Postmodern Blackness. *Postmodern Culture* 1(1). https://muse.jhu.edu/journal/160

63 Gilroy, *Black Atlantic,* 102.

64 Kennedy, R. (2008) *Sellout: The Politics of Racial Betrayal.* New York: Pantheon Books.

65 Willie, S. (2003) *Acting Black: College, Identity, and the Performance of Race.* New York: Routledge.

66 Malcolm X, Message to the grassroots.

67 Ibid.

68 Ibid.

69 Andrews, K. (2014) From the Bad Nigger to the Good Nigga: An unintended legacy of the Black Power movement. *Race and Class* 55(3): 22–37.

70 Wright, *Physics,* 45.

71 Newton, H.P. (1970) The women's liberation and gay liberation movements. Speech, 15 August.

72 Nero, C. (2005) Queering the souls of Black folk. *Public Culture* 17(2): 255–276.

73 Wright, *Physics,* 14.

74 Malcolm X, Ballot or the bullet.

75 Crenshaw, K. and Ritchie, A. (2015) *Say Her Name: Resisting Police Brutality against Black Women.* New York: African American Policy Forum.

76 Wright, M. (2004) *Becoming Black: Creating Identity in the African Diaspora.* Durham, NC: Duke University Press: 3.

77 Cruse, H. (1967) *The Crisis of the Negro Intellectual: An Historical Analysis of the Failure of Black Leadership.* New York: New York Review of Books.

Chapter 6

1   Marx, K. and Engels, F. (2002) *The Communist Manifesto.* London: Penguin Books, 233.
2   Freire, P. (1972) *The Pedagogy of the Oppressed.* Harmondsworth: Penguin Education.
3   Malcolm X, Ballot or the bullet.
4   Layne, J. (2014) *We Move Tonight: The Making of the Grenada Revolution.* CreateSpace Independent Publishing Platform.
5   Cabral, A. (1982) *Unity and Struggle: Speeches and Writings.* London: Heinemann Educational.
6   Nyerere, J.K. (1971) African Socialism: Ujaaama in practice. *The Black Scholar* 2(6): 2–7.
7   Robinson, C.J. (1983) *Black Marxism: The Making of the Black Radical Tradition.* London: Zed Books.
8   Hall, S. (1983) The problem of ideology: Marxism without guarantees. In Matthews, B. (ed.) *Marx 100 Years On*, 57–84. London: Lawrence and Wishart.
9   Hall, S. (1986) Gramsci's relevance for the study of race and ethnicity. *Journal of Communication Inquiry* 10(2): 5–27.
10 DuBois, W.E.B. (1998) *Black Reconstruction in America:1860–1880.* New York: The Free Press.
11 Adi, H. (2013) *Pan-Africanism and Communism: The Communist International, African and the Diaspora, 1919–1939.* London: Africa World Press, 30.
12 Ibid., 23.
13 Ibid., 23.
14 Marx, K. (n.d.) *The Poverty of Philosophy: A Reply to M. Proudhon's Philosophy of Poverty.* New York: International Publisher, 4–5.
15 Robinson, C. (1992) CLR James and the world-system. *Race and Class* 34(2): 49–62, 61.
16 Wallerstein, I. (2007) *World-System Analysis: An Introduction.* Chapel Hill, NC: Duke University Press.
17 Gladwell, M. (2008) *Outliers: The Story of Success.* New York: Little, Brown and Company, 282.

18 Stack, L. (2017) Debunking a myth: The Irish were not slaves, too. *New York Times*, 17 March.

19 Williams, *Capitalism and Slavery*.

20 In Allsop, J. (1984) *Health Policy and the National Health Service*. Harlow: Longman, 37.

21 Virdee, S. (2000) A Marxist critique of Black radical theories of trade-union racism. *Sociology* 34(3): 545–565, 547.

22 Ibid.

23 Taylor, *From #BlackLivesMatter*.

24 Srnicek, N. and Williams, A. (2016) *Inventing the Future: Postcapitalism and a World Without Work*. London: Verso.

25 Standing, G. (2017) *Basic Income: And How We Can Make It Happen*. London: Penguin.

26 Andrews, The psychosis of whiteness.

27 In Niro, B. (2003) *Race*. Houndmills: Palgrave Macmillan, 65.

28 Guyatt, *Bind us Apart*.

29 Harris, C.I. (1993). Whiteness as property. *Harvard Law Review* 106: 1707–1791.

30 Roediger, D. (1992). *The Wages of Whiteness: Race and the Making of the American Working Class*. London: Verso.

31 Warren, J. and Twine, F. (1997). White Americans, the new minority? Non-Blacks and the ever expanding boundaries of whiteness. *Journal of Black Studies* 28: 200–218.

32 Allen, R.L. (2001). The globalization of white supremacy: Toward a critical discourse on the racialization of the world. *Educational Theory* 51: 467–485.

33 Aveling, N. (2004). Critical whiteness studies and the challenges of learning to be a 'white ally'. *Borderlands* 3: 1–43.

34 Owen, D.S. (2007). Towards a critical theory of whiteness. *Philosophy & Social Criticism* 33: 203–222, 203.

35 Ignatiev, N. (1997). The point is not to interpret whiteness but to abolish it. *Race Traitor*. http://racetraitor.org/abolishthepoint.pdf

36 Ignatiev, N. (1995). *How the Irish Became White*. New York, NY: Routledge.

37 Harris, A.L. (1925) A white and Black world in American labour politics. *Social Forces* 4(2): 376–383, 380.

38 Adi, *Pan-Africanism.*

39 Harris, A.L. (1927) Economic foundations of American race division. *Social Forces* 5(3): 468–478, 470.

40 Williams, *Capitalism & Slavery*, 7.

41 Ibid., 18.

42 Ibid., 5.

43 Omi, M. and Winant, O. (1989) *Racial Formation in the United States: From the 1960s to the 1980s.* London: Routledge.

44 Fanon, *Wretched of the Earth*, 62.

45 Guevara, E. (2000) *The African Dream: The Diaries of the Revolutionary War in the Congo.* New York: Grove Press.

46 Cabral, A. (1973) *Revolution in Guinea: An African People's Struggle.* London: Stage 1, 56.

47 Ibid., 50.

48 Ibid., 58.

49 Sankara, T. (2015) *We are the Heirs of the World's Revolutions.* London: Pathfinder.

50 Cabral, *Revolution*, 60.

51 Carmody, P. (2011) *The New Scramble for Africa.* Cambridge: Polity.

52 M'Buyinga, *Pan-Africanism*, 156.

53 Nyerere, African Socialism, 2.

54 Seale, *Seize the Time.*

55 Haas, J. (2009) *The Assassination of Fred Hampton: How the FBI and Chicago Police Murdered a Black Panther.* Chicago: Chicago Review Press.

56 Hampton, F. (1969) I'm free. Speech at People's Church Chicago, August.

57 Cleaver, E. (1972) On lumpen ideology. *The Black Scholar* 4: 2–10.

58 Marx, *Communist Manifesto*, 48.

59 Newton, H. (1980) *War against the Panthers: A Study of Repression in America.* Unpublished doctoral thesis, University of California, Santa Cruz.

60 Miles, R. and Phizacklea, A. (1977) Class, race, ethnicity and political action. *Political Studies* 25(4): 491–507.

61 Ishmail, M. (2016) Malcolm X was the progenitor Panther, Bobby Seale says so. *Rolling Out*, 22 May.

62 Johnson, G.T. and Lubin, A. (eds) (2017) *Futures of Black Radicalism*. London: Verso.

Chapter 7

1 Jackson, G. (1970) *Soledad Brother: The Prison Letters of George Jackson*. New York: Coward-McCann.

2 Carrier, J. (2015) *Hard Right Turn: The History and the Assassination of the American Left*. New York: Algora Press, 39.

3 Davis, A. (2003) *Are Prisons Obsolete?* New York: Seven Stories Press.

4 Davis, A. (2015) The refugee movement. Speech in Tosco, Belgium, 14 May.

5 United Nations Refugee Agency (2017) Figures at glance. http://www.unhcr.org/uk/figures-at-a-glance.html

6 Sue, D. (2010) *Microaggressions in Everyday Life: Race, Gender, and Sexual Orientation*. London: Wiley.

7 Wilson, A. (1994) *Black on Black Violence: The Psychodynamics of Black Self-annihilation in the Service of White Domination*. New York: Afrikan World Infosystems.

8 Dionne, E. (2015) For Black women, self-care is a radical act. Ravishly. http://www.ravishly.com/2015/03/06/radical-act-self-care-black-women-feminism

9 Shakur, A. (2014) *Assata: An Autobiography*. London: Zed Books.

10 Newton, H.P. (2009) *Revolutionary Suicide*. London: Penguin.

11 Malcolm X, Message to the grassroots.

12 Ibid.

13 Roberts, *Freedom as Marronage*, 11.

14 Kent, R. (1965) Palmares: An African state in Brazil. *Journal of African History* 6(2): 161–175.

15 Roberts, *Freedom*, 104.

16 Edmonds, E.B. (1998) Dread 'I'" in-a-Babylon: Ideological resistance and cultural revitalization. In Murrell, N.S., Spencer, W.D.

and McFarlane, A.A. (eds) *Chanting Down Babylon: The Rastafari Reader*, 23–35. Philadelphia: Temple University Press.

17 Ibid., 23.

18 CCCS (1978) *Policing the Crisis: Mugging, the State, and Law and Order*. Houndsmills: Macmillan.

19 Shakur, *An Autobiography*.

20 On 'A Song for Assata' by Common (1997) *One Day It'll All Make Sense*. Relativity Records.

21 Malcolm X, Ballot or the bullet.

22 Malcolm X, Message to the grassroots.

23 Kelley, R. (2002) *Freedom Dreams: The Black Radical Imagination*. Boston: Beacon Press, 181.

24 Moten, F. (2003) *In the Break: The Aesthetics of the Black Radical Tradition*. Minneapolis: University of Minnesota Press, 24.

25 Kelley, *Freedom Dreams*, 164.

26 Ibid., 191.

27 Lee, S. (2010) *Erotic Revolutionaries: Black Women, Sexuality and Popular Culture*. Lanham, MD: Hamilton Books, xiv.

28 Washington, *Up From Slavery*.

29 For a complete discussion of Cosby's politics see Dyson, M.E. (2005) *Is Bill Cosby Right? Or Has the Black Middle Class Lost Its Mind?* New York: Basic Civitas Books.

30 Younge, G. (1999) *No Place Like Home: A Black Briton's Journey through the American South*. London: Picador.

31 Thompson, L. (2009) *Beyond the Black Lady: Sexuality and the New African American Middle Class*. Urbana: University of Illinois Press, 2.

32 Hill Collins, P. (2000) *Black Feminist Thought: Knowledge, Consciousness, and the Politics of Empowerment*. London: Routledge, 69.

33 Williams-Forson, P. (2006) *Building Houses out of Chicken Legs: Black Women, Food, and Power*. Durham: University of North Carolina Press.

34 Malcolm X, Militant Labor Forum.

35 Jones, R. (2012) Martin Luther King Jr's Agape and World House. In Birt, R. (ed.) *The Liberatory Thought of Martin Luther King,*

Jr: Critical Essays on the Philosopher King, 135–156. Plymouth: Lexington Books, 137.

36 Malcolm X, Message to the grassroots.

37 Ibid.

38 Jamal Joseph, former Black Panther in an interview with Shadow and Act, April 2017. https://shadowandact.com/panther-baby-an-interview-with-jamal-joseph

39 Cook, A.E. (1995) Beyond critical legal studies: The reconstructive theology of Dr. Martin Luther King, Jr. In Crenshaw, K.W., Gotanda, N., Peller, G. and Thomas, K (eds) *Critical Race Theory: The Key Writings that Formed the Movement,* 85–102, New York: The New Press.

40 Bell, D. (1992) *Faces at the Bottom of the Well: The Permanence of Racism.* New York: Basic Books, 12.

41 Ibid., 3.

42 Parsons, C. (2009) Explaining sustained inequalities in ethnic minority school exclusion in England — passive racism in a neoliberal grip. *Race, Ethnicity and Education* 35(2): 249–265, 262; emphasis original.

43 Gillborn, D. (2008) *Racism and Education: Coincidence or Conspiracy.* Abingdon, Oxon: Routledge, 9.

44 Milner, H.R. (2007) Race, culture, and research positionality: Working through dangers seen, unseen, and unforeseen, *Educational Researcher* 6: 388–400.

45 Tupper, J.A. and Cappello, M. (2008) Teaching treaties as (un)usual narratives: Disrupting the curricular commonsense. *Curriculum Inquiry* 38(5): 559–578, 574.

46 Vaught, S.E. and Castagno, A.E. (2008) 'I don't think I'm a racist': Critical Race Theory, teacher attitudes and structural racism. *Race, Ethnicity & Education* 11(2): 95–113, 110.

47 Milner, H.R (2008) Critical Race Theory and interest convergence as analytic tools in teacher education policies and practices. *Journal of Teacher Education* 59: 332–346, 338.

48 Ibid., 240.

49 Bell., 198.

50 Osuna, S. (2017) Class suicide: The Black radical tradition, radical

scholarship and the neoliberal turn. In Johnson, G.T. and Lubin, A. (eds) *Futures of Black Radicalism.* London: Verso [Kindle], Loc 437.

51 Ladson-Billings, G. (2004) New directions in multicultural education: Complexities, boundaries and critical race theory. In Banks, J.A. and Banks, C.A.M. (eds) *Handbook of Research on Multicultural Education*, 2nd ed., 50–65. San Francisco: Jossey-Bass, 59.

52 Patterson, O. (1982) *Slavery and Social Death: A Comparative Study.* Cambridge, MA: Harvard University Press.

53 Sexton, J (2011) The social life of social death: On Afro-pessimism and Black optimism. *InTensions* 5. Online journal. http://www.yorku.ca/intent/issue5/articles/jaredsexton.php

54 Moten, F. (2008) The case of Blackness. *Criticism* 50(2): 177–218.

55 Malcolm X, Ballot or the bullet.

Chapter 8

1 Fukuyama, F. (1992) *The End of History and the Last Man.* London: Penguin.

2 West, C. (2002) The paradox of the African American rebellion. In Glaude, E. (ed.) *Is it Nation Time? Contemporary Essays on Black Power and Black Nationalism*, 22–38. Chicago: University of Chicago Press, 35.

3 McGhee, D. (2008) *End of Multiculturalism? Terrorism, Integration and Human Rights.* Maidenhead: Open University Press.

4 Male, G.A. (1980) Multicultural education and education policy: The British experience. *Comparative Education Review* 24(3): 291–301.

5 Jackson, N. (2016) The ties that bind: Questions of empire and belonging in Black British educational activism. In Andrews, K. and Palmer, L. (2016) *Blackness in Britain*, 117–129. London: Routledge.

6 Delmont, M. (2016) *Why Busing Failed: Race, Media and the National Resistance to School Desegregation.* Oakland: University of California Press.

7 Parekh, B. (2000) *The Future of Multi-Ethnic Britain: The Parekh Report.* London: Runnymede Trust, xv.

8   Kundani, A. (2002) The death of multiculturalism. *Race and Class* 43(4): 67–72.

9   Andrews, The problem of political blackness.

10   Rex, J. and Moore, R. (1971) *Race, Community and Conflict: A Study of Sparkbrook.* London: Oxford University Press.

11   Orfield, G. (2009) *Reviving the Goal of an Integrated Society: A 21st Century Challenge.* Los Angeles, CA: The Civil Rights Project/ Proyecto Derechos Civiles.

12   Sunak, R. and Rajeswaran, S. (2014). *A Portrait of Modern Britain.* London: The Policy Exchange.

13   Wilson, A. (1998) *Blueprint for Black Power: A Moral, Political, and Economic Imperative for the Twenty-First Century.* New York: Afrikan World Infosystems.

14   Upchurch, D. (2016) *Pyrrhic Victory: The Cost of Integration.* Charlotte: Information Age Publishing.

15   Malcolm X, *The End of White World*, 9.

16   Lennard, N. and Mirzoeff, N. (2016) What protest looks like. *New York Times*, 3 August.

17   Adams, K. (2017) Smartphones play crucial role for Black Lives Matter. *Marketplace*, 11 July. https://www.marketplace. org/2016/07/11/wealth-poverty/smartphones-play-crucial-role-black-lives-matter

18   Kelly, A. (2016) Children as young as seven mining cobalt used in smartphones, says Amnesty. *The Guardian*, 19 January.

19   Lorde, *Sister Outsider*, 110.

20   Malcolm X, 2nd Founding Rally.

21   Ibid.

22   Andrews, K. (2013) *Resisting Racism: Race, Inequality and the Black Supplementary School Movement.* London: Institute of Education Press.

23   Stone, M. (1981) *The Education of the Black Child in Britain.* London: Fontana.

24   Malcolm, 2nd Founding Rally.

25   Ibid.

26   Malcolm X, Ballot or the bullet.

27   Newton, *Revolutionary Suicide*, 57.

28 Burrough, R. (2015) *Days of Rage: America's Radical Underground, the FBI and the Forgotten Age of Revolutionary Violence*. New York: Penguin.

29 Grady-Willis, W. (1998) The Black Panther Party: State repression and political prisoners. In Jones, C. (ed.) *The Black Panther Party Reconsidered*, 363–390. Baltimore: Black Classic Press, 366.

30 Smith, R. (2002) *A Huey P. Newton Story*. Documentary, Public Broadcasting Service.

31 Reed, J. (1971) Newton-Cleaver rift threatens Panthers. *Harvard Crimson*, 23 March.

32 Marable, M. (2011) *Living Black History: How Reimagining the African-American Past Can Remake America's Racial Future*. New York: Basic Civitas.

Epilogue

1 Malcolm X, Ballot or the bullet.

2 Newton, *Revolutionary Suicide*, 333.

3 Malcolm X, Ballot or the bullet.

4 Lorde, *Sister Outsider*, 138.

5 Malcolm X, Ballot or the bullet.

6 Davis, A. (1981) *Women, Race and Class*. New York: Random House.

7 Mandela, *Long Walk to Freedom*, 698.

8 Walker, *When We Ruled*.

9 Higman, B. (1976) *Slave Population and Economy in Jamaica, 1807–1834*. Kingston: Press of the University of the West Indies.

10 Pilkington, E. (2014) Caribbean nations prepare demand for slavery reparations. *Guardian*, 9 March.

11 Williams, *Capitalism and Slavery*.

12 Craemer, T. (2015) Estimating slavery reparations: Present value comparisons of historical multigenerational reparations policies. *Social Science Quarterly* 96(2): 639–655.

13 Bell, *Faces at the Bottom*, 3.

14 Ture, K. (1983) Black Power and the need to organise. Speech, Handsworth Birmingham.

Index

ZED

Zed is a platform for marginalised voices across the globe.

It is the world's largest publishing collective and a world leading example of alternative, non-hierarchical business practice.

It has no CEO, no MD and no bosses and is owned and managed by its workers who are all on equal pay.

It makes its content available in as many languages as possible.

It publishes content critical of oppressive power structures and regimes.

It publishes content that changes its readers' thinking.

It publishes content that other publishers won't and that the establishment finds threatening.

It has been subject to repeated acts of censorship by states and corporations.

It fights all forms of censorship.

It is financially and ideologically independent of any party, corporation, state or individual.

Its books are shared all over the world.

www.zedbooks.net

@ZedBooks